Regional politics
in Russia

Regional politics in Russia

Edited by
Cameron Ross

Manchester University Press

Manchester and New York

distributed exclusively in the USA by Palgrave

Published by Manchester University Press
Oxford Road, Manchester M13 9NR, UK
and Room 400, 175 Fifth Avenue, New York, NY 10010, USA
www.manchesteruniversitypress.co.uk

Distributed exclusively in the USA by
Palgrave, 175 Fifth Avenue, New York NY 10010, USA

Distributed exclusively in Canada by
UBC Press, University of British Columbia, 2029 West Mall,
Vancouver, BC, Canada V6T 1Z2

British Library Cataloguing-in-Publication Data
A catalogue record for this book is available from the British Library

Library of Congress Cataloging-in-Publication Data
A catalog record for this book is available from the Library of Congress

ISBN 13: 978 0 7190 8117 0

First published in hardback 2002 by Manchester University Press
This edition first published 2009

Printed by Lightning Source

Contents

Tables and appendices

Tables

Appendices

Contributors

James Alexander   Department of Political Science, Northeastern State University, USA.

Midkhat Farukhshin   Department of Political Science, Kazan' University, Russian Federation.

Vladimir Gel'man   Faculty of Political Science and Sociology, European Institute at St. Petersburg, Russian Federation.

Grigorii Golosov   Faculty of Political Science and Sociology, European Institute at St. Petersburg, Russian Federation.

Vadim Goncharov   St. Petersburg State University of Telecommunications, Russian Federation.

Jörn Grävingholt   Federal Institute of Eastern Affairs and International Studies, Cologne, Germany.

Jeffrey W. Hahn   Department of Political Science, Villanova University, USA.

Daniel N. Lussier   Analyst with the East–West Institute, New York, USA.

Ian McAllister   Research School of the Social Sciences, Australian National University, Canberra.

Sarah Oates   Department of Politics, University of Glasgow, UK.

Nikolai N. Petro   Department of Political Science, University of Rhode Island, USA.

Cameron Ross   Department of Politics, University of Dundee, UK.

Richard Sakwa   Department of Politics and International Relations, University of Kent at Canterbury, UK.

Elizabeth Teague   Senior Research Officer, Eastern Research Group, Foreign and Commonwealth Office, London, UK.

Stephen White   Department of Politics, University of Glasgow, UK.

Matthew Wyman   School of Politics, International Relations and the Environment, University of Keele, UK.

Acknowledgements

The editor would like to thank the British Academy, the British Council, and the Foreign and Commonwealth Office for their generous financial support for the Conference 'Regional Politics and Democratisation in Russia', which took place at the University of Dundee 13–15 May 2000. The majority of the chapters in this book were first presented as papers at this conference.

Abbreviations

APR	Agrarian Party of Russia (*Agrarnaya Partiya Rossii*)
CO	Honour and Fatherland (*Chest' i Otechestvo*)
DVR	Russia's Democratic Choice (*Demokraticheskii Vybor Rossii*)
FD	Federal District
FDI	foreign direct investment
FSB	Federal Security Service (*Federal'naya Sluzhba Bezopasnosti*)
IPU	Index of Party Utility
IREX	International Research and Exchanges Board
KEDR	Ecological Party of Russia (*Ekologicheskaya Partiya Rossii*)
KPRF	Communist Party of the Russian Federation (*Kommunisticheskaya Partiya Rossiiskoi Federatsii*)
KPSS	Communist Party of the Soviet Union (*Kommunisticheskaya Partiya Sovetskovo Soyuza*)
KRO	Congress of Russian Communities (*Kongress Russkikh Obshchin*)
LDPR	Liberal Democratic Party of Russia (*Liberal'no Demokraticheskaya Partiya Rossii*)
MVD	Ministry of the Interior (*Ministerstvo Vnutrennikh Del*)
NDR	Our Home is Russia (*Nash Dom – Rossiya*)
NGO	non-governmental organisation
NPR	People's Party of Russia (*Narodnaya Partiya Rossii*)
NPSR	National Patriotic Union of Russia (*Narodno Patriotischeskii Soyuz Rossii*)
OSCE	Organisation for Security and Cooperation in Europe
OVR	Fatherland – All Russia (*Otechestvo – Vsya Rossiya*)
PK	Primorskii Krai
PL	party list
PST	Party of Independent Workers (*Partiya Samoupravleniya Trudyashchikhsya*)
RDV	Russian Far East (*Rossiiskii Dal'nii Vostok*)
RFE/RL	Radio Free Europe/Radio Liberty
RKRP	Russian Communist Workers' Party (*Rossiiskaya*

	Kommunisticheskaya Rabochaya Partiya)
ROS	Russian National Union (*Rossiiskii Obshchenarodnyi Soyuz*)
RP	Republican Party (*Respublikanskaya Partiya*)
RSFSR	Russian Soviet Federative Socialist Republic (*Rossiiskaya Sovetskaya Federativnaya Sotsialisticheskaya Respublika*), the largest republic of the former USSR
RSP	Russian Socialist Party (*Russkaya Sotsialisticheskaya Partiya*)
SM	single member list
SPS	Union of Right Forces (*Soyuz Pravo Sil'*)
USSR	Union of Soviet Socialist Republics (*Soyuz Sovyeticheskikh Sotsialisticheskikh Respublik*)
VTsIOM	All-Union Centre for Public Opinion Research (*Vserossiiskii Tsentr Izucheniya Obshchestvennovo Mneniya*)
Zhir	Zhirinovsky Bloc

1 *Richard Sakwa*

Federalism, sovereignty and democracy

The spatial element in post-communist Russian politics is now a political fact, but the scope and nature of regional autonomy and initiative is far less clear.[1] In the 1990s the old hyper-centralised Soviet state gave way to the fragmentation of political authority and contesting definitions of sovereignty. Under President Boris Yeltsin a complex and unstable balance was drawn between the claimed prerogatives of the centre and the normative and de facto powers of the regions. The tension between central and regional claims concerned not only practical issues of governance and finances, but also focused on fundamental competing sovereignty claims. In that context the evolving practice of 'asymmetrical federalism' concerned the very definition of the state. A distinctive type of 'segmented regionalism' emerged, whereby Russia in effect had ninety governments. The federal authorities at the centre entered into asymmetrical bargaining relations with the other eighty-nine 'subjects of the federation', one of which (Chechnya) claimed outright independence.

This was the situation facing the incoming president, Vladimir Putin, on coming to office in early 2000. His response was to appeal to the principle of 'the dictatorship of law', and in particular the unimpeded flow of constitutional and juridical authority throughout the territory of the Russian Federation. Subnational sovereignty claims were thereby rendered illegitimate, even though federalism as a principle is all about shared sovereignty. Fundamental issues were occluded by Putin's attempts to reconstitute the state, above all the question of the form of state sovereignty. Was Russia to become a genuine federation, in which law would be defined in accordance with the normative spatial division of sovereignty?; or would it take the form of de facto regionalism, where an effectively unitary state grants rights to devolved units, in which case a very different definition of sovereignty would operate.

Statism, federalism and regionalism

The debate over federalism and regionalism is at the same time a question of the type of state that Russia will become. It is a question of the nature of the sovereignty that will be exercised by the federal authorities and the degree to which sovereignty will be shared with the subjects of the federation. Russia now finds itself in a period identified by Robert Jackson: 'We should probably regard periodical reshuffling of the title to sovereignty, even major redistribution, as something to be expected from time to time.'[2] The disintegration of the USSR represented a major reshuffling, but federalists in Russia insisted that the process was far from complete. Statists, however, responded that instead of federalism emerging in Russia, a fragmented regionalism (what we call segmented regionalism) had become established that threatened the very integrity of the state.

Under Yeltsin regional regimes came to exert considerable autonomous authority over their 'fiefdoms'. Putin's reassertion of central authority in defence of the writ of the Constitution represented the defence of a particular vision of democracy. His aim, literally, was to reconstitute the state, to place the Constitution at the centre of the political process in regional relations. For some this was no more than a new form of Russia's traditional tendency towards recentralisation; but the case could be made with equal plausibility that it offered an opportunity to move away from asymmetrical federalism towards a more balanced form. Asymmetrical federalism not only granted differential rights to regional leaderships, but effectively established different gradations of democratic citizenship to those living in different parts of the country. The attempt to achieve a universal and homogeneous type of citizenship lay at the heart of Putin's attempt to reconstitute the state.

Segmented regionalism versus compacted statism

In the 1990s the federal separation of authority was undermined by spontaneous processes of segmented regionalism.[3] The development of asymmetrical federalism may well have provided a framework for the flexible negotiation of individual tailor-made solutions to Russia's diverse ethnic and political composition,[4] but it failed to do this within the framework of universal norms of citizenship. Instead, segmented regionalism fragmented the country juridically, economically and, implicitly, in terms of sovereignty. By the end of Yeltsin's term in office Russia was beginning to become not only a multinational state, but also a multi-state state, with numerous proto-state formations making sovereignty claims vis-à-vis Moscow.[5] The country was increasingly divided into segments, not only spatially but also in terms of the fragmentation of political authority. In contrast to the European Union, where the pooling of sovereignty began to create a single political community, Russia was moving in the opposite direction, towards what some called the 'medievalisation' of politics where overlapping jurisdictions fragmented administrative and legal practices. The development of a national party system was undermined by the proto-state claims made by regional executives, their ability to control patronage resources and to influence electoral outcomes. The emergence of a single national community was impeded by the segmented regionalisation of political authority.

Putin's response to segmented regionalism was to reconstitute the state. However, this attempt to place the Constitution at the centre of relations between the centre and the regions was torn between at least two forms. The Constitution of 1993 is capable of varying interpretations, above all between a permissive and a constrictive reading of federal relations. The permissive inter-pretation sustained what could be called 'pluralistic statism'; while a more con-strictive reading gives rise to what we call 'compacted statism'. It is compacted not so much because of any notional agreement between the parties, although as we see this element does play a part, but above all because through compac-tion the relative pluralism, media freedom and regional diversity of the country that had emerged under Yeltsin was threatened. The resurgence of the state is thus torn between two forms: compacted statism, using the rhetoric of the defence of constitutional norms and the uniform application of law throughout the country but threatening the development of a genuine federal separation of powers; while pluralistic statism defends the unimpeded flow of law and individ-ual rights while respecting the diversity of civil society and federalist norms.

Federalism

Caught between segmented regionalism and the Putinite normative reconstitu-tion of the state, federalism itself as the legal separation of powers in the spatial context is under threat. According to Preston King, the defining feature of fed-eralism is that 'central government incorporates regional units in its decision procedure on some constitutionally entrenched basis.'[6] Although Smith is correct to stress that the defining feature of federal policy making is the 'politics of accommodation',[7] the problem everywhere, but particularly acute in Russia, is that the resources available to the various actors in the bargaining process are far from equal, and it is these power asymmetries that shape Russia's distinctive type of federalism and encourage the development of segmented regionalism. Stavrakis noted one aspect of this, namely 'the fundamental economic disparity between Moscow and the provinces is emerging as the defining characteristic of post-Soviet society.'[8] Moscow city alone generates over a third of Russia's GDP, absorbing a large proportion of the revenues generated from the primary mate-rials industries.

Attempts in the 1990s to build federalism from the top down were countered by the regions which managed, *de facto* if not yet *de jure*, to ensure a significant bottom up devolution of power.[9] All federations are designed to constrain central political power, but not all do so with equal effect. In Russia, whatever the nature of the local regimes themselves, regions acted as a check on the central author-ities; a type of spatial separation of powers emerged that to a degree compensated for the inadequacy of the vertical separation of power in the constitutional order established in December 1993. In this context – however democratic the reconsti-tution of the Russian state may be – the weakening, if not the removal, of this 'fourth pivot' in Russian government (in addition to the classical trinity of the executive, legislative and judiciary) could weaken the overall democratism of the Russian constitutional order. Russian regionalism emerged as a more effective check, if not a democratic balance, on executive authority than the relatively weak legislature and judiciary.

The demise of the USSR in December 1991 brought the issue of the territorial arrangements for Russia into sharp focus. Known collectively as the Federation Treaty, the signing of the three federal treaties on 31 March 1992 allowed a significant degree of decentralisation, providing for joint jurisdiction over education, environmental protection and conservation, health care and natural resources, while recognising certain areas as the sole prerogative of the subjects. The Federation Treaty failed to reconcile the positions of the centre and the regions, but in adopting at times mutually contradictory positions the differences in viewpoints were made clear. The treaties were excluded from the 12 December 1993 Constitution, although the basic principles of decentralisation, joint and sole jurisdictions, remained. The new Constitution, which took precedence over the Federation Treaty, took a more restrictive view of these rights. Although the definition of the republics as 'sovereign states' was struck out of the new text, the federation structure continued to apply different criteria to various units despite the formal claim that all federal components are equal (Article 5.1).

While a number of European countries have an asymmetrical state structure (with the autonomous regions in Italy, for example, enjoying certain extra competencies, and in Spain between the normal provinces and the so-called nationalities, above all Catalonia), there is no example of asymmetrical federalism in the rest of Europe, and indeed it is often argued that the success of Swiss and German federalism lies in symmetry. As Lane and Ersson note, 'Asymmetrical federalism may lead to dual federalism, where one state or region is entirely distinct from the others.'[10] Dual federalism has an implicit state building dynamic and can lead to the break-up of federations, as was the case with Czechoslovakia earlier. Asymmetry establishes a competitive dynamic where federal relations are in a state of constant flux. In Russia under Yeltsin a concession granted to one region was immediately demanded by others, while the republics insisted on preserving their differentials vis-à-vis the regions. While no federation can be completely symmetrical (for example, in terms of population and area), very few give political form to asymmetries.

In Russia there was a formal power asymmetry enshrined in the differing prerogatives granted to republics and regions and further codified in power-sharing agreements (see below). There were, in addition, informal asymmetries, focused above all on personal networks and ties between regional leaders and the central government. Under Yeltsin, regional governors sought to establish good relations with the current prime minister but frequent changes jeopardised these links and the ability to plan constructively. With Putin's rise and the reinvigoration of the Kremlin these asymmetries focused largely on personal relations with the president.

Regionalism

Segmented regionalism in Russia appealed to the language of federalism but in practice undermined the capacity of the state and the legal-normative prerogatives of the federal authorities. Undoubtedly elements of federalism emerged, but in a highly ambiguous way. Part of the ambiguity derives from the historical legacy. The Soviet institution of ethno-federalism provided Russia with two very different constituent elements:

1 the republics based on a titular nationality (or group of nationalities in the case of Dagestan, Kabardino-Balkariya and others) and based on a specific territory; and
2 regions, based on territory alone.

This provided a powerful impetus to the segmentation of regionalism along the lines of this division. A second historical factor promoting segmentation was the weakness of autonomous rational bureaucratic administration and civic association in the regions themselves, a factor stemming from both the Tsarist and Soviet past. The attempt to establish a federal system in a context where civil society is weak could not but exaggerate the autonomy of regional leaders, and encouraged them to view themselves as quasi-sovereign actors, a tendency reinforced in the ethno-federal republics by appeal to the national histories of the titular nationalities.

Regionalism has deep roots in Russia. During the Civil War various regionalist movements sought power in Siberia and the Urals, while industrial administration during the Stalinist five-year plans was riven by regional influences.[11] Yet regionalism was the great under-rated force of early post-communist Russian politics.[12] Much attention was devoted to the analysis of civil society and political parties, but it was the regional element that took on substantive form in the early post-communist period. The notion of civil society is embedded in the idea of the self-determining individual joining voluntarily in associational life to pursue material and psychological advantages, but this is very far from the world of dependency networks typical of Russia, rooted in local production and supply communities, and regional identities. There is a regional dimension to the politics of civil society formation, with regional conflicts cutting across trade-union and other movements.

Post-communist Russian regionalism expressed specific bureaucratic and social interests that became increasingly deeply entrenched, deploying political resources against the centre and other federal subjects to ensure freedom of action to attract investment (above all foreign) and to exploit regional resources, and to ensure relative autonomy from popular accountability (by diminishing the authority of local legislatures, manipulating electoral contests and establishing regional 'parties of power'). Although the regional institutions of the USSR created powerful patronage and political networks, their persistence was determined by specific regional coalitions able to exploit the new political and economic conditions.

As with the development of civil society, it is assumed that the development of regionalism requires economic autonomy for regional-level actors. The main components of regional elites are, in various combinations, the managers of former state enterprises, the new business class (which in many cases has swapped the tyranny of the old state planners for the arbitrary exploitativeness of the financial–industrial oligarchs), the agrarian sector and the world of small and medium businesses. Regions dependent on heavy industry suffered the most from Russia's economic decline, the agricultural sector suffered from the lack of financing and depressed prices, while entrepreneurialism was choked by heavy taxes and oppressive bureaucracy. Everywhere regional leaderships imposed various types of administrative controls over the local economy, including complicated registration procedures for exports, sanitation inspections, and controls on the pricing and movement of goods, something that intensified after the August 1998 crisis (see below). Regional governors, moreover, consolidated their power by taking over partial ownership in enterprises. Banks were offered tax breaks and contracts to service regional budgets in exchange for transferring a controlling stake to the regional authorities (for example, in Sverdlovsk and St. Petersburg). The republics were the most active in this direction, with Bashkortostan, for example, creating a state-run monopoly in the cash-rich energy sector.[13]

In regional elections the premium was less on ideological debate than on defining sustainable regional development strategies and establishing effective working relationships with Moscow. This was particularly evident in the case of Pskov, where the Liberal Democratic Party of Russia (LDPR; headed by Vladimir Zhirinovsky) scored its sole electoral success in the gubernatorial elections of late 1996. Once elected, however, the victor, Yevgenii Mikhailov, soon toned down the LDPR's grand geopolitical rhetoric and set about managing the local economy and establishing good relations with his neighbours (Estonia and Latvia), including the resolution of border disputes.[14]

Regionalism is not just a passive actor in the evolution of post-communist Russia. Russia's regions have now become one of the main sites for policy innovation, and in some cases are able to diffuse their experience to the rest of the country. During the first Chechen war, for example, the governor of Nizhnii Novgorod, Boris Nemtsov, forbade the sending of local conscripts to the Caucasus, and in February 1999 the same region under a new governor defied the Constitutional Court by ordering local companies to pay wages before paying taxes, directly contradicting a federal ruling. Numerous regions adopted administrative measures against what was perceived as hostile proselytising by foreign religious bodies, acts that fed into the adoption of restrictive national legislation on religious associations in September 1997. Segmentation and federal asymmetries derived, therefore, not only from Yeltsin's distinctive leadership style but reflected objective differences in historical traditions, economic resources and elite representations of regional interests.

Segmented regionalism, democracy and state sovereignty

Mikhail Alexseev notes that 'The spectre of regional separatism has haunted Russian politics since the collapse of the Soviet Union in 1991.'[15] Segmented regionalism was underpinned by competing sovereignty claims. On 5 August 1990, on a visit to Kazan', Yeltsin had urged the federation subjects to 'take as much sovereignty as you can swallow', an injunction that he repeated on the eve of his impeachment vote in the Duma in May 1999. Consistent in this if in little else, the sovereignty of the centre was eroded in a process called by Katznelson, in a different context, the 'parcelisation of sovereignty'.[16] The continuing crisis of the state and the economy allowed some of the republics to expand their *de facto* sovereignty by adopting laws that created a legal space that became increasingly distinct from that established by Moscow. In the vanguard of this process, dubbed 'disassociation by default', were Tatarstan, Bashkortostan, Khakasiya, and Sakha (Yakutiya). The unifying role of the military was lost and, indeed, the army became increasingly dependent on the regional authorities. The federal authorities were unable to guarantee basic civil rights in the regions, and even lost control over regional branches of state agencies. The local branches of the procuracy, the Ministry of the Interior (MVD) and other ministries fell into the hands of governors and local presidents. Only the KGB's successor, the Federal Security Service (FSB), appeared able to withstand 'capture' by regional authorities.

Yeltsin-style authoritarianism never quite developed into full-blown dictatorship but equally never quite submitted itself to popular accountability and constitutional and legal restraints. The phenomenon was replicated at the regional level. An extremely heterogeneous pattern of regime types emerged, ranging from the relatively democratic in Novgorod, Arkhangel'sk, Samara and St. Petersburg, to the outright authoritarian in Primorskii Krai under Yevgenii Nazdratenko and Kalmykiya under president Kirsan Ilyumzhinov. There was also diversity in types of state-political structure. Udmurtiya was a parliamentary republic (until a referendum in early 2000), Samara was a fully fledged presidential republic, Dagestan was governed by a form of consociational democracy in which a State Council sought to balance and represent the ethnic diversity of the republic, while Moscow city replicated the 'super-presidentialism' of the central government itself. This diversity in part reflected local traditions, the dynamic of elite relations, and the ethnic and social composition of a particular republic, and in turn affected policy outcomes.[17]

Segmented regionalism was generated by historical, material and social factors and not simply by the strategic choices of post-communist central and regional elites. However, while federal asymmetry reflected the diversity of the country, it did not explain the precise legal and juridical disparities between the country's regions. In the 1990s federal relations developed largely as a function of the immediate political needs of the presidency. The lack of genuine reciprocal and transparent relations between the centre and the localities was one of the most significant failures of Yeltsin's presidency. As his regime gave way to Putin's, a whole series of issues remained problematical. We examine some of them below.

1 Subject-level constitutions and charters

At least fifty of the eighty-nine local constitutions and charters contradicted the federal one, while a third of local legislation violated federal legislation in one way or another. The constitution of Bashkortostan, Tatarstan and the regional charter of Tula Oblast were exemplary cases of subjects claiming rights not allowed for in the national Constitution, derogating from the principle of equality between subjects of the federation. Article 1 of Bashkortostan's constitution, adopted in December 1993, stated that 'The Republic of Bashkortostan has supreme authority on its territory, independently defining and conducting domestic and foreign policies, adopting the Bashkortostan constitution and its laws, which have supremacy on its entire territory.' Komi's constitution granted special rights to citizens of the republic who were ethnic Komi, stipulating that the head of the republic and deputies to the Legislative Assembly had to be citizens of Komi, while its citizenship laws themselves contravened the national Constitution. Already a ruling of the Constitutional Court in December 1997 condemned the Tambov Oblast charter, adopted by the regional legislature as part of its long-standing struggle with the governor, Alexander Ryabov. One of Putin's immediate concerns was to bring the republican constitutions and regional charters into line with the Russian Constitution.

2 The fragmentation of legal space

According to the Justice Ministry, an examination of 44,000 regional legal acts, including laws, gubernatorial orders and similar documents, found that nearly half did not conform with the Constitution or federal legislation.[18] Sergei Stepashin, at the time Minister of Justice, in December 1997 noted that his ministry had analysed 9,000 laws adopted in the regions, and claimed that a third contradicted either the Russian Constitution or federal legislation. By January he announced that about one-third of the 16,000 regional laws examined by the Justice Ministry since the summer of 1995 were found to have violated federal legislation. On the same theme, the Prosecutor General, Yurii Skuratov, noted that nearly 2,000 regional laws had been revoked for contradicting the Constitution, but warned that Russia lacked sufficient 'levers' to ensure compliance at the regional level with the rulings of the Constitutional Court.[19] It was under the premiership of Stepashin (May–August 1999) that the long-awaited law 'On the Principles of Dividing Power Between the Russian Federation Government and the Regions' was finally adopted,[20] stipulating that all new federal and regional laws had to be adopted in conformity with this law, and that all previously adopted legislation and treaties had to be brought into line within set periods.

The 1993 Constitution established a unified national system of the administration of justice. The judicial system includes the procuracy, the *arbitrazh* courts (dealing with disputes between economic and other legally-constituted organisations), and the normal criminal courts. The Constitutional Court of nineteen judges gives judgements interpreting the writ of the Constitution in specific cases. The national judicial system acted as a barrier, however weak in some places, to the emergence of regional despotisms. It was this obstacle to the medieval fragmentation of law that Putin sought to strengthen.

3   Power-sharing bilateral treaties

During Yeltsin's presidency forty-six power-sharing treaties were signed between the leaders (not, it should be noted, by the subjects as a whole) of individual regions and the federal authorities. The treaties formalised the emergence of asymmetrical federalism where the rights of separate regions were negotiated on an *ad hoc* and often conjunctural basis. The terms of many of these treaties, especially various annexes and annual supplements, were not made public, but their net result was to accentuate the asymmetries in federal relations. The bilateral treaties allowed customised deals between the centre and the subjects. To that degree Yeltsin had a case in arguing that they 'strengthened Russian statehood',[21] yet they could not but undermine basic principles of constitutional equality and political transparency. The formal bilateral treaties, moreover, were supplemented by numerous treaties dealing with sectoral issues. For example, five treaties with Tatarstan dealt with banking, currency, oil refining, foreign economic, ownership and related issues, while Sakha (Yakutiya) alone signed fifteen agreements of that type with the federal authorities. Most were not published in the press and, although the federal authorities insisted that these were not international treaties, their precise juridical status was not specified.

The relative hierarchy of laws in Russia appeared to be in question. Did these various treaties take priority over federal laws, supplement them, or trump them? In addition, subjects of the federation signed agreements amongst themselves, bypassing the centre, which further fragmented Russian economic and political space. The law 'On the Principles of Dividing Power . . .' of June 1999, mentioned above, formalised the procedures for the adoption of power-sharing treaties, stressing above all that everything was to be done openly, thus forbidding secret clauses and sub-treaties.

4   Fiscal federalism

The asymmetry in federal relations is reflected in budgetary matters, although fiscal matters can never be fully symmetrical. There is a long way to go before the procedure for distributing transfers among regions becomes both transparent and accurate, with the clear enunciation of the formulae whereby budget revenues are collected and distributed.[22] The allocation of tax revenues at the point of collection and from the federal budget became the defining indicator of Russia's failure to establish itself as a genuine federation.

The principles underlying inter-regional transfers have been the subject of considerable debate.[23] The whole notion of 'donor' or 'subsidised' region depends to a large degree on definitions, on what is included and what is left out in making these calculations. By May 1999 there were only thirteen donor regions,[24] but this did not mean that all the others were recipients: about a third received nothing from the centre. In addition, the various bilateral agreements discussed above allowed differences to emerge in the amounts of tax revenue transferred to the centre. Tatarstan, for example, passed on only 50 per cent of its VAT revenues to the federal budget, while other regions transferred 75 per cent of what is the most effectively collected tax in Russia.

The fundamental fact of fiscal dependency for most remained, although there is little evidence to suggest that the centre used the system of transfer payments for overtly political purposes.[25] Indeed, Daniel Treisman has argued that during Yeltsin's rule transfers were used as 'bribes' to encourage loyalty among the more fractious regions rather than as 'rewards' for those who demonstrated loyalty.[26] Others have argued, however, that transfers to a large degree were depoliticised and reflected relatively objective criteria of need rather than a mechanism of punishment and rewards.[27] Regions dependent on the centre for subsidies, whatever their political complexion, were forced to establish good relations with the Kremlin to ensure the continued flow of funds. The adoption of the budget provided an annual spectacle of bargaining and deals. It was Moscow's enduring control over the allocation and disbursement of funds to the regions that was often considered the main cement holding the federation together.

5   The fragmentation of the national market

Federalism in Russia was undermined by arbitrariness and political inequality. In addition, there was a growing economic divergence between regions that provided an economic basis to federal asymmetries. Some regions have access to world markets through the sale of energy, raw materials or basic finished industrial goods, giving them an independent resource in the federal bargaining game. In this context, it is difficult to talk of 'the regions' as a single unified actor, since that would suggest unified and purposive collective action that would be far from reality.

Central to the development of segmented regionalism is the political economy of the post-Soviet period. Economic 'reform' in the 1990s was not so much a transition from the Soviet forms of economic planning to the market but rather endless exploitation of the opportunities opened up by the transition process itself. Martin Nicholson notes:

> From heady beginnings, when they acquired control over the wealth-creating assets of the former Soviet Union, regional leaders have become locked into an economic system that is neither 'socialist' nor 'capitalist', but a battle of vested interests in which normal economic indicators, including money, play little part.[28]

Joel Hellman characterised this as a 'partial reform equilibrium',[29] although quite why this is considered an 'equilibrium' is unclear. As in politics, the political economy of Yeltsinism looked both forwards (towards the effective liberalisation of the economy and its integration into the global economy) and backwards (towards bureaucratic regulation and arbitrary state interventions). This tension helps in part explain why regions like Primorskii Krai, bordering on China, Korea and Japan, failed to take advantage of the opportunities to integrate into the Pacific Rim market but instead focused on an *oblastnichestvo* ('regionalism') that sparred with the federal authorities but which ultimately remained dependent on Moscow.[30] The regional leadership here (above all the governor, Nazdratenko) and elsewhere concentrated on the expanded opportunities for rent-seeking and other pathologies of a semi-marketised economy to maintain their grip on power. These relations were far from stable, even from the point of view of economic competitiveness, and at some point would give way to a more coherent, although not necessarily more marketised, order.

In this context it should be noted that non-governmental actors were an increasingly important element framing Russia's political and economic space. Above all, the large energy producers and primary materials exporters negotiated directly with subject-level leaderships, and indeed appeared to conduct their own foreign policies. The sectoral fragmentation of Russia, with powerful lobbies enjoying direct access to government at all levels, was reminiscent of the old Soviet economic ministries.[31]

The August 1998 financial crisis stimulated further the 'economisation' of regional politics. Regions and republics, forced back on to their own resources, saw themselves increasingly as autonomous economic subjects and less as part of a single national market.[32] Regional responses fell into two categories:

- measures designed to take control of financial flows, including the refusal to pay taxes to the central budget; and
- laws that tried to control the market by regulating prices and the movement of goods.

Many regions stopped remitting tax revenues to Moscow, and a number introduced price and other controls over their economies. Krasnoyarsk Krai governor Alexander Lebed' and Kemerovo Oblast governor Aman Tuleev, and some others, placed limits on food price rises and imposed restrictions on the movement of foodstuffs, something explicitly banned by federal law, while in Pskov protectionist barriers were established against goods from other regions or neighbouring countries.[33] Many other non-market responses were implemented as regions took advantage of the crisis in the payments system to increase their autonomy. The national market appeared to be breaking down. Some of these measures were temporary and primarily defensive in character as the interdependence of central and regional economies became clear. Nevertheless, an underlying trend towards the imposition of regional administrative controls remained. On 24 June 1999, for example, Kirov Oblast became the third region in Russia, after Khabarovsk Krai and Tyumen' Oblast, to impose price controls on selected food products, industrial goods and services like rented housing, heating and public transport.[34]

The attempt to recreate a national market became one of the central planks of Putin's regional policy. The general weakening of the power of individual regions during his presidency had important economic consequences, particularly in the struggle against Russia's 'virtual economy' (the network of barter and non-payments) that was very much regionally based. At the same time, the federal government began to revoke many of the tax concessions that it had granted under Yeltsin.

6 The regionalisation of foreign policy

Regions began to emerge as international actors in their own right. Between 1991 and 1995 alone, Russian regions signed over 300 agreements on trade, economic and humanitarian cooperation with foreign countries, undermining Moscow's monopoly on foreign relations and shifting attention away from high diplomacy to the pressing needs of Russia's regions. While some regions inhibited problem-solving, particularly those in the Far East that opposed the border settlement with China, others like Kareliya, Pskov and Kaliningrad acted to stabilise their regional foreign relations. Over half of Russia's regions are borderlands, and need the support of the federal authorities in dealing with their neighbours.

Regions were able effectively to impose a veto on foreign-policy initiatives by the centre. This was particularly in evidence during the Kosovo war of 1999, when president Mintimer Shaimiev of Tatarstan threatened to send Tatar volunteers to support the Moslem Albanians if Russian nationalists sent volunteers to assist the Serbian oppressors. The prospect of Russian fighting Russian in the Balkans, in the context where some thirty million Russian citizens had some Islamic heritage, brought the government and public opinion back from the brink of ethnicising Russian foreign policy.[35] The preferences of Russia's regional leaders became part of the complex tapestry of Russia's foreign relations.

The long-term trend for regional elites to try to enter the global market on their own remained, with intensifying attempts to bypass Moscow. Despite the rhetoric of globalisation, however, there are limits to the ability of a region to enter the world market. The conventions of the international financial system, for example, do not allow regions to have a higher credit rating than that of the country as a whole. Thus, when Moscow sneezes, the regions catch a cold. Nevertheless, regions actively sought foreign investment. By 2000 Tatarstan had twenty representations abroad, dealing mainly with economic issues, and the republic had signed fifty-six agreements with foreign institutions. Of course, neither Tatarstan nor Chechnya had achieved anything like external recognition since, as Alan James stresses, 'the concept of state sovereignty – in the sense of constitutional independence – is of fundamental importance for the maintenance of international order.'[36] No country wanted to be seen as supporting the break-up of an existing state – if only out of fear that such an action might boomerang back on itself.

To coordinate regional and federal foreign policy, in October 1997 the Duma adopted a law ensuring that regional authorities liased with the Foreign Ministry over any negotiations with a foreign government.[37] A special department was established by the ministry dealing with inter-regional affairs with branch offices in regions and republics that were particularly active in foreign affairs. The principle that only the federal government had the right to sign international treaties (*dogovory*), however, was jealously guarded, and upheld by numerous judgements of the Constitutional Court.[38]

In these six spheres the Yeltsin system threatened the very viability of the state. The ambiguities in the federal system were exploited by actors in the regions to enhance their privileges and powers, while the central leadership was more concerned with political advantage than the coherence of the state. Segmented regionalism cut across all processes of state building, undermining the emergence of a unified national market, legal space and Russia's coherence as an international actor. There was, moreover, a great variety in regime types, with some taking on increasingly authoritarian forms, something that impeded Russia's development as a democracy. Peter Kirkow, for example, identified the emergence of a type of local corporatism in the regions (on evidence drawn largely from Primorskii Krai), marked by 'the institutional entanglement of politics and economics.'[39] It is this segmentation of political, economic and juridical development against which Putin set his face.

State reconstitution: compacted or pluralistic statism?

The Yeltsinite regional bargain basically suggested to the regions and republics that they had a free hand as long as they did not threaten secession.[40] As in the Ottoman and Habsburg empires, local privileges were granted in return for loyalty. The development of civil society was inhibited since these were privileges granted not to individuals but to corporate groups. The free hand extended to the manipulation of elections (until the abrogation of the results of the elections for the head of Karachaevo-Cherkesiya in May 1999, no election result had been rescinded), allowed the political elites of titular ethnic groups to consolidate their dominance and permitted various types of authoritarian regimes elsewhere. In the context of the segmentation of regional politics, the individual had little recourse.[41] Segmented regionalism threatened the rights of minorities and of individuals. It was in response to this that the countervailing universalistic agenda represented by the national state was asserted.

On coming to power Putin committed himself to the reconstitution of the state. We have suggested that this could take two main forms:

- compacted statism, where the pluralism of civil society and the federal elements in territorial arrangements were threatened; or
- a more pluralistic statism guaranteeing the unimpeded writ of the Constitution, individual rights and the legal division of sovereignty between the centre and the regions.

Segmented regionalism had emerged as one of the greatest threats to the political integrity of the country, but under Putin two processes were in uneasy tension:

- the assertion of state management of the socio-economic and political life of the country; and
- the demands for a genuine devolution of authority to the regions.

Was there a way of making the two processes – state reconstitution and federal decentralisation – not only compatible, but also mutually supportive? Alan James had long asserted that one of the central features of sovereignty 'is that it is an absolute condition.'[42] He had in mind external relations, but the apostles of compacted statism sought to apply the principle of sovereign absolutism to internal affairs as well. Is there, indeed, a zero-sum game involved, in which state reconstitution in the centre will undermine federalism in the regions?

The ambiguous status of regional governors reflected this tension. Although enjoying an autonomous political legitimacy derived from popular election, according to the Constitution (Articles 5.3 and 77.2) they were part of a single vertically-integrated executive structure. In recognition of this, some regional governors themselves called for the abolition of direct elections and the formal resubordination of regional executives to the federal authorities. The attempt by the regions in 1999 to 'storm the Kremlin' through the creation of various governors' blocs was repulsed and then followed by a counter-attack from the centre.

Yeltsin's traditional style of managing the regions, where relative independence and selective privileges had been granted in return for support for the Kremlin at the federal level, now gave way to a period of federal activism. The centrepiece of the new 'state gathering' policy was Putin's decree of 13 May 2000 dividing Russia's eighty-nine regions into seven larger administrative districts. The establishment of an administrative layer between the federal centre and the regions reduced the significance of the latter. The new regions were headed by presidential appointees and were directly subordinate to the president. Instead of restoring the 'executive vertical' as intended, the reform appeared to have established a 'triangle' with the new Federal District (FD) capitals added to relations between the regions and Moscow.

The seven new representatives were responsible for organising the work of federal agencies in the regions (with particular attention to the law-enforcement bodies), monitoring the implementation of federal policy, providing the federal authorities with information on what was going on in the regions, and advising and making recommendations on federal appointments in the region. They were also to work with the eight inter-regional associations to devise social and economic policies. As part of the reform the system of presidential representatives was also abolished. They had not been notably successful in restoring presidential authority; indeed, many had been 'coopted' by the very regional authorities that they had been intended to monitor. The new system would make the emergence of these regional 'policy communities' much more difficult since each of the new presidential representatives would be responsible for a dozen-odd regions. The measure ensured regional conformity to national laws, but in addition the reform had a straightforward administrative rationale: to stop the 'capture' of federal agencies by regional executives, who had often supplied the former with offices, transport and other facilities. The aim was clearly to reassert central control over its own agencies.

The powers of the new 'governors general' soon became clear, and they became an essential element ensuring the development of political and economic reforms. They coordinated the work of federal agencies in the regions, of which there were between thirty-six and fifty-three employing a total staff of 380,000. At last the giant army of federal employees and federal agencies in the regions were resubordinated to Moscow. The seven Federal Districts gradually took on a range of functions. The government as a whole adapted its work to conform to the new administrative pattern. The MVD reorganised its key departments along the lines of the seven super-regions, with new offices established in each of the regions in charge of preliminary investigations. Similarly, the Procurator General set up office in each of the new federal districts, as did the Justice Ministry and the judicial system as a whole. Federal District branches of the Justice Ministry not only examined regional legislation but also ensured that it complied with federal norms. Important federal-level agencies like the treasury and the tax ministry all adapted themselves to the new structure of government. The influence of vested regional interests was diluted as the supremacy of federal legislation was asserted throughout Russia.

Three additional measures confirmed the new model of federal relations. The first changed the way that the Federation Council was formed. The new 'senators' would be delegates of the regional authorities rather than popular representatives. A governor's appointment of a representative could be blocked by a two-thirds majority in the regional legislative assembly within two weeks. Dismissal was also to be approved by a two-thirds majority of the local legislature. There was also a 'soft turnover' of Federation Council members, with governors leaving the Federation Council as their terms expired or by 1 January 2002 at the latest. A large number of governors faced election in autumn 2000, and were not able to return to the upper chamber. Although Putin had made some concessions, the overall package was in line with his aspiration to create a full-time working upper chamber. Thus the Federation Council was replaced by two permanent representatives, one nominated by each region's executive branch and one by the legislature. The new representatives were to be dismissed in the same way as they were selected. The current members of the Federation Council who were not members of local legislatures lost their immunity from criminal prosecution after 1 January 2002.

The second law provided a mechanism whereby the heads of regions could be removed and regional legislatures dissolved if they adopted laws that contradicted federal legislation. Although in principle the courts already enjoyed the power to dismiss governors, two court decisions were required stating that the governor had violated federal law. The attempt to strengthen this right by Putin proved difficult, especially since it had to be approved by the Federation Council, the very body whose membership was under threat. The new law gave the president the right to dismiss governors who had violated federal laws on more than one occasion. A court ruling that the official had broken the law and a letter from the Prosecutor General that a case had been opened against a regional leader regarding a serious crime was required to confirm that a regional leader was facing criminal charges. To dissolve a regional legislature, the president had to submit a bill to the State Duma. The third measure acted as a compensatory mechanism, granting the regional leaders or the president the right to dismiss local authorities subordinate to them.

These three measures were adopted within the framework of the constitution and demonstrated Putin's political skills. Their sum effect was to reduce the influence of regional leaders on federal policy. Conflicts between the federal centre and the regions was now to a degree displaced to the level of relations between the federal districts and individual regions. Centre–regional conflicts were no longer so politicised, and, instead, the courts played a more active role in constitutionalising federal relations. A notable case was the attempt by the head of the Central Federal District, Georgii Poltavchenko, to get Moscow city to abolish its registration (*propiska*) laws. Similar conflicts emerged elsewhere. In the Southern FD, for example, Viktor Kazantsev was confronted with a dispute over control over the electoral system in Ingushetiya, where the republic's authorities effectively cancelled a Duma by-election.

In his book *First Person*, Putin had stressed the importance of an independent judiciary together with greater federal control over the regions,[43] and now he implemented this programme. The reassertion of federal law sought to ensure that Russia became a single legal space, with the principles of legality and individual rights enshrined in the constitution enforced throughout the country. This legal offensive against segmented regionalism brought regional charters, republican constitutions and all other normative acts into conformity with the constitution and federal law.

Regional authorities had long been condemned for transforming their territories into separate fiefdoms where they ruled like the boyars of old, apparently insulated from the writ of federal laws and the constitution. The vote for Putin in March 2000 had been for strong authority which could defend people from the arbitrariness of bureaucrats and ensure the supremacy of law at all levels. Putin's attempts to rein in the regions were not only about the reassertion of federal authority but about the defence of the rights of citizens. The country now was to live according to one constitution and one set of laws regardless of the region where one lived. The era of special privileges for territorial entities was over.

Putin and the regions: evaluation

Thus, the stick, which had bent so strongly towards the republics in the period of the 'parade of sovereignties' in 1990–91, was now pushed back the other way.

As we have suggested above, however, the defence of centralisation to ensure the uniformity of law and legal standards throughout the federation ran perilously close to becoming defederalisation. The presidential representative to the Constitutional Court, Mikhail Mityukov, noted that the reforms 'drew a line as it were under the so-called ideology of the sovereignisation of the subjects of the federation. Their sovereignty is not unlimited.' However, in stressing that their sovereignty 'has limits, strictly defined in the country's Basic Law',[44] he implicitly accepted the concept of shared sovereignty. Putin himself conceded, in a brief visit to Kazan' on 23–24 June 2000, that the normative reconstitution of the state was not all a one-way street, and that while regional laws had to be brought into conformity with federal legislation, in some cases regional laws might be superior to federal norms, in which case the latter should be brought into line with regional practices.[45] Regions like Bashkortostan insisted that its republican laws corresponded more closely to the standards of European law than did the Russian Constitution, and condemned Russia's development as a 'unitary enclave state'.[46] The case of land ownership and sale was a major case where regional legislation had moved far beyond the restrictions exercised at the federal level, and would be very difficult to reverse. Above all, the status of Russia's regions was not clearly defined in the Constitution, while there were numerous ambiguities concerning the delineation of competencies between the centre and the regions and over the definition of the sphere of joint authority. Pressure began to build up in the regions for constitutional amendments that would clarify the rights and the status of the regions.

The manner in which Putin approached the regions is also noteworthy. As he reminded his audience in his televised address of 17 May, in his inaugural speech of 7 May 'I promised you that there would be open government, with policy aims and specific steps clearly explained to citizens.'[47] The use of direct public addresses sought to ensure a popular base for his reforms, but he avoided populistic sloganeering. At the same time, he sought to forge a reform consensus that would include the governors themselves, and thus in his public speeches he did not make broad condemnatory statements against them of the sort that Mikhail Gorbachev had made against his own officials during perestroika. It was clear that Putin went out of his way to demonstrate his openness to enter into dialogue with regional elites.[48] This conciliatory approach was vividly in evidence in the St. Petersburg gubernatorial elections in early 2000, where the Kremlin's favoured candidate, Valentina Matvienko, was dropped once it became clear that she had little chance of beating the incumbent, Vladimir Yakovlev. Instead, Putin reconciled himself to Yakovlev, including a personal visit. Putin kept open channels of communication with other regional and republican leaders who would be prominent in any attempt to reassert the authority of the federal authorities, for example Murtaza Rakhimov in Bashkortostan and Shaimiev in Tatarstan.

In all of his initiatives, Putin tried to avoid alienating the regional leaders by eschewing populistic forms of mobilisation and anti-elite rhetoric. In his television broadcast of 17 May Putin was at pains to stress that his recently announced package of draft laws was 'not directed against regional leaders'; on the contrary, he insisted that 'regional leaders are the most important support for the president and will act as such in the strengthening of our state.'[49] As he put it on a later occasion, the 'management reforms' (*'upravlenchenskoi reformy'*, as he called them), are 'not to limit the rights of the regions. Our historical experience proves that super centralisation and the attempt to manage "all and everything" from Moscow is ineffective . . . I am convinced that the real self-dependency (*samostoyate'nost'*) of the regions is one of the most important achievements of the last decade.'[50]

Although Putin sought to avoid a direct confrontation with regional leaders, the clear effect of the creation of a presidential federal administration was to shift power away from regional elites. As more and more federal agencies shifted their main regional offices to the seven new FD capitals, regional governors lost one of their main sources of local control. As one report put it, they were now reduced to 'ordinary medium-rank officials'.[51] It was not surprising that after an initial calm reaction, there were signs of growing unease in the regions,[52] while the speaker of the Federation Council, Yegor Stroev, criticised several features of Putin's planned reform of the upper chamber.[53] Boris Berezovsky argued that the creation of the seven federal districts would divide regional leaders into first and second classes and could ultimately provoke the disintegration of the country.[54] The fact that five out of seven of the first cohort of 'governors general' came from a security background suggested that the necessary political skills to establish good working relationships with the existing regional leaders might be lacking. Used to military methods, subordination rather than consensus could be their approach.

Fears that the reassertion of federal authority would lead to defederalisation were focused on the implications of the first strand of Putin's policy, the re-establishment of the presidential 'vertical'. Would recentralisation be the same as defederalisation? In his book *First Person* Putin noted: 'But from the very beginning, Russia was created as a super centralised state. That's practically laid down in its genetic code, its traditions, and the mentality of its people.'[55] Were these policies vis-à-vis the regions now a concrete manifestation of these traditions?

The question can be considered within the framework of theories of sovereignty and their relationship to Russian practices. For the republics in Russia, sovereignty came to be equated with federal non-interference in their internal affairs and a degree of economic autonomy. As we have seen above, however, instead of developing a sustained legal framework for federalism, under Yeltsin a segmented regionalism had emerged reflecting not so much the spatial separation of powers but the fragmentation of political authority. Sovereignty claims by regional leaders, including in the republics, gained little support among the non-titular peoples, and even titular groups were divided. The fragmentation of citizenship was particularly resented. A survey in Komi revealed that 60 per cent of the ethnic Russians considered themselves primarily citizens of Russia rather than of the republic.[56]

Regional authorities had long been condemned for transforming their territories into separate fiefdoms where they ruled like the boyars of old, apparently
insulated from the writ of federal laws and the Constitution. The vote for Putin
in March 2000 had been, according to one observer, for 'the instilling of order in
the country and for strong authority which could defend everyone from the high-
handedness of bureaucrats and ensure the supremacy and dictatorship of law at
all levels.'[57] The decrees concerning Bashkortostan and the other regions, in this
light, were not only about the reassertion of federal authority but also about the
defence of the rights of citizens. While the strengthening of the 'vertical power
hierarchy' could be seen as a simple power bid by the centre, it also suggested
that the country was to live according to one constitution and one set of laws
regardless of the region where one lived. It was not surprising, therefore, that
Putin's initiatives were welcomed by regional democratic movements, hoping
that Putin would force regional leaders to live up to international standards of
human rights and democratic accountability.[58] The strengthening of the independence of the judiciary represented an important step on this road. As noted,
however, there remained valid concerns whether the attempt to undermine the
powers of regional leaders would in fact represent an increase in the democratic
rights of citizens. The regional authorities had acted as an important 'check and
balance' against the overweening power of the centre; now this federal element
in the separation of powers had been undermined.[59]

Conclusions

The presidential regime was much weakened in the late Yeltsin years, and the
regional executives sought to fill the vacuum of central authority. The Kremlin
in late 1999 was able to repulse the efforts of the regions to take over the centre,
and then launched a counter-offensive. The Putin phenomenon represented
(among other things) a ground swell of popular revolt against the exploitation
of the rent-seeking opportunities provided by an economy stuck halfway
between the plan and the market and of a political system that institutionalised
competing sovereignty claims and which fragmented the universality of citizen
rights in the nascent national political community.

Segmented regionalism was characterised by the erosion of constitutional
principles of a single legal and economic space. Regional authorities took
advantage of the weakness of the Russian state under Yeltsin to develop a
highly variegated set of policies and political regimes. The concept of asymmetrical federalism disguised the way that national norms guaranteeing individual rights, legal standards and the development of a national market were
undermined by strong regional executives, often little constrained by their own
representative assemblies. It was this segmented regionalism that Putin sought
to reverse, but his attempts to reconstitute the state were torn between compacted and more pluralistic forms of statism. The struggle against segmented
regionalism could easily undermine the development of federalism, and in

taking the form of traditional centralism would threaten the development of Russian democracy.

Notes

1 Some of the themes in the first part of this chapter have been examined in my 'Russian regionalism, policy-making and state development', in Stefanie Harter and Gerald Easter (eds.), *Shaping the Economic Space in Russia: Decision Making Processes, Institutions and Adjustment to Change in the Yeltsin Era* (Aldershot: Ashgate, 2000), Chapter 1, pp. 11–34.

2 Robert Jackson, 'Sovereignty in world politics: a glance at the conceptual and historical landscape', *Political Studies*, 47:3 (1999), 434.

3 For a useful discussion, see S. D. Valentei, *Federalizm: Rossiiskaya Istoriya i Rossiiskaya Real'nost'* (Moscow: Institute of the Economy, Centre for the Socio-Economic Problems of Federalism, RAS, 1998).

4 This is argued, for example, by James Hughes, 'Moscow's bilateral treaties add to confusion', *Transition*, 20 September (1996), 39–43.

5 Richard Sakwa, 'The republicanisation of Russia: federalism and democratisation in transition I', in Chris Pierson and Simon Tormey (eds.), *Politics at the Edge, The PSA Yearbook 1999* (Basingstoke: Macmillan, 1999), Chapter 16, pp. 215–26. See also the second part of the article by Cameron Ross in the same volume, Chapter 17, pp. 227–40.

6 Preston King, *Federalism and Federation* (London: Croom Helm, 1982), p. 77.

7 Graham Smith, 'Mapping the federal condition', in Graham Smith (ed.), *Federalism: The Multiethnic Challenge* (London and New York: Longman, 1995), p. 7.

8 Peter J. Stavrakis, 'Introduction', in Peter J. Stavrakis, Joan DeBardeleben and Larry Blank (eds.), *Beyond the Monolith: The Emergence of Regionalism in Post-Soviet Russia* (Baltimore, MD: Johns Hopkins University Press, 1977), p. 4.

9 Kathryn Stoner-Weiss, 'Central weakness and provincial autonomy: observations on the devolution process in Russia', *Post-Soviet Affairs*, 15:1 (1999), 87–106.

10 Jan-Erik Lane and Svante O. Ersson, *European Politics: An Introduction* (London: Sage, 1996), p. 100.

11 David R. Shearer, *Industry, State, and Society in Stalin's Russia, 1926–1934* (Ithaca, NY: Cornell University Press, 1996).

12 Although see Peter J. Stavrakis, Joan DeBardeleben and Larry Blank (eds.), *Beyond the Monolith*.

13 Radoslav Petkov and Natan M. Shklyar, 'Power to the regions', *Transitions* (March 1999), 40.

14 Mikhail A. Alexseev and Vladimir Vagin, 'Russian regions in expanding Europe: the Pskov connection', *Europe–Asia Studies*, 51:1 (1999), 43–64. See also Mikhail Alexseev and Vladimir Vagin, 'Fortress Russia or gateway to Europe? The Pskov connection', in Mikhail A. Alexseev (ed.), *Center–Periphery Conflict in Post-Soviet Russia: A Federation Imperilled* (Basingstoke: Macmillan, 1999), Chapter 5, pp. 167–204.

15 Mikhail A. Alexseev, 'Introduction: Challenges to the Russian Federation', in Alexseev, *Center–Periphery Conflict*, p. 1.

16 I. Katznelson, *City Trenches* (Chicago, IL: Chicago University Press, 1981).

17 A theme explored by Kathryn Stoner-Weiss, *Local Heroes: The Political Economy of Russian Regional Governance* (Princeton, NJ: Princeton University Press, 1997).

18 *Izvestiya* (4 November 1997); East–West Institute, *Russian Regional Report*, 2:38 (6 November 1997) (hereafter, EWI, *Russian Regional Report*).

19 *RFE/RL Newsline* (20 January 1998).

20 *Rossiiskaya gazeta* (30 June 1999).

21 James Hughes, 'Moscow's bilateral treaties add to confusion', *Transition* (20 September 1996), 43.

22 Aleksei Salmin noted that the margin of error in the calculation of transfers in some cases reached 100 per cent, allowing great scope for bureaucratic arbitrariness and encouraging corruption. Press conference with Sergei Karaganov and other Foreign and Defence Policy Council officials, in *Johnson's Russia List*, 4255 (14 April 2000).

23 The issue is examined in A. Lavrov (ed.), *Federal'nyi Byudzhet i Regiony: Opyt Aanaliza Finansovykh Potokov* (Moscow: Dialog-MGU, 1999). See also S. D. Valentei (ed.), *Ekonomicheskie Problemy Stanovleniya Rossiiskogo Federalizma* (Moscow: Nauka, 1999).

24 EWI, *Russian Regional Report*, 4:20 (27 May 1999).

25 For example, in Pskov, see Darrell Slider, 'Pskov under the LDPR: elections and dysfunctional federalism in one region', *Europe–Asia Studies*, 51:5 (1999), 764.

26 Daniel Treisman, 'The politics of intergovernmental transfers in post-soviet Russia', *British Journal of Political Science*, 26:3 (July 1996), 299–335. See also his 'Deciphering Russia's federal finance: fiscal appeasement in 1995 and 1996', *Europe–Asia Studies*, 50:5 (July 1998), 893–906.

27 Alistair McAuley, 'The determinants of Russian federal–regional fiscal relations: equity or political influence', *Europe–Asia Studies*, 49:3 (May 1997), 431–44.

28 Martin Nicholson, *Towards a Russia of the Regions*, Adelphi Paper, 330 (London: International Institute for Strategic Studies, 1999), p. 35.

29 Joel S. Hellman, 'Winners take all: the politics of partial reform in postcommunist transitions', *World Politics*, 50 (1998), 203–34.

30 Mikhail S. Alexseev and Tamara Troyakova, 'A mirage of the "Amur California": regional identity and economic incentives for political separatism in Primorskii Krai', in Alexseev, *Center–Periphery Conflict*, Chapter 6, pp. 205–46.

31 See Neil Robinson, 'The global economy, reform and crisis in Russia', *Review of International Political Economy*, 6:4 (Winter 1999), 531–64.

32 Robert McIntyre, 'Regional stabilisation policy under transitional period conditions in Russia: price controls, regional trade barriers and other local-level measures', *Europe–Asia Studies*, 50:5 (July 1998), 859–72.

33 Darrell Slider, 'Pskov under the LDPR: elections and dysfunctional federalism in one region', *Europe–Asia Studies*, 51:5 (1999), 761.

34 EWI, *Russian Regional Report*, 4:24 (24 June 1999).

35 *Nezavisimaya gazeta* (26 June 1999); *Izvestiya* (30 June 1999).

36 Alan James, 'The practice of sovereign statehood in contemporary international society', *Political Studies*, 47:3 (1999), 472.

37 *Kommersant-Daily* (31 October 1997).

38 For example, in the case of Gorno-Altai, discussed below, *Rossiiskaya gazeta* (21 June 2000), pp. 5–6.

39 Peter Kirkow, *Russia's Provinces: Authoritarian Transformation versus Local Autonomy?* (Basingstoke: Macmillan, 1998), p. 125.

40 Some of the arguments of this section were outlined in Richard Sakwa, 'Putin's new federalism', EWI, *Russian Regional Report*, 5:21 (31 May 2000), 12–17.
41 For a critique of this, see Grigorii Yavlinskii, 'The last phase of agony', *Obshchaya gazeta* (10–16 June 1999).
42 James, 'The practice of sovereign statehood', 463.
43 Vladimir Putin, *First Person: An Astonishingly Frank Self-Portrait by Russia's President Vladimir Putin*, with Nataliya Gevorkyan, Natalya Timakova, and Andrei Kolesnikov, translated by Catherine A. Fitzpatrick (London: Hutchinson, 2000), pp. 182–3.
44 Aleksandr Shipkin, 'Altai perebral: suvereniteta', *Rossiiskaya gazeta* (10 June 2000), p. 3.
45 EWI, *Russian Regional Report*, 5:25 (28 June 2000).
46 This at least was the view of Zufar Yenikeev, a deputy to the Bashkortiostan State Assembly and Russia's representative to the European Chamber of the Regions, EWI, *Russian Regional Report*, 5:25 (28 June 2000).
47 *Obschchestvennoe Rossiiskoe Televidenie* (ORT), 17 May 2000, 1700 GMT; Sarah Karush and Catherine Belton, 'Putin to tighten grip on regions', *Moscow Times* (18 May 2000).
48 See Mikhail Zherebiatev, 'Yeltsin's successor agrees to early gubernatorial elections', *The Jamestown Foundation, Prism*, 2, Part 1 (February 2000).
49 www.president.kremlin.ru/events/34.html
50 Interview with *Welt am Sontag*, June 2000 (www.president.kremlin.ru/events/38.html).
51 *Moskovskii komsomolets* (24 May 2000).
52 For example, in *Nezavisimaya gazeta* (25 May 2000).
53 *Nezavisimaya gazeta* (6 May 2000).
54 *Kommersant Daily* (31 May 2000).
55 Putin, *First Person*, p. 186.
56 EWI, *Russian Regional Report*, 5:21 (31 May 2000).
57 Mikhail Kushtapin, 'The long expected. and the unexpected', *Rossiiskaya gazeta* (16 May 2000).
58 This, for example, was the case in Tatarstan, as reported by Robert Orttung and Peter Reddaway, EWI, *Russian Regional Report*, 5:25 (28 June 2000).
59 As *Obshchaya gazeta* put it on 25 May 2000, Putin's measures were 'a series of blows against the independence . . . of the regional leaders, who under the conditions of the extreme weakness of the legislative and judicial branches are the single real counterweight to the authoritarianism of the Centre.' Cited in Jamestown Foundation, *Monitor* (25 May 2000).

2 *Matthew Wyman, Stephen White, Ian McAllister and Sarah Oates*

Regional voting patterns in post-communist Russia

Russian elections, a decade into post-communist rule, are less of a mystery than they used to be. Survey-based inquiries, certainly, have found strong and apparently consistent relationships between social characteristics, attitudes and voting behaviour.[1] There is general agreement, across such inquiries, that the old are more pro-communist than the young, that supporters of the Yeltsin administration were better off than their opponents, and that the pro-reform opposition does better among the highly educated and more widely travelled sections of the electorate. Several prominent students of post-communist electoral politics have nonetheless argued that associations of this kind may not be durable, and that political forces of various kinds will find it difficult to establish a distinct social base of a kind that will support them on a continuing basis. To put it another way, a social base that happens to exist at a particular point in time is not the same as a cleavage.[2]

One aspect of Russian voting behaviour that has been relatively neglected in this discussion is its regional dimension. This is in part a result of the fact that it is difficult to shed much light on wider patterns by survey methods because the samples involved are rarely large enough.[3] This chapter suggests an alternative approach, based upon aggregate rather than survey data, to explore the extent to which 'region matters' in Russian voting: or in other words, to establish the extent to which a distinctive regional effect beyond that which can be explained by socio-economic factors exists. To do this, we examine the extent to which observed differences in regional voting patterns can be accounted for by the socio-economic characteristics of the regions with which they are associated. Given the limitations of official data, we have sought to minimise error by creating composite measures of the characteristics in which we are interested. We use factor analysis to identify the relevant variables and then construct four scales representing urbanisation, ethnic composition, age structure, and a combination of prosperity and educational levels. We employ multiple regression to examine the effects of region, once we have controlled for these socio-economic variations; and then we move to the regions themselves, identifying which of them have behaved electorally in a way we would not have expected on the basis of their socio-economic characteristics. We conclude with some reflections on the implications of these findings for Russian electoral politics.

Voting patterns in the regions

Observed regional voting trends show some clear patterns. Communist candidates do best in the northern Caucasus and in the central Russian regions that have become known as the 'red belt'. Yabloko has been particularly successful in the Far East, and in the north-west, including the city of St. Petersburg; it has also done well in regions that have embraced market reforms with more enthusiasm than others. Liberal Democrats have tended to do best in regions that were economically depressed, and badly in regions with an ethnically mixed population. In the 1996 presidential contest Boris Yeltsin emerged with particularly high levels of support in northern Russia, and in his home region of the Urals. The Yabloko leader Grigorii Yavlinsky was also successful in the reformist north. Support for Yedinstvo (Unity) and for Vladimir Putin has been more evenly distributed, but appears notably lower in Siberia and the Far East.

To what extent, therefore, do these patterns simply reflect social differences among the regions, rather than the characteristics of the regions themselves? For example, were regions that supported pro-Kremlin forces distinctive in themselves, or was it simply that richer or better educated parts of the country were more inclined to support the current administration, while poorer ones were more likely to identify with Communists and other oppositional forces? Equally, if there were distinctive patterns, did these persist across elections, and from parliamentary to presidential contests? In comparative perspective we would certainly expect the latter.[4] In the USA, for instance, Southern politics have a character of their own as a result of historical and cultural as well as socio-economic differences. In the United Kingdom, patterns of electoral support for the Labour Party are closely related to the historical strength of non-conformist religions;[5] and in Italy, support for parties of the left is stronger in northern parts of the country that experienced civic self-government in medieval times, and weaker in cities and regions that were under Vatican or monarchical authority.[6]

In order to investigate these relationships, we began by producing workable measures of social structure (details of how the measures were constructed may be found in Appendix 2.1). It should be noted that our measures are for the most part based on data from 1994, when a limited national census was conducted, although data about ethnic composition come from 1989, when the last full-scale census took place in what was then still the USSR.[7] There had clearly been changes in all the relevant parameters by the time of the 1999/2000 elections, but they were rarely of such a magnitude as to alter the position of the regions in relation to each other. It should also be noted that the Chechen and Ingush republics are not incorporated within our calculations, owing to missing data, and that in some of the scales important data are missing for the autonomous regions, which have accordingly been excluded. Collectively the measures used account for around 75 per cent of the variation in constituency characteristics.

The first scale is a measure of the extent to which a particular region is urban and industrial. This is a composite measure consisting of the percentage living in urban areas, the proportion of the workforce employed in industry, the proportion of homes with running water, and the proportion of the workforce not engaged in agriculture. The measure (in this and in the other three cases) was rescaled to run from zero to 100, and was constructed so that a region that scored 100 had the highest scores on these four variables – that is, it had more city dwellers, industrial workers and homes with running water, and the highest proportion of non-agricultural workers – and the region which scored zero was the lowest in all of these. It should be noted that this was simply a way of ranking the regions: quantitative differences among them did not have any particular significance. As it happens, the region that ranked highest on this scale was St. Petersburg, followed by Vladimir, Murmansk, Sverdlovsk and Kemerevo regions. The city of Moscow ranked sixth because, while it scored highly on most of the variables, the proportion of the workforce employed in industry was relatively low. The least urban/industrial parts of Russia were all ethnic areas: the republics of Kalmykiya, Tyva and Dagestan, the Altai republic, and the Agin-Buryat autonomous area.

The second scale can be interpreted as a measure of prosperity and regional educational achievement. It consists of nominal and real incomes, the proportion of households with telephones, the proportion of the population with a higher education, and the proportion employed in education, science or the arts. Intuitively the combination of these factors makes sense, since higher educational achievement tends to be associated with larger incomes, and regions that are richer can afford to spend more on education. The more prosperous and better educated regions, on these measures, were Moscow and St. Petersburg (by a very large margin), and then Kamchatka, the Koryak autonomous area, and the oil-rich republic of Sakha (Yakutiya); the poorest and least educated were the Kurgan, Volgograd, Tambov, Orenburg and Kirov regions.

The third scale takes account of ethnic differences, combining the percentage of Russians in a region, average family size and the proportion of the population unemployed, since it turns out that many of Russia's ethnic regions have also been disproportionately affected by unemployment. On this scale, the highest ranked were the Dagestan, Kabardino-Balkariya, Tyva, Kalmyk and Karachaevo-Cherkass republics; the lowest-ranking were the central Russian heartland regions of Lipetsk, Kaluga, Voronezh, Tver' and Belgorod. The fourth measure reflects the age structure of the region, combining as it does the proportion of a region's population aged between sixty and seventy-two, the percentage of pensioners, and the proportion of the population above working age. The regions with the oldest populations were Tula, Pskov, Tver', the Moscow region and Yaroslavl'. The rich west Siberian region of Tyumen', its two autonomous areas Khanty-Mansiisk and Yamalo-Nenets, as well as Magadan and the Koryak autonomous areas, were the least elderly, these being places where younger Russians went to earn higher wages but certainly not to retire. It should be noted that regions, of course, vary enormously in size and population, and many contain differences on the dimensions in which we are interested that are greater than those that exist between the regions themselves.

Regional differences in voting patterns

Having defined our scales, the next task is to investigate their relationship to voting behaviour. This is done by means of a simple OLS regression equation of the following form:

$$\text{VOTE} = \text{URBAN} + \text{WEALTH} + \text{ETHNIC} + \text{OLD} + \text{REGION},$$

where REGION involves six 'dummy' variables, for the North-West, North Caucasus, Volga, Urals, Siberian and Far East federal districts. We expected that Yeltsin/pro-government regions would be those in which levels of wealth and urbanicity were the highest, and in which average ages were relatively low. We were uncertain about the effects of ethnicity. Where levels of support for the Communists were at their highest we expected levels of urbanicity and wealth would be low, but that average ages would be relatively high. We were less sure, again, about the effects of ethnicity, which has been associated with oppositional voting in the past but which is most often relevant in regions where the local leadership has shown a consistent ability to mobilise support for a party or candidate of its own choosing.

Tables 2.1–2.2 apply our model to Communist and to pro-Kremlin voting from 1993–2000. The tables should be read as follows. The figures represent the constant term (a) and partial regression (b) coefficients, as well as the percentage of the variation explained by each of the independent variables. For each of the four scales, the b-coefficient represents the change in the vote that is equivalent to a one-point move on the 1–100 scale. So, for example, looking at the 2000 presidential election, Vladimir Putin was predicted to obtain a 0.21 per cent greater share of the vote in a region that was 1 per cent more ethnic or, to put it another way, the most non-Russian region was expected to vote 21 per cent more in favour of Putin, all other characteristics of the region being held constant. For the regional variable, the figure is an actual percentage. In that election, regional location in the North-Western federal district gave Putin an 8.7 per cent improvement in his share of the vote compared with what might have been expected given the region's socio-economic characteristics.

What do these data tell us about the relative importance of the various social structural factors in explaining regional voting patterns in the last decade? Overall, the model is a reasonable fit in most cases, explaining from one third to just over two thirds of the variance in regional voting. In comparative perspective, this is not an especially large figure: for example, in their analysis of the United Kingdom in the 1970s, Rose and McAllister were able to use social structural variables to explain around three quarters of the vote for the Labour and Conservative parties. A combination of factors may be responsible. First, this kind of analysis is still new for Russia, and there is little consensus about precisely what the significant independent variables are. Some error may accordingly have been introduced by our having omitted particular variables. Second, the data that are available to us have serious shortcomings. Not all data are available for all regions, and they relate to 1989 and 1994 rather than to the years in which voting was taking place, which may have modified their effect. There are also reasons to suppose that the social structural characteristics of regions might have had less effect in the 1990s than at other times and in other societies, given that the period was one of rapid and unsettling change in long-established patterns.

Nevertheless, it is still possible to identify social-structural factors that do underlie voting patterns for most of the more significant political forces in post-communist Russia. Let us first consider voting for the candidates who were broadly referred to as 'the party of power' at the time of the votes in question. What stands out most from these data is how very different the regional bases of support were in each of the three rounds of elections, 1993, 1995–96 and 1999–2000. Russia's Choice in 1993, as a firmly pro-market party, gained the strongest support in more urban/educated and wealthier parts of Russia. However, the degree of urbanicity made very little difference to support for Yeltsin or Putin, except in the second round of the 1996 vote, when we can assume that supporters of the democratic opposition voted for Yeltsin as the lesser of two evils. The data also emphasise how fundamentally different the regional support patterns for Yeltsin and for Putin are. Regional prosperity was the best explanation of pro-Yeltsin voting, but Putin's strongest support came from ethnic republics. Not surprisingly, Siberia and the Far East show a consistently higher degree of hostility to the occupants of the Kremlin than other parts of Russia.

The regional basis of voting for the Communist Party of the Russian Federation (KPRF) also appears to have differed from election to election. In 1993, the non-Russian parts of the country had been more pro-Communist even than their socio-economic status would lead us to expect, but in the last two presidential elections, their support had moved away towards the Kremlin's favourites. In the 1995 Duma election, the relative wealth and ethnic composition of a region appear to have been relatively unimportant factors. The most significant variable turns out to be age, with regions that have a higher proportion of older people favouring the Communists. Once again, location in some regions did appear to have made a difference beyond that which might be explained by social-structural factors. Voting patterns for Genadii Zyuganov are much more consistent. The most important explanatory variables underlying them in the first round of the presidential election were rurality, wealth and age structure, and, once again, location in the North-West of Russia. The patterns became still more pronounced in round two. Zyuganov was consolidating the votes of

Table 2.1 Voting for the Communist Party and Zyuganov, 1993–99

	Duma elections						Presidential elections					
	1993		1995		1999		1996 round 1		1996 round 2		2000	
	B	% variance explained	B	% variance explained	B	% variance explained	B	% variance explained	B	% variance explained	B	% variance explained
Urban	-0.13*	9	-0.1	6	-0.07	6	-0.19**	13	-0.18**	11	-0.14**	10
Money	-0.1	6	-0.1	5	-0.16**	12	-0.19*	10	-0.3**	15	-0.17**	10
Ethnic	0.23**	14	0.11	6	0.02	1	0.14*	8	-0.09	5	-0.12*	7
Age	0.07	4	0.23*	11	0.11	8	0.19	10	0.12	6	0.02	1
North-West	-9.9**	11	-7.3*	7	-8.3**	11	-13.1**	13	-11.0**	10	-10.4**	12
North Caucasus	0.4	–	2.6	2	3.9	5	0.1	–	-1.6	2	-2.6	3
Volga	-1.3	2	-1.1	1	-0.7	1	2.3	3	0.5	1	-1.4	2
Urals	-6.3	4	-5.9	3	-3.9	3	-7.1	5	-7.3	5	-3.4	3
Siberia	-7.3*	9	1.3	1	0.8	1	-0.2	–	3.1	3	1.9	2
Far East	-7.6	9	4.3	3	3.0	4	-0.9	1	2.8	3	2.7	3
Constant	26.8		14.8		26.4		36.6		54.9		45.2	
r²	.68		.46		.53		.63		.61		.52	

Notes: * p<0.05; ** p<0.01

Table 2.2 Pro-Kremlin voting, 1993–2000

| | Duma elections | | | | | | Presidential elections | | | | | |
| | Russia's Choice 1993 | | NDR 1995 | | Yedinstvo 1999 | | Yeltsin 1996 round 1 | | Yeltsin 1996 round 2 | | Putin 2000 | |
	B	% variance explained	B	% variance explained	B	% variance explained	B	% variance explained	B	% variance explained	B	% variance explained
Urban	0.11**	16	-0.02	1	-0.04	2	0.01	–	0.15*	9	0.03	2
Money	0.12**	14	0.12**	6	-0.13	4	0.32**	16	0.32**	16	0.05	2
Ethnic	-0.06	7	0.09*	5	-0.05	2	0.05	3	0.11	5	0.21**	11
Age	-0.02	3	-0.07	4	-0.29**	10	-0.09	4	-0.1	5	-0.09	5
North-West	2.4	5	-0.9	1	3.9	2	5.5	5	9.9**	9	8.7**	8
North Caucasus	-0.9	2	-1.4	1	-3.9	2	-0.9	1	2.4	2	0.3	–
Volga	–	–	-0.2	–	-8.5*	6	0.7	1	-0.4	–	-1.6	1
Urals	2.5	4	-3.4	2	-6.0	2	7.4	4	7.4	4	-1.0	1
Siberia	-0.6	2	-5.2*	5	-2.4	2	-3.3	3	-3.6	4	-12.4**	12
Far East	-4.7*	10	-9.1**	8	-2.6	2	-6.7	6	-4.2	4	-8.5	7
Constant	8.4		13.6		54.3		31.5		39.3		54.1	
r²	0.64		0.35		0.34		0.43		0.59		0.50	

Notes: * p < 0.05; ** p < 0.01; NDR = Our Home is Russia

regions that were relatively worse off, but which in the first round had cast their votes for other opponents of the existing government. The presidential contest of the spring of 2000 showed identical patterns of regional support.

A couple of points are worth making about the overall findings. First, it is striking in comparative terms that no single variable is dominant in its effect. Rather, the most important components of the regional vote differ across political groupings and over time. Our findings tend accordingly to support the views of those who argue that divisions within Russian politics are still highly fluid and not yet anchored in structural cleavages in the way that analysts of elections in longer-established democracies might otherwise have expected.[8] Our findings also suggest that region as an independent variable does matter. Regional cultural and political differences are clearly a factor that can influence voting behaviour, even at the relatively high level of aggregation that we have employed.

Regions and their deviations

In the final stage of our analysis we consider 'deviant regions' in which levels of support in the various elections were substantially above or below the levels predicted by our model (see Tables 2.3–2.5). These are less wealthy regions that, for instance, voted for Yeltsin, or more industrial ones that voted for Zyuganov. We have sought to do no more than identify such deviant regions; a convincing analysis of the reasons for their electoral behaviour would of course require a detailed, case by case discussion of a kind that cannot be attempted within the confines of this chapter. Our central concern, in this final section, is whether there are conditions in each of these regions that make them behave in an unusual way.

If one looks at the list of deviant regions, a number of points stand out. First, the behaviour of several of the predominantly non-Russian republics is highly distinctive. For example, Tyva and Kalmykiya were considerably more pro-Kremlin than might have been expected given their socio-economic characteristics. It might, of course, be that the political orientations of Tyvans and Kalmyks are different from those of a comparable group within the wider population, or that the same is true of the Russian minorities that live in those republics. But it is much more likely that the distinctive voting patterns that we observe in these republics reflect the particular conditions within which their political life is conducted. All Russian regions, even those that are net contributors to the national budget, have reasons to seek the favour of the Kremlin administration. But in some, whether through a network of patron–client relations or through open intimidation, leaders are in a particularly good position to ensure that the local population votes in accordance with their wishes. Some particularly striking examples of this kind have taken place in Bashkortostan and Tatarstan. Nationally, for instance, there were sixty electoral districts with a turnout of more than 90 per cent in the first round of the 1996 presidential contest; twenty-five of these were in Bashkortostan, and twenty-four in Tatarstan.[9] In many of them, the voting results 'strikingly coincided with the current interests of local

Table 2.3 Yeltsin over/underprediction, 1996 round 2

Underprediction	%	Overprediction	%
Kalmykiya	25.3	North Osetiya	−18.4
Sverdlovsk	21.8	Chuvashiya	−15.1
Perm'	19.3	Kemerovo	−13.5
Vologda	16.2	Penza	−12.1
Tuva	14.8	Adygeya	−10.6
Tatarstan	12.0	Ulyanovsk	−9.8
Leningrad Region	11.3	Mari El	−9.8
Novgorod	10.7	Bryansk	−9.7
Kareliya	10.4	Orel	−8.9
Kabardino-Balkarya	10.3	Altai Krai	−8.8
Kaliningrad	9.2	Belgorod	−8.7
Arkhangel	8.9	Novosibirsk	−8.5
Moscow Region	8.5	Kamchatka	−8.5
Yaroslavl'	7.6	Amur	−8.5
Murmansk	7.3	Smolensk	−8.4
Tver'	6.7	Tambov	−7.6
Chelyabinsk	5.7	Khakasiya	−6.9
Kirov	5.3	Kursk	−6.7
Rostov	5.3	Buryatiya	−6.7
Krasnodar Krai	4.3	Voronezh	−6.5
Tomsk	4.1	Sakhalin	−6.2
Komi Republic	4.1	Magadan	−5.7
City of St. Petersburg	3.8	Lipetsk	−5.7
Kurgan	3.8	Chita	−5.6
Bashkortostan	3.5	Mordoviya	−5.0
Tula	3.2	Karachai-Cherkesiya	−4.1
Dagestan	2.9	Krasnoyarsk Krai	−3.3
Pskov	2.7	Irkutsk	−3.1
Ivanovo	2.5	Ryazan'	−3.0
Kostroma	2.4	Kaluga	−2.9
Sakha (Yakutiya)	1.9	Omsk	−2.8
Khabarovsk Krai	0.4	Tyumen'	−2.7
Vladimir	0.2	Orenburg	−2.6
Volgograd	0.2	Stavropol' Krai	−2.1
Chukot Autonomous Okrug	0.1	City of Moscow	−2.0
		Udmurtiya	−1.7
		Saratov	−1.6
		Astrakhan	−1.5
		Jewish Autonomous Oblast	−0.6
		Primorskii Krai	−0.3
		Samara	−0.3
		Nizhnii Novgorod	−0.2
		Altai Republic	−0.1

Table 2.4 Yedinstvo over/underprediction, 1999

Underprediction	%	Overprediction	%
Tuva	38.4	Chuvashiya	−14.9
Pskov	13.0	Bashkortostan	−14.2
Kostroma	11.0	City of Moscow	−12.1
Magadan	10.8	Tatarstan	−11.5
Chukot Autonomous Okrug	10.6	Karachai-Cherkesiya	−10.9
Yaroslavl'	9.6	Moscow Region	−10.6
Kemerovo	9.6	Mordoviya	−10.0
Udmurtiya	9.4	Tomsk	−9.6
Kaliningrad	8.9	Omsk	−8.3
Kareliya	8.2	Lipetsk	−8.2
Kirov	7.2	Jewish Autonomous Oblast	−8.1
Ivanovo	7.1	Samara	−7.0
Voronezh	6.8	Perm'	−6.9
Novgorod	6.7	Novosibirsk	−6.9
Leningrad Region	6.6	Orenburg	−6.5
Tver'	5.6	Sakha (Yakutiya)	−6.4
Komi Republic	4.9	Mari El	−5.9
Kursk	4.8	Altai Republic	−5.6
Vologda	4.8	Altai Krai	−5.6
Irkutsk	4.6	Buryatiya	−5.5
Astrakhan	4.6	Saratov	−5.3
Rostov	4.5	Kurgan	−5.2
Murmansk	4.3	Tyumen'	−5.2
Amur	3.1	Chelyabinsk	−4.8
Vladimir	3.1	Ulyanovsk	−4.5
Sverdlovsk	2.7	Kabardino-Balkariya	−4.1
Smolensk	2.6	Adygeya	−2.6
Khakasiya	2.4	Primorskii Krai	−2.5
Volgograd	2.3	Kaluga	−2.0
North Osetiya	2.2	Chita	−1.9
Tula	2.2	Nizhnii Novgorod	−1.8
Penza	2.1	Belgorod	−1.5
Arkhangel	1.2	Khabarovsk Krai	−1.5
Dagestan	0.3	Ryazan'	−1.4
Krasnoyarsk Krai	0.0	City of St. Petersburg	−1.3
		Krasnodar Krai	−1.3
		Tambov	−1.1
		Stavropol' Krai	−1.0
		Sakhalin	−0.9
		Bryansk	−0.8
		Kamchatka	−0.5
		Orel	−0.3
		Kalmykiya	−0.2

Table 2.5   Putin over/underprediction, 2000

Underprediction	%	Overprediction	%
Vologda	16.8	Kemerovo	−27.1
Chukot Autonomous Okrug	15.6	Altai Republic	−14.8
Tatarstan	15.4	Buryatiya	−12.7
Novgorod	14.1	Chuvashiya	−12.6
Leningrad Region	13.4	Omsk	−12.2
Dagestan	11.8	Mari El	−12.0
Murmansk	11.4	Novosibirsk	−11.6
Kabardino-Balkariya	11.2	Jewish Autonomous Oblast	−11.5
Pskov	11.2	City of Moscow	−11.1
Sverdlovsk	9.5	Primorskii Krai	−11.0
Yaroslavl'	9.3	Adygeya	−10.3
Perm'	9.2	Samara	−10.2
Magadan	9.1	Khakasiya	−9.9
Kareliya	8.1	Sakhalin	−9.4
Kirov	8.0	Bryansk	−8.2
Kostroma	7.8	Karachai-Cherkesiya	−7.7
Saratov	7.7	North Osetiya	−7.7
Kaliningrad	7.4	Lipetsk	−7.5
Tver'	7.0	Moscow Region	−6.8
Voronezh	6.8	Altai Krai	−6.0
Astrakhan	6.7	Orenburg	−5.1
Arkhangel	6.4	Tula	−4.5
Bashkortostan	5.7	Kamchatka	−4.1
Mordoviya	5.4	Chelyabinsk	−3.9
Udmurtiya	5.3	Orel	−3.7
Tuva	4.1	Krasnoyarsk Krai	−3.5
Tyumen'	3.8	Ulyanovsk	−3.4
City of St. Petersburg	3.7	Penza	−3.3
Komi Republic	3.1	Ivanovo	−3.0
Kalmykiya	2.8	Khabarovsk Krai	−2.9
Rostov	2.3	Tambov	−2.6
Krasnodar Krai	2.2	Sakha (Yakutiya)	−1.8
Stavropol' Krai	1.9	Irkutsk	−1.6
Volgograd	1.9	Kaluga	−1.5
Kursk	1.2	Amur	−1.5
Nizhnii Novgorod	1.2	Ryazan'	−1.4
Tomsk	1.0	Chita	−0.9
Kurgan	0.7	Vladimir	−0.9
Smolensk	0.4	Belgorod	−0.7

elites'. Equally, there were many cases in which there had been dramatic shifts of electoral loyalty from the Duma to the presidential election, or between the two rounds of the 1996 presidential contest. The methods that were employed in such circumstances were strongly reminiscent of those of Soviet times.

Another, more predictable feature of the data in Table 2.3 is that it reflects a bonus for Yeltsin in his home region of the Urals, particularly in Sverdlovsk and Perm'. Interestingly, however, Zyuganov did not do very much better in his home region of Orel than might have been expected from its socio-economic characteristics. The appeal was far more party based and less individually based in his case. The parts of the country where the then President Yeltsin did worse than expected were for the most part more remote and included a number of ethnic republics, such as Mari-El, Mordoviya and Chuvashiya, which unlike Tyva and Kalmykiya are republics where Russians make up the majority of the population. A few of the Siberian regions were also particularly hostile to the President, such as the coal-mining centre of Kemerovo, where economic conditions are particularly difficult and the local governor was closely associated with the opposition cause, and Magadan. As well as the republics already discussed, the regions where Zyuganov did worse than expected were almost all more northerly. Again, what it is that caused the greater degree of hostility to Zyuganov and the Communist Party in these parts of the world is less well understood by analysts than it should be (it is unlikely to be temperature).

Overall then, there is little doubt that we are in a position to identify a regional effect above and beyond that which we might expect to exist on the basis of their social and economic characteristics. What remains unclear is what precisely it is about the different areas that causes these clearly identifiable differences to occur. This reflects our lack of knowledge about regional cultural differences and our limited ability to identify and assess differences in local political conditions, two areas that are highly promising fields for future research of both a case-study nature and a more broadly comparative nature. We note, for instance, that 'regional effects' are in fact confined to relatively few parts of this vast and heterogeneous country, notably to the north-west and to the areas east of the Urals. In comparative terms, it may be this relative lack of diversity that is the most striking feature of post-communist Russia's electoral geography.

Appendix 2.1 Scale construction

Since one of the major problems of regression analysis is multicollinearity, that is to say the interdependence of independent variables – and also because of the potential inaccuracies of taking any one measure as a proxy for a particular social structural category, we decided to create composite measures for our social-structural categories – using variables indicated by a prior-factor analysis. In each case the variables were converted to standard scores, according to the following formula:

$$\text{new value} = \frac{\text{old value} - \text{mean value}}{\text{standard deviation}}$$

This transformation was carried out in order to ensure that each item made the same contribution to the overall scale. If this had not been done then, for example, the income variable (varying between 91 and 691) would have overwhelmed, say, the education variable (measured in percentages). Then, to try to minimise problems caused by skewed distributions, cases that were more than ±2.5 standard deviations from the sample mean were recoded as ±2.5. The scales were then constructed as follows (with each variable expressed in standard scores):

$$URBAN = \frac{\% \text{ urban} + (100 - \% \text{ farm workers}) + \% \text{ industrial workers} + \% \text{ homes with running water}}{4}$$

$$WEALTH = \frac{\text{nominal income} + \text{real income} + \% \text{ of homes with own phone} + \% \text{ of adult population with higher education} + \% \text{ employed in education, science or culture}}{5}$$

$$ETHNICITY = \frac{\% \text{ non-Russian} + \text{average family size} + \% \text{ unemployed}}{3}$$

$$OLD = \frac{\% \text{ aged } 60\text{–}72 + \% \text{ pensioners} + \% \text{ of population above working age}}{3}$$

Since the resulting scales were difficult to interpret, they were then manipulated in such a way that the region which was highest on the scale would score 100, and the lowest would score zero. This was achieved by subtracting the minimum score from each value of the scale, dividing by the range throughout and then multiplying by 100. The scales were not designed to be completely independent, but are sufficiently so for a regression to be interpretable. Their covariation is:

	Age	Ethnic	Money	Urban
Age	1.0000 (85)	−0.5270 (84) $p=.000$	−0.2357 (84) $p=.031$	0.3088 (84) $p=.004$
Ethnic	−0.5270 (84) $P=.000$	1.0000 (86)	0.0381 (83) $p=.733$	−0.4617 (84) $p=.000$
Money	−0.2357 (84) $P=.031$	0.0381 (83) $P=.733$	1.0000 (84)	0.3258 (84) $p=.002$
Urban	0.3088 (84) $p=.004$	−0.4617 (84) $p=.000$	0.3258 (84) $p=.002$	1.0000 (85)

Notes

1 See, for example, M. Wyman, 'Developments in Russian voting behaviour: 1993 and 1995 compared', *Journal of Communist Studies and Transition Politics*, 12:3 (1996),

277–92; S. White, R. Rose and I. McAllister, *How Russia Votes* (Chatham, NJ: Chatham House, 1997); M. Wyman, S. White and S. Oates (eds.), *Elections and Voters in Post-Communist Russia* (Cheltenham and Northampton, MA: Elgar, 1998); and T. J. Colton, *Transitional Citizens* (Cambridge, MA: Harvard University Press, 2000).

2 G. Evans and S. Whitefield, 'Identifying the bases of party competition in East Central Europe', *British Journal of Political Science*, 23:4 (October 1993), 521–48; and P. Mair, 'What is different about post-communist party systems?' in Mair, *Party System Change: Approaches and Interpretations* (Oxford: Clarendon Press, 1997), pp. 175–98.

3 Although see, for example, R. S. Clem and P. R. Craumer, 'The regional dimension', in L. Belin and R. W. Orttung, *The Russian Parliamentary Elections of 1995* (Armonk, NY and London: M. E. Sharp, 1997), Chapter 8.

4 Relevant to the UK are I. McAllister and R. Rose, *The Nationwide Competition for Votes* (London: Frances Pinter, 1984); and W. L. Miller, *Electoral Dynamics* (London and Basingstoke: Macmillan, 1977).

5 See P. Pulzer, *Political Representation and Elections in Britain*, 3rd edition (London: George Allen and Unwin, 1975).

6 R. Putnum, *Making Democracy Work* (Princeton, NJ: Princeton University Press, 1993).

7 For the 1989 census see *Itogi Vsesoiznoi perepisi naseleniya 1989 g.* (Minneapolis, MN: East View Publications, 1991–93).

8 R. Rose, N. Munro and S. White, *The 1999 Duma Vote: A Floating Party System* (Glasgow: Centre for the Study of Public Policy, University of Strathclyde, SPP 331, 2000).

9 *Vybory Prezidenta Rossiiskoi Federatsii 1996. Eleektoral'naya statistika* (Moscow: Ves' mir, 1996), pp. 188, 190.

Political parties and regional democracy

Role and function of political parties: importance for democracy

Whilst there is some debate about the importance of parties in contemporary industrial societies, most scholars would still agree with Geoffrey Pridham that, 'parties and party systems must remain a basic if not the central theme for examining not only the quality of the liberal democracy in question but also its progress towards and achievement of democratic consolidation.'[1] As Juan J. Linz notes, 'Today, in all countries of the world, there is no alternative to political parties in the establishment of democracy. No form of nonparty representation that has been advocated has ever produced democratic government.'[2] And Peter Mair adds that, 'However fragmented, weak, or undisciplined, however poorly rooted in society, however unstable and vociferous, parties are a very real and necessary part of the politics of new democracies. Democracy cannot be sustained without competing political parties.'[3] Parties are particularly important during regime transitions and the consolidation of democracy where they play a vital role in bolstering system legitimacy at a time of political uncertainty.[4] And strong and cohesive national parties have an important integrative function in federal states binding together the diverse subjects of the federation.

According to Hague, Harrop and Breslin, parties perform four vital functions in modern democracies:

1 as agents of elite recruitment, parties serve as the major mechanism for preparing and recruiting candidates for public office;
2 as agents of interest aggregation parties transform a multitude of specific demands into more manageable packages of proposals . . .
3 parties serve as a point of reference for many supporters and voters, giving people a key to interpreting a complicated political world; and
4 modern parties offer direction to government, performing the vital task of steering the ship of state.[5]

Scholars in the field have traditionally been divided over which prerequisites are necessary for the creation of a strong party system. One group stresses the external environment in which parties operate: the political culture and the strength of civil society. From this perspective, parties are seen as dependent variables, and their ability to develop successfully is determined by these external cultural factors. As Karen Dawisha notes, 'a strong civil society is a necessary but not sufficient condition for a strong party and system and it is difficult to find examples where parties have been established in states with weak civil cultures.'[6] In contrast, a second group of scholars focus on the internal structures, leadership and operational behaviour of parties. In this second approach, parties are seen as independent variables whose actions can positively or negatively shape civil society and culture. Here, institutions matter: change the institutions, change the culture. Strong cohesive parties can bring about consolidated democracies even in hostile cultural environments. Democratic parties can create democrats. But, just as equally, weakly institutionalised parties and party systems can allow authoritarianism to take root. Hence, before parties can play their vital role in the process of consolidating democracy, parties themselves must be institutionalised and consolidated.

According to Scott Mainwaring, institutionalisation 'means the process by which a practice or organisation becomes well established and widely known, if not universally accepted'. Strongly institutionalised parties exhibit the following characteristics:

1   high degrees of stability of interparty competition and low electoral volatility;
2   strong roots in society;
3   'unassailable support and legitimacy from elites and citizenry who believe them to be fundamental, necessary and desirable';
4   strong, disciplined and territorially comprehensive organisations with well established structures and procedures; significant material and human resources, and an independent status not overshadowed by a personalistic leader or coterie.

Mainwaring contrasts the highly institutionalised parties largely to be found in Western Europe and North America with the weakly institutionalised 'inchoate' parties of the 'third wave democracies' in Eastern Europe and Russia.[7]

Political parties in Russia

There has already been a significant body of work devoted to the study of parties in Russia at the national level[8] but very little has, as yet, been published on the development of parties at the regional level.[9] In this chapter I focus on the participation of 'national' parties[10] in elections for regional assemblies and governors. In contrast to previous studies, based on a small sample of case studies, I provide a macro-level analysis covering all eighty-nine of Russia's regions. In addition to the study of national parties in elections at the regional level I also examine the territorial comprehensiveness of national parties as indicated by their participation in the December 1999 elections to the State Duma.

Political parties and democratisation in Russia

Since the adoption of the Russian Constitution in December 1993, Russian citizens have been given the opportunity to engage in three rounds of national
elections (1993, 1995 and 1999) and two rounds of presidential elections (in
1996 and 2000). In addition, two rounds of elections have now also been held
for the vast majority of Russia's eighty-nine regional executive and legislative
bodies. As I demonstrate below, Russia is still a long way from creating a
viable and stable party system. Whilst there has been some progress in the
consolidation and solidification of political parties at the national level,[11]
their participation in regional level politics, if anything, has declined since
1995. As is documented below, the vast majority of elections for regional
assemblies and executive bodies have been, and continue to be, largely partyless. All four of Mainwaring's factors of institutionalisation are still very weak
in Russia.

Elections to regional assemblies

Of the 3,481 deputies elected to eighty-three of Russia's eighty-nine republics
and regions, in post as of January 1998, only 635 (18.4 per cent) were members
of national political parties. A study of individual legislatures shows that party
representation is very weak, with seventeen of Russia's regional assemblies
having no party representation at all.[12] Moreover, in only five assemblies did
party members comprise a majority of the deputies corps: in Krasnoyarsk Krai
(80.4 per cent), Novosibirsk Oblast (55.1 per cent), Kemerovo Oblast (57.1 per
cent), Ryazan' Oblast (50.0 per cent) and Sverdlovsk Oblast (69.3 per cent) (see
Appendix 3.1). No party held a majority of the seats in any of Russia's eighty-
nine regional assemblies, and there were only ten chairs of assemblies with a
party affiliation.[13]

The political orientations of legislative assemblies

Of those 635 deputies with a party affiliation in January 1998 by far the largest
number belonged to the Communist Party of the Russian Federation (KPRF)
(279 deputies or 44.0 per cent) which won seats in forty-two regions. However,
overall the Communists' 279 seats made up only 8.0 per cent of the total (see
Table 3.1). All of the other political parties had a minimal presence, none comprising even as much as 1 per cent of the total number of deputies. Thus, for
example, the Agrarian Party of Russia (APR) won a mere twenty-eight seats in
seven assemblies, the National Patriotic Union of Russia (NPSR) won twenty-
six seats in three assemblies, Yabloko won twenty-two seats in eight assemblies;
Our Home is Russia (NDR) won eighteen seats in twelve assemblies, and the
Liberal Democratic Party of Russia (LDPR) won fifteen seats in just six assemblies.

Table 3.1 Number of seats won by candidates of national parties and number of assemblies in which parties held seats in January 1998

Name of party	Total no. of seats	No. of assemblies
KPRF	279	42
APR	28	7
KEDR	1	1
DVR	2	1
CO	11	4
RP	1	1
RKRP	9	5
LDPR	15	6
NPSR	26	3
NDR	18	12
YABLOKO	22	8
PST	1	1
NPR	1	1
KRO	2	1
Others	219	45

Source: 'Parties in Assemblies', special report prepared for the author by the Russian Central Electoral Commission, no author, January 1998.

Notes: KPRF = Communist Party of the Russian Federation; APR = Agrarian Party of Russia; KEDR = Ecological Party of Russia; DVR = Russia's Democratic Choice; CO = Honour and Fatherland; RP = Republican Party; RKRP = Russian Communist Workers' Party; LDPR = Liberal Democratic Party of Russia; NPSR = National Patriotic Union of Russia; NDR = Our Home is Russia; PST = Party of Independent Workers; NPR = People's Party of Russia; KRO = Congress of Russian Communities

Participation of public associations and blocks 1995–97

There has been a proliferation of parties and political movements in Russia. Over the period 1991–97 a total of 5,000 parties and 60,000 public organisations were registered with the Ministry of Justice.[14] There are wide regional variations in the political activism of public associations ('obshchestvennykh ob'edinenii') and blocks. In the statistics that follow I have taken data from elections to seventy-two regional assemblies conducted over the period 1995–97 (here we include information about national and regional parties/associations). Of the 17,900 candidates, 4,600 (or 25.7 per cent) were nominated by such associations.[15] And public associations participated in sixty-four of the seventy-two elections examined.

The most active public associations were to be found in Moscow City, where forty-four associations nominated candidates for elections to the City Duma, followed by Krasnoyarsk Krai which nominated forty-one candidates; Kemerovo Oblast (36 candidates); Novosibirsk Oblast (24); Udmurtiya republic (23); The State Council of the Republic of Komi (22).[16] A positive development in party institutionalisation has been the formation of electoral coalitions and blocks. Over the period 1995–97 fifty-five blocks (uniting 187 public associations) were created in twenty-four regions. The largest number were registered in Krasnoyarsk Krai where twenty-five associations were united in nine electoral blocs.[17] However, one of the problems with this data is that under the umbrella term 'public association' are included not just parties, but a whole host of other political movements and civic organisations, many of which should more precisely be classified as interest or occupational groups. Thus, we find, for example, such groups as the 'Union of Young Jurists' (Penza Oblast), the 'Capital Housing Movement' and 'Medics for the Rebirth of Health' (Moscow City), the 'Fund for the Mentally Ill' (Saratov Oblast), even the football club 'Saliut' (Saratov Oblast) and – what appears to be a contradiction in terms – the 'Bloc of Non-Party Independents' (Krasnoyarsk Krai).

The decline in participation of public associations and electoral blocks 1995–97

However, whilst we have undoubtedly witnessed a vast expansion in the formation and registration of public associations and electoral blocs, their participation in regional elections declined over the period 1995–97. Indeed, the vast majority of public associations did not participate in the elections: only 712 of the 4,600 registered associations (or 15.5 per cent) put forward candidates. In eight regions there were no candidates nominated by public associations.[18] And only 18.6 per cent of all candidates with a party affiliation won seats in the regional assemblies.[19]

Furthermore, the participation of electoral associations dropped over the period 1995–97 from a participation rate of 23.2 per cent in 1995 (17.1 per cent in 1996) to just 13.2 per cent in 1997. The higher participation rates in 1995 and 1996 are no doubt related to the fact that national parliamentary and presidential elections took place over these two years, and there was much more party activism in general. But, it would appear that this increased activism around national elections did not feed into the subsequent elections for regional assemblies in 1997 and beyond. Finally, despite the general rise in the overall number of electoral blocs, the percentage of public associations which entered into such blocs has also declined. Thus, in 1995, 5.7 per cent of public associations entered blocs, but this fell to just 3.2 per cent in 1997.[20]

Elections for governors

In 1996 Boris Yeltsin, under pressure from regional elites, relinquished his powers of appointment over chief executives in the regions, and he gave the go ahead for governors to be elected by popular mandate. But, if, as we have demonstrated, party affiliation in regional assemblies is weak, in the governors corps it is even more inchoate and transient. Thus, for example, of the 4,000 public associations which had the right to nominate candidates in seventy 'gubernatorial' elections, over the period from August 1995 to April 1997, only 100 (or 2.5 per cent) actual participated in just forty-eight regions.[21] And these public associations put forward just 18.8 per cent (eighty candidates) of the total number of candidates. Finally, of the seventy chief executives who were finally elected, just ten (14.3 per cent) had a party affiliation.

The majority of regional governors and republican presidents have, for the most part, rejected any party affiliation or allegiance to a particular ideology, tending to portray themselves as strong 'economic managers' whose deep concern for the welfare of their regions transcends party politics. Indeed, it would appear that governors are prepared to change their political affiliation at the drop of a hat; see Table 4.1 (on pages 60–3), which shows the political affiliation of governors in October 1999. However, it is clear that in the wake of the December 1999 elections many governors have already shifted their political allegiances and have jumped onto the political bandwagon of President Vladimir Putin.

The weak political affiliation of regional governors is graphically illustrated by the colourful career of Aleksandr Rutskoi, the former Russian Vice President, who moved rapidly from being a staunch ally of Yeltsin in 1991 to being his arch enemy by September 1993. After his release from prison for his leading role in the 'October 1993 events', Rutskoi was elected to the post of Governor of Kursk with the support of the KPRF and the National Patriotic Union of Russia (NPSR). However, it was not long before Rutskoi soon abandoned any supposed loyalty to these left-wing parties, becoming one of Yeltsin's staunchest supporters in the Federal Council (the upper chamber of the national parliament). Moreover, Rutskoi is now a member of Yedinstvo (Unity), the new Kremlin 'party of power'. In a similar manner, once in office, even such hard line communists as the President of Mordoviya (Merkushkin), and the governors of Ul'yanovsk (Gorachev), Smolensk (Glushenkov) and Lipetsk (Narolin) Oblasts, quickly abandoned any pretence of party loyalty in order to curry favour with the federal government.[22]

The new governors' parties

Rather than governors joining parties in order to promote their election prospects, it is more often the case that parties are forced to turn to governors to help them bring home the regional votes. Regional presidents and governors have considerable control over electoral finances, the local media, courts and electoral commissions. There are many instances of governors resorting to outright manipulation of the electoral rules in order to ensure their victory in gubernatorial elections or to pack regional assemblies with their own appointed officials.[23]

A new and worrying development, in 1999 and 2000, has been the creation of Governors' parties (for example, Fatherland – All Russia or Voice of Russia) set up by regional governors to promote their interests in the Duma. The creation of these artificial top-down 'parties of government' has been a major blow to the

Table 3.2 Variations in the level of governors' support of parties, 1999

Bloc	No. of subjects (Russian Federation)	No. of Electoral districts	No. of voters (millions)	Share of electorate (%)
OVR	18	74	34.6	32.0
KPRF	16	40	20.6	19.1
Yedinstvo	23	40	17.7	16.4
NDR	10	20	10.2	9.5
SPS	1	5	2.5	2.3
LDPR	1	1	0.6	0.6
Yabloko	0	0	0.0	0.0
Not stated	20	45	21.7	20.1
Total	89	225	108.0	100.0

Source: Vladimir Kozlov and Dmitrii Oreshkin, 'Bluzhdaiushchie zvezdy rossiiskoi politiki (o politicheskikh migratsiiakh regional'nykh liderov)' *Golos Rossii*, 6 (1 November 1999), 6, 4.
Notes: OVR=Fatherland – All Russia; KPRF = Communist Party of the Russian Federation; NDR =Our Home is Russia; LDRR =Liberal Democratic Pary of Russia

development of grass-roots democracy in the regions. As Daniel Slider notes, these governors' blocs are in effect, 'anti-party parties' that have been set up specifically to preclude effective national party building in the regions.[24] The Kremlin-backed 'party of power', Yedinstvo, also has the support of a number of powerful governors. Table 3.2 shows variations in the level of governors' support for parties in 1999. However, as note above, we must be careful to take such declarations of party allegiance with a large pinch of salt.

Factors explaining Russia's weakly institutionalised party system

How can we explain the chronically low levels of party activism and electoral participation and representation, demonstrated in the data above? I would argue that the following five factors have thwarted the institutionalisation of political parties in Russia:

1 the legacy of an authoritarian political culture;
2 the weak development of social and economic cleavages;
3 the negative impact of Russia's mixed electoral system;
4 the presidential system; and
5 Russia's weak asymmetrical form of federalism.

1 The legacy of an authoritarian political culture
Seventy years of communist rule have left an authoritarian legacy, a very weak and inchoate civil society and massive citizen distrust in political institutions.[25] Political parties still command very little trust in Russian society. In a VTsIOM

survey of public opinion, carried out in March 1999, only 3 per cent of respondents declared full confidence in parties.[26]

2   The weak development of social and economic cleavages

As Michael McFaul notes, 'Whereas most countries in transition seek to change only their system of governance, Russia had to create a new state, a new political system, and a new economic system simultaneously.'[27] But which reforms should be implemented first? Linz and Stepan have argued that political reform should come first 'because democracy legitimates the market, not the reverse'.[28] However, without comparable economic reforms accompanying political change, transitional states cannot generate the necessary social cleavages around which parties need to coalesce and compete for power. As Smolar observes, in state socialist societies, the typical citizen identified with only two levels of community, one was family and friends, and the other was the nation. Identification with any intermediate structures was lacking altogether. In addition, the proletarianisation of these societies made it difficult for individuals to recognize differences of interests.'[29] In the first years of Russia's transition, the implementation of political reforms far outpaced the development of economic reforms. This has led to a situation in which we have seen the formation of a multitude of parties with very shallow roots in civil society. Thus, for example, we have witnessed a proliferation of right-of-centre parties which were founded long before there was any sizeable property owning bourgeoisie to support them. Where sharp cleavages did emerge, they were much more likely to be based on ethnic and regional conflicts rather than economics and class.

The lack of well developed social cleavages has meant that Russian parties are more often based around personalities than policies. Many parties in post-communist states are classic 'insider parties' formed from loose coalitions of deputies in the national parliament, or they are top-down elite organisations with no real grass-roots support (for example, the 'parties of power'). Not surprisingly, party identification is extremely low in Russia. As Stephen White notes, 'according to survey evidence, just 22 per cent of Russians identified to some degree with a political party, compared with 87 per cent of the electorate of the United States of America and more than 92 per cent in the United Kingdom.'[30] And electoral volatility in Russia is, according to Matthew Wyman, six times higher than in Western Europe and twice as high as in Eastern Europe.[31]

3   The negative impact of Russia's mixed electoral system

Russia's electoral system has also tended to work against the development of nationwide parties. Sartori has described the electoral system as the most specific manipulative instrument of politics; as Robert Moser observes, 'if this is true, then decisions involving electoral arrangements of new democracies in the post-communist world are among the most important decisions leaders of these new states will make.'[32] Russia's choice of electoral system for the national parliament has worked against the development of a truly national party system. In the Duma, there is a mixed electoral system in operation. Half the members are elected by proportional representation using a party list system (with a 5 per cent threshold), and half by a first-past-the-post system, in single member districts. The first-past-the-post electoral system in single member districts is also the most common system for elections at the regional level.[33]

In elections to the single member districts (for both the Duma and regional assemblies), the first-past-the-post system has clearly benefited local notables standing as independents, over and above the less well known candidates of national parties. Indeed, most of the candidates competing in the single member districts for national elections stand as independents. Independents won most of the seats in the 1993 Duma elections and came second to the Communists in 1995 and 1999.[34] In sharp contrast, the highest level of party representation is to be found in Krasnoyarsk Krai (8 per cent), which is one of only four regions that rejected the norm of the Westminster first-past-the-post system (see Appendix 3.1) and instead opted for a mixed majoritarian and proportional party list system.[35] Adopting this system nationwide would have a positive impact on party building and consolidation.

Turning to the party lists, Richard Sakwa notes that procedures which were designed to help consolidate Russia's parties accelerated the fragmentation of the party system. The 1995 electoral rules, by allowing only twelve Moscow politicians on the party list, encouraged those lower down the list to break away and form their own electoral blocs.[36]

Russia's adoption of nationally drafted party lists in a single nationwide electoral district, rather than regionally drafted lists in multi-member districts (as is the case in Germany), has also worked against the development of strong nationally integrated parties. As Remington notes, the choice of one single nationwide electoral district rather than a larger number of multi-member districts, was a deliberate one, 'designed to reduce the chances that parties with a strong regional or ethnic appeal might win seats and weaken the state's unity'.[37] As a solution Russell Bova argues that abolishing the party list vote in the Duma and electing all the seats in single member districts would give Russia's developing parties greater incentives to form coalitions or even to merge in order to acquire the majority or plurality required for election; it would also 'destroy the illusion that one can win elections and govern entirely from Moscow'.[38]

4 The presidential system

Party cohesion is much more difficult to achieve in presidential systems than in parliamentary regimes. Russia's choice of a hybrid presidential–parliamentary system at the national level has further weakened the development of strong cohesive parties. As Karen Dawisha writes, 'Presidentialism by focusing on the election of a single individual to an all powerful post diminishes the influence of the party system.' In contrast, 'parliamentary systems require the formation of disciplined parties and coalitions in order to keep the executive in power.'[39] Legislative stalemate and deadlock are also much more common in presidential systems. In Russia, such stalemate turned into outright hostilities between the parliament and the president, and ultimately to the forced dissolution of the White House in September 1993. Moreover, Yeltsin's claim to 'stand above party' has hindered the consolidation of parties at the national level. It was clearly not in Yeltsin's (and now Putin's) interest to support the development of strong disciplined parties which could rise up and challenge his authority: a divided and fragmented parliament is a weak parliament.

5 Russia's Weak asymmetrical form of federalism

Russian federalism has impacted negatively on the development of national parties. The federal structure has strengthened authoritarianism and made it far more difficult for democracy to take root. This is seen in the chronically weak and divided party system in Russia where, on the one hand, the major parties represented in the Duma are poorly organized outside of Moscow and St. Petersburg and, on the other hand, there are scores of regionally based public associations and electoral blocs that are peculiar to only one particular region or republic. As Michael Burgess notes:

> Where there is a political party 'symmetry' between the federal (central) government and the governments of the constituent units of the federation, we can expect the relative partisan harmony to have a binding impact upon the federation. Conversely, where there is a notable and resilient 'asymmetry' between the central authorities and the local party elites and organisations, the resulting differences of interest may have a centrifugal effect leading to political mobilisation for decentralist reforms. Ultimately such enduring 'asymmetry' could conceivably lead to pressures for secession from the union.[40]

The weak political affiliation of regional governors, and chairs of regional assemblies is also important for party consolidation in the Federation Council where these two groups are ex-officio members. In a vicious circle, weak levels of party affiliation at the regional level feed into weak party consolidation at the national level.

The importance of national parties that cross ethnic and regional divisions is also important for the consolidation of democracy. As David Laitin notes:

> National parties that seek to build alliances that crosscut cultural groups in all regions tend to modulate the demands from regionally based autonomy movements. In Nigeria, the constitutional drafters recognised this issue and required that in order to become accredited parties must have significant membership across a variety of regions.[41]

However, no such electoral rule exists in Russia. As Table 3.3 shows, in the 1999 elections for the Duma even the KPRF could field candidates in only 62.2 per cent of the single member election districts. Yabloko and NDR fielded candidates in approximately 60 per cent; OVR and SPS in about half, and Yedinstvo in just 18 per cent.[42] Zhirinovsky's Bloc failed to contest a single seat.[43] Turning to the party list elections, even here none of the parties fielded candidates in all of the

Table 3.3   Regional distribution of parties in the December 1999 Duma elections

	SM candidates	PL candidates	Percentage of party members		SM* reside in Moscow/ St. Petersburg	PL* reside in Moscow/ St. Petersburg
			SM	PL		
KPRF	140 (62.2%)	84	86.4	78.0	27.0	30.3
Yedinstvo	41 (18.2%)	53	–	–	46.3	41.8
OVR	118 (52.4%)	68	25.3	62.1	34.8	41.4
URF	108 (48.0%)	63	51.4	49.4	34.2	27.8
Yabloko	135 (60.0%)	57	60.8	73.2	28.9	32.2
Zhir	–	–	–	92.6	–	–
NDR	118 (52.4%)	86	7.1	3.1	31.0	16.0

Notes: KPRF = Communist Party of the Russian Federation; OVR = Our Fatherland – All Russia; SPS = Union of Right Forces;[46] Zhir = Zhirinovsky Bloc; NDR = Our Home is Russia; SM = single member list; PL = party list. *Candidates residing in Moscow and St. Petersburg Oblasts and the cities, Moscow and St. Petersburg.

regions; NDR's candidates competed in 84 of Russia's 89 regions; the KPRF (84 regions), OVR (68), SPS (63), Yabloko (57) and Yedinstvo (53).[44]

The territorial distribution of members of national parties in the regions and republics is also very low. With the exception of the KPRF and the LDPR, most national parties are based largely in Moscow and St. Petersburg and have very weak ties with their regional branches. Thus, for example, approximately one third of all candidates nominated by national parties in December 1999 came from elites residing in the cities of Moscow and St. Petersburg (see Table 3.3).

The weak organisational base of national parties in the regions is also revealed by the stark fact that a significant number of the candidates registered for election, even in the party lists (PL), are not in fact members of these parties. LDPR had the highest percentage of its own party members on its party list (92.6 per cent), followed by the KPRF (78 per cent), Yabloko (73.2 per cent), OVR (62.1 per cent), SPS (49.4 per cent). The former 'party of power' NDR had an incredibly low figure of only 3.1 per cent and should clearly more properly be classified as a loose political movement, rather than as a political party.[45] See Table 3.3, which also shows similar wide variations in the single member lists (SM).

Elites, clientelism and corporatism

As O'Donnell observes, when democratic institutions are weak and inchoate their place is soon taken over by informal practices, such as clientelism, patrimonialism and corruption.[47] The chronic weakness of parties has left open the door for other groups to enter politics. Two of the most powerful are industrial executives and state bureaucrats. In a new post-communist corporatist alliance, regional economic and political elites (many of whom were formerly members of the Soviet nomenklatura) have joined forces to plunder the wealth of their regions. Key members of the Soviet economic and administrative elites now dominate and control the work of Russia's local assemblies.[48]

Members of the economic elite in regional assemblies

In his 1998 study of twenty-seven regional assemblies Turovskii concluded that by far the largest groupings in the assemblies were directors of industrial enterprises and chairs of collective farms. In ten of the assemblies entrepreneurs made up a majority or near majority of the deputies corps. Indeed, so great is the representation of business interests that the list of deputies in some assemblies reads like a 'Whose Who?' of local business[49]. For example, 80 per cent of the members of the legislature of Kabardino-Balkariya represented the economic elite of factory directors and businessmen.[50] In Sakha's (Yakutiya's) regional assembly, the firm 'Russian Diamonds' was represented not only by its President but also by two vice presidents, and there were also two managers of the 'Sakha Gold' company. In Tyumen' Oblast at least five deputies, including the speaker of the assembly, belonged to the top leadership of the gas giant 'Gazprom'.[51] In 1998 representatives of large business concerns won twenty of thirty seats in the Ishevsk City Duma.

The new members of the legislature control two of the largest banks in the city, all the private television stations, 90 per cent of private newspapers, two thirds of the market for oil products, all three large construction companies and the two trading companies that control produce sales in the city. Among the winners was the Chairman of 'Udmurtneft', which extracts 80 per cent of the oil in the region. No political party member was elected.[52]

Members of the regional administrative elite in regional assemblies

A number of republican presidents and regional governors have also been successful in creating weak ceremonial parliaments. In a flagrant violation of the democratic principle of the separation of powers they have packed legislative bodies with their subordinates from the state administration. Thus, for example, in elections conducted over the period 1995–97, 332 heads of city and district administrations won seats in forty-five regional assemblies. The highest representation of such officials was to be found in: Bashkortostan (50.0 per cent); Novgorod (46.2 per cent); Sverdlovsk Oblast (35 per cent); Kabardino-Balkariya, Tatarstan and Komi (30 per cent in each).[53] Indeed, in some cases where there are two chamber assemblies the upper chamber was specially created to include heads of local administrations (for example, Bashkortostan, Kareliya). As Farukshin observes, 'in Tatarstan we find what would appear to be a contradiction in terms, a "bureaucratic parliament" where 78 of the 130 members of the legislature (the State Council) hold full-time posts in the state apparat. Moreover, the majority of these state officials were directly appointed to their posts by the President'.[54] According to Article 111 of Tatarstan's Constitution, the President has the right to nominate candidates for half the members of the Constitutional Court, and half the members of the Central Electoral Commission. These candidacies are then placed before the Tatarstan Parliament for ratification.[55] By packing the parliament with his administrative subordinates, the Tatarstan President can maintain control over the judiciary and the electoral process in the republic, which in turn guarantees his complete domination of the legislature.

Conclusions

The problem of party building in Russia's regions comes not so much from what Sartori calls 'polarized pluralism' or the danger of 'anti-system parties' threatening the stability of the party system. Russia's problem is that, with the exception of the KPRF, and the transient 'parties of power' (Russia's Choice, Our Home is Russia, Yedinstvo), there are no other national parties with sufficient organisational capacity and financial resources to compete effectively in federal-wide elections. Thus, one of the striking features of local politics in Russia is the almost total partyless nature of regional election campaigns and the dismal representation of political parties in regional assemblies. Politics at the regional level is highly fragmented. In the majority of cases, competition is not between disciplined nationwide parties with competing policies, but rather between a host of competing individuals and personalities. If you are a communist candidate in the 'red belt' this may very well be an advantage, but in most other regions a party label is more liable to scare away potential voters.

The absence of strong institutionalised parties in the regions has intensified the clientalistic and corporatist nature of politics in Russia. State officials and economic elites have benefited from the partyless nature of regional politics and the fragmented and divided nature of politics in the assemblies. As Liebert notes:

> empirical studies on Third World legislatures . . . have pointed out that legislatures are far more vulnerable to extra-constitutional attacks against their prerogatives in systems where political parties are weak; stronger parties help the legislature to generate the support it needs from mass publics to withstand challenges from bureaucratic elites.[56]

Populist regional governors have tapped into the vacuum of power in Russia's partyless regions, creating regional autocracies. As Mainwaring notes:

> The weakness of parties' social roots means that democratic political competition, rather than being channelled through parties and other democratic institutions, assumes a personalized character . . . populism and 'antipolitics' are more common in countries with weak institutionalised systems.[57]

However, fragmented and divided assemblies have also led to legislative deadlock. Governors often cannot guarantee majority support for their policies, and often they are forced to enter into a 'war of laws' with the regional assemblies.

Just as Yeltsin found himself caught in a deadly stalemate with the Russian parliament in 1993, so republican presidents and regional governors (mini-
presidencies) have found themselves in similar predicaments.

In recent years we have also seen the worrying development of governors'
parties, created from above, thwarting the development of grass-roots parties,
from below. The Federation Council is also likely to continue as a largely partyless chamber with an ever changing set of personal alliances and cliques. As the
centrifugal power of the regions have expanded, the need for strong unifying
parties has become more pressing. Yet, as Alfred Stepan observes, 'No other
federal system has a party system that to date has contributed so little to producing polity wide programmatic discipline.'[58] It is very difficult to consolidate
parties in weak and fragmented federal systems, but it is even more difficult to
build federal systems in the absence of strong and territorially comprehensive
parties. In conclusion, there can be no consolidation of democracy in Russia
without a nationwide consolidation of parties and the party system.

Appendix 3.1   Party membership of regional assemblies, January 1998

Federal subject	Total number of deputies	No. of party members	Percentage of party members
Krasnoyarsk Krai	41	33	80
Sverdlovsk Oblast	49	34	69
Kemerovo Oblast	21	12	57
Novosibirsk Oblast	49	27	55
Ryazan' Oblast	26	13	50
Bryansk Oblast	49	24	49
Adegeya Republic	45	22	49
Kamchatka Oblast	43	20	47
Kaluga Oblast	40	18	45
Koryak Autonomous Okrug	9	4	44
Altai Krai	50	22	44
Belgorod Oblast	35	14	40
Penza Oblast	45	17	38
Udmurtiya Republic	100	37	37
Stavropol' Krai	25	9	36
Khabarovsk Krai	23	8	35
Kaliningrad Oblast	32	11	34
Omsk Oblast	30	10	33
Smolensk Oblast	30	10	33
Kirov Oblast	54	17	31
Pskov Oblast	20	6	30
Orel Oblast	50	14	28
Tambov Oblast	50	14	28
Astrakhan Oblast	29	8	28
Kareliya Republic	56	15	27

Federal subject	Total number of deputies	No. of party members	Percentage of party members
Jewish Autonomous Oblast	15	4	27
Voronezh Oblast	45	12	27
Tula Oblast	48	11	23
Moscow City	35	8	23
Rostov Oblast	45	10	22
Volgograd Oblast	47	10	21
Ust'-Orda Buryat Autonomous Okrug	19	4	21
Karachaevo-Cherkesiya Republic	73	15	21
Ivanovo Oblast	35	7	20
Ul'yanovsk Oblast	25	5	20
Orenburg Oblast	47	9	19
Lipetsk Oblast	38	7	18
Murmansk Oblast	24	4	17
Irkutsk Oblast	44	7	16
Chuvashiya Republic	63	9	14
Kabardino-Balkar Republic	36	5	14
Kursk Oblast	44	6	14
Vladimir Oblast	37	5	14
Aginsk-Buryat Autonomous Okrug	15	2	13
Moscow Oblast	50	6	12
Sakhalin Oblast	27	3	11
Marii-El Republic	66	7	11
Tatarstan Republic	130	13	10
Yaroslavl' Oblast	50	5	10
Severo-Osetiya-Alaniya Republic	73	7	10
Tyva Republic	21	2	10
Sakha Republic (Yakutiya)	66	6	9
Saratov Oblast	35	3	9
Komi Republic	50	4	8
Samara Oblast	25	2	8
Tomsk Oblast	42	3	7
Vologda Oblast	30	2	7
Khakasiya Republic	75	4	5
Altai Republic	41	2	5
Yamalo-Nenets Autonomous Okrug	21	1	5
Tyumen' Oblast	25	1	4
Kurgan Oblast	33	1	3
Tver' Oblast	33	1	3
Arkhangelsk Oblast	36	1	3
Nizhegorod Oblast	45	1	2
Leningrad Oblast	50	1	2
Amur Oblast	30	0	0
Bashkortostan Republic	185	0	0
Buryatiya Republic	64	0	0
Chelyabinsk Oblast	41	0	0

Federal subject	Total number of deputies	No. of party members	Percentage of party members
Chita Oblast	39	0	0
Chukotka Autonomous Okrug	13	0	0
Dagestan Republic	121	0	0
Khanty-Mansi Autonomous Okrug	23	0	0
Komi-Permyak Autonomous Okrug	15	0	0
Kostroma Oblast	19	0	0
Magadan Oblast	17	0	0
Nenets Autonomous Okrug	15	0	0
Novgorod Oblast	26	0	0
Perm' Oblast	40	0	0
Primorskii Krai	39	0	0
Taimyr Autonomous Okrug	11	0	0
Evenki Autonomous Okrug	23	0	0

Source: 'Parties in Assemblies', special report prepared for the author by the Russian Central Electoral Commission, no author, January 1998.

Notes

1 Geoffrey Pridham, 'Southern European democracies on the road to consolidation: a comparative assessment of the role of political parties', in Geoffrey Pridham (ed.), *Securing Democracy: Political Parties and Democratic Consolidation in Southern Europe* (London and New York: Routledge, 1990), p. 2.
2 Paper delivered to the Conference 'Political Parties and Democracy', 18–19 November 1996, Washington, DC sponsored by the International Forum for Democratic Studies. See www.ned.org
3 *Ibid.*
4 G. Pridham and P. Lewis, 'Introduction: stabilising fragile democracies and party system development', in Geoffrey Pridham and Paul Lewis (eds.), *Stabilising Fragile Democracies: Comparing New Party Systems in Southern and Eastern Europe* (London and New York: Routledge, 1996), p. 5.
5 R. Hague, M. Harrop and S. Breslin, *Comparative Government and Politics: An Introduction* (London: Macmillan, 4th edition, 1998), p. 131.
6 K. Dawisha, 'Democratisation and political participation: research concepts and methodologies', chapter 2 of K. Dawisha and B. Parrot (eds.), *The Consolidation of Democracy in East-Central Europe* (Cambridge: Cambridge Uuniversity Press, 1997), p. 55.
7 S. Mainwaring, 'Party systems in the third wave', *Journal of Democracy*, 4 (December 1999), 69–71.
8 John Lowenhardt (ed.), *Party Politics in Post-Communist Russia* (London: Frank Cass, 1998); John T. Ishiyama, 'The Russian proto-parties and the national republics', *Communist and Post-Communist Studies*, 29:4 (1996), 395–411; also by Ishiyama, 'Political parties and candidate recruitment in post-soviet Russian politics', *Journal of Communist Studies and Transition Politics*, 15:4 (1999), 41–69; Peter. C. Ordeshook,

'Russia's party system: is Russian federalism viable?', *Post-Soviet Affairs*, 12:3 (1996), 195–217; Peter C. Ordeshook and Olga Shevtsova, 'Federalism and constitutional design', *Journal of Democracy*, 1 (1997), 27–36; M. Makfol, S. Markov i A. Riabov (eds.), *Formirovanie Partiino-Politicheskoi Sistemy v Rossii* (Moscow: Carnegie Endowment for International Peace, 1998); G. V. Golosov, *Partiinye Sistemy Rossii i Stran Vostochnoi Evropy* (Moscow: Ves' mir, 1999).

 9 See Vladimir Gel'man and Grigorii V. Golosov, 'Regional party system formation in Russia: the deviant case of Sverdlovsk oblast', in Lowenhardt, *Party Politics*; Alexei Kuzmin, 'Partii v regionakh', in M. Makfola *et al.*, *Formirovanie*; D. Slider, 'National political parties in Russia's regions', paper delivered to the 31st National Convention of the AAASS, St. Louis, 20 November 1999.

10 As Richard Sakwa notes, 'According to the draft Law on Political Parties adopted by the Duma on 8 December 1995 three types of political parties may be established: national, with regional organisations in at least forty-five components of the Russian Federation; interregional, with membership from at least two components; and regional.' R. Sakwa, *Russian Politics and Society* (1996), p. 90. In this study national parties are defined simply as those parties which compete for power at the national level (see my list in Table 3.1). Regional parties by contrast compete for power only at the regional level.

11 Forty-three parties and political movements contested the Duma elections in 1995 and twenty-six did so in 1999.

12 No parties were represented in the republics of Bashkortostan, Buryatiya, Dagestan; Primorskii Krai; Amur, Chelyabinsk, Chita, Kostroma, Magadan, Novgorod and Perm' Oblasts; Komi-Permyak, Nenetsk, Taimyr, Khanty Mansi, Chukotka and Yevenk Autonomous Okrugs. Here we need to note that these figures refer to the party affiliation of candidates at the time of the election campaign and do not count changes after the assemblies were formed. Many candidates do not declare their party affiliations during the election campaigns for fear that it will impact negatively on their electoral prospects. Thus, the party affiliation of assemblies is probably higher than the data presented here.

13 In the regions of the so-called 'red belt' (for example, Stavropol' Krai, Belgorod, Vologda, Ryazan', Smolensk, Tambov, Bryansk and Penza Oblasts), the communists were able to achieve a plurality, if not a majority, in coalition with other parties such as the Agrarian Party of Russia (APR) and the National Patriotic Union of Russia (NPUR).

14 S. V. Alekseev, V. A. Kalamanov and A. G. Chernenko, *Ideologicheskie Orientiry Rossii* (Moscow: Kniga i Biznes: 1998), pp. 320–1.

15 *Vybory v Zakonodatel'nye (Predstavitel'nye) Organy Gosudarstvennoi Vlasti Sub'ekov Rossiiskoi Federatsii 1995–1997* (Moscow: Ves' mir: 1998) p. 584.

16 *Ibid.*, p. 584.

17 *Ibid.*, pp. 587–9.

18 Republic of Dagestan; Amur Oblast; Komi-Perm', Nenetsk, Taimyr, Khanty-Mansi, Chukotka and Yevenk Autonomous Okrugs.

19 In seven assemblies there were no deputies elected from public associations; Primorskii Krai, and Kostroma, Magadan, Novgorod, Perm', Chelyabinsk and Chita Oblasts.

20 *Vybory v Zakonodatel'nye*, p. 585.

21 *Vybory Glav Ispolnitel'noi Vlasti Sub'ektov Rossiiskoi Federatsii 1995–1997*

(Moscow: Ves' mir: 1997), p. 40. The largest number of such organisations were registered with the Ministry of Justice in Moscow (456), Orenburg (250), Perm' (124), Sverdlovsk (120), Samara (127), Rostov (112), Kaliningrad (107), Amur (105) and Arkhangel'sk (103) Oblasts.

22 Vladimir Kozlov, Dmitrii Oreshkin, 'Bluzhdaiushchie zvezdy rossiiskoi politiki (o politicheskikh migratsiiakh regional'nykh liderov)' *Golos Rossii*, 6 (1 November 1999), pp. 1–6, 3.

23 See Cameron Ross, 'Federalizm i demokratizatsiya v Rossii', *Polis*, 3 (1999), 16–29.

24 Daniel Slider, 'National political parties', p. 6.

25 K. Dawisha, 'Democratisation and political participation', p. 55.

26 Nationwide VTsIOM survey, March 6–21 ($n = 2,385$), as reported at www.russiavotes.org/Duma_poll_cur.htm#109, Strathclyde University, December 1999.

27 Michael McFaul, 'Russia's transition', in *Consolidating the Third Wave Democracies*, Larry Diamond, Marc F. Platter, Yun-han Chu and Hung-mao Tien (eds.) (Baltimore, MD and London: Johns Hopkins University Press, 1997), pp. 64–94, p. 65.

28 Juan Linz and Alfred Stepan, *Problems of Democratic Transition and Consolidation* (Johns Hopkins University Press: 1996), p. 436, quoted by Zvi Gitelman in *Developments in Russian Politics*, 4, Stephen White, Alex Pravda and Zvi Gitelman (eds.) (Basingstoke: Macmillan, 1999), p. 275.

29 Aleksander Smolar, paper delivered to the Conference 'Political parties and democracy', 18–19 November 1996, Washington, DC, sponsored by the International Forum for Democratic Studies.

30 S. White, 'Political parties', chapter 3 of Mike Bowker and Cameron Ross (eds.), *Russia After the Cold War* (London: Longman, 1999), pp. 82–3.

31 Matthew Wyman, 'Elections and voting behaviour', chapter 6 of Stephen White, Alex Pravda and Zvi Gitelman (eds.), *Developments in Russia Politics*, 4, (Basingstoke: Macmillan, 1999), p. 119.

32 Robert G. Moser, 'The impact of parliamentary electoral systems in Russia', *Post-Soviet Affairs*, 13:3 (1997), 284–302.

33 In some regions, to win a candidate requires a majority of the votes cast, and there are two rounds of elections. In other regions candidates can win in single round contests with a plurality of the votes cast. In four of the seventy-two regions where elections for regional assemblies were held 1995–97 (Krasnoyarsk Krai, Kaliningrad Oblast, Koryak, and Ust'-Orda Buryat Autonomous Okrugs) there was a mixed electoral system, similar to that used in the State Duma. In Sverdlovsk Oblast the lower chamber (Legislative Assembly) was elected by proportional representation and the upper chamber (Assembly of Representatives) by the first-past-the-post system. In a number of regions there are multi-mandate constituencies.

34 Stephen White, Richard Rose and Ian McAllister, *How Russia Votes* (Chatham, NJ: Chatham House, 1997), p. 123 (for 1993 Duma elections) and pp. 224–5 (for results of 1995 elections) and www.rferl.org/elections/russia99results/index.html (for the 1999 election results).

35 The other three are Kaliningrad Oblast (34 per cent), Koryak (44 per cent) and Ust'-Orda Buriatiya (21 per cent) Autonomous Okrugs).

36 Sakwa, *Russian Politics*, p. 92.

37 T. F. Remmington, *Politics in Russia* (London: Longman, 1999) p. 151.

38 R. Bova, 'Political culture, authority patterns, and the architecture of the new Russian

democracy', chapter 7 of H. Eckstein, F. Fleron, E. Hoffmann and W. Reisinger (eds.), *Can Democracy Take Root in Post-Soviet Russia?* (Lanham, MD: Rowman and Littlefield, 1998), pp. 177–200, 195.

39 K. Dawisha, 'Democratisation and political participation', p. 56.

40 Michael Burgess and Alain-G. Gagnon (eds.), *Comparative Federalism and Federation* (London: Harvester Wheatsheaf, 1993), p. 107.

41 David Laitin, 'Transitions to democracy and territorial integrity', in Adam Przeworski (ed.), *Sustainable Democracy* (Cambridge: Cambridge University Press, 1995), p. 24.

42 Data in Table 3.3 is from Aleksandr Strokhanov, 'Who is who on the parties lists?', www.panorama.ru. These figures refer to candidates registered by the Central Electoral Commission (August–October 1999) as eligible to stand for elections to the Duma, and not those who actually took part in the December 1999 elections.

43 A large number of LDPR candidates were rejected by the Central Electoral Commission.

44 Aleksandr Strokanov, 'Who is who'. Here we only have figures for number of regions, rather than number of electoral districts.

45 I could find no comparable data for the party of power, Yedinstvo.

46 Of the 108 candidates on the single member list of the movement, Union of Right Forces (URF), Democratic Choice of Russia made up 24.1 per cent (24.6 per cent of party list), New Force made up 8.3 per cent (5.3 per cent of party list), Democratic Russia, 6.5 per cent (4.2 per cent of party list), Young Russia, 6.5 per cent (–). Other organisations belonging to the block have just one or two candidates.

47 G. O'Donnell, 'Delegative democracy', *Journal of Democracy*, 5:1 (January 1994), 55–69, 59.

48 See David Lane and Cameron Ross, *The Transformation from Communism to Capitalism: Ruling Elites from Gorbachev to Yeltsin* (New York: St. Martin's Press, 1999).

49 R. F. Turovskii, 'Gubernatory nachinaiut i vyigryvayut?', chapter 3 of R. F. Turovskii (ed.), *Politicheskie Protsessy v Regionakh Rossii* (Moscow: Tsentr Politicheskikh Tekhnologii, 1998), pp. 182–245, 203.

50 R. Orttung, 'Directors, Businessmen Dominate Kabardino-Balkariya Returns', East–West Institute, *Russian Regional Report*, 2:44 (18 December, 1997), 13 (hereafter, EWI, *Russian Regional Report*).

51 Turovskii, 'Gubernatory', p. 204.

52 'Mayor, Businessmen Win Local Elections in Izhevsk', EWI, *Russian Regional Report*, 3:16 (23 April 1998), 382 (no author noted).

53 V. N. Kozlov and D. B. Oreshkin, *Vybory v Zakonodatel'nye Predstavitel'nye Organy Syb'ektov Rossiiskoi Federatsii 1995–1997* (Moscow: Ves' mir, 1998), p. 636.

54 M. Farukshin, 'Federalizm i demokratiia: slozhnyi balans', *Polis*, 6:42 (1997), 164–73, 170.

55 E. V. Filippova (ed.), *Tatarstan Osnovy Politicheskovo Ustroistva i Kratkaia Kharakteristika Ekonomiki (Spravochnik)* (Moscow: Fond Razvitiia Parliamentarizma v Rossii, 1996), p. 265.

56 U. Liebert, 'Parliament as a central site in democratic consolidation: a preliminary exploration', chapter 1 of Ulrike Liebert and Maurizio Cotta (eds.), *Parliament and Democratic Consolidation in Southern Europe* (London and New York: Pinter, 1990), pp. 3–30, p. 21.

57 Mainwaring, 'Party systems', 75.
58 Alfred Stepan, 'Russian federalism in comparative perspective: problems of power creation and power deflation', paper delivered to the 31st National Convention of the AAASS, St. Louis, MO, 18–21 November 1999, p. 36. See also Stepan's 'Federalism and democracy: beyond the U.S. model', *Journal of Democracy*, 10:4 (October 1999), 19–34.

The role of Russia's governors in the 1999–2000 federal elections

Following the August 1998 economic crisis, Russia's federal centre lost much of its power to control regional executives.[1] The centre had less to offer the regions economically, leaving regional governments to define their own survival strategies. Likewise, Boris Yeltsin's deteriorating health and the constant stream of prime ministers that marked the end of the Yeltsin era left regional executives room to strengthen their positions vis-à-vis Moscow. By the end of the year, regional leaders had proven to be both firm and vocal in their positions while the federal centre was becoming more and more incapable of exerting any real influence over the governors.

Heading into the 1999–2000 campaign season, Russia's governors appeared ready to capitalise on the power vacuum that had developed in the Kremlin. The political and economic crisis created a window of opportunity for a well-organised regionally-based movement to take power in post-Yeltsin Russia. Regional executives, who were accustomed to equating centre–periphery relations to their relationships with Yeltsin, began looking past Yeltsin to cast their lots with potential successors. The governors also seemed to learn the lessons of the 1995 elections in which too many parties failed to work together and therefore did not cross the 5 per cent barrier.

The governors' desire to put an ally in office as president is understandable since the Russian constitution clearly concentrates most federal power in the hands of the country's chief executive. But the governors also wanted to have a greater say in the Duma. Many of them were frustrated with the obstructionist actions of the Communist Duma elected in 1995. Since laws were slowly becoming more important than presidential decrees, the governors wanted to have a voice in writing them. In 1995 the governors had often used the State Duma elections as a way of removing potentially powerful opponents from their home district and sending them to Moscow.[2] In 1999 they clearly wanted to elect allies to the Duma with whom they could work on future legislation.

The governors' involvement in the 1999–2000 federal election season can be divided into two stages. The first stage is from December 1998 to September 1999. During this period governors tried to increase their influence on the federal political scene by forming alliances with the goal of promoting their groups and candidates to become the next party of power. Since the Kremlin was viewed as weak and inactive, governors often broke from their traditional methods of courting Yeltsin and entered into open confrontation with the federal government. Fatherland – All Russia (OVR) was the most powerful regionally-based coalition to emerge in this period.

The situation began to change in September 1999, when the Kremlin announced the formation of Yedinstvo, (Unity), a new party of power that would run with the support of newly appointed Prime Minister Vladimir Putin. While the party seemed laughably weak at first, the initial success of the autumn 1999 Chechen offensive improved the federal government's standing and boosted Putin to instant popularity. The party went on to win second place in the Duma race and set the stage for Yeltsin's 31 December 1999 resignation, which ensured Putin's subsequent election as president. With their defeat in the December Duma elections, the governors fell back into their traditional methods of aligning loyally behind the chief executive.

Overall, coalition building among regional executives was unsuccessful in the 1999–2000 election cycle. The only bond holding the governors together was their collective sense of who would be the country's next president. The most powerful regional alliance, OVR, fell apart when it was clear that its candidate would not be the president. Additionally, the limited success regional alliances did achieve in the election did not evolve into the establishment of effective factions within the Duma. For example, deputies elected from the OVR party list quickly broke into several smaller factions rather than remaining a unified force.

However, although regional alliances did not outperform the Kremlin-backed Yedinstvo and the Communists in party-list voting, the governors were very successful in influencing the results of single seat races. Candidates supported by regional executives were victorious in 99 of the 168 races in which we were able to identify the governor's preference.[3] This trend demonstrates the authority of governors in their home districts. They managed to campaign effectively for their chosen candidates, successfully employing their control over regional bureaucracy and the media to provide support for their candidates. In this respect, the governors have managed to establish a certain level of meaningful representation in the State Duma.

The federal elections of 1999–2000 demonstrate the increased importance of Russia's regional elite in the country's federal government. The governors naturally played a much larger independent role in this electoral cycle than they did in the 1995–96 elections because this time around they had all been popularly elected rather than merely appointed by the president. This chapter explores the role of regional executives in the 1999–2000 election season and the impact of this role on both federal and regional structures. First, we discuss the history of the formation of the regional parties and alliances. Then we analyse the results of the 1999 State Duma elections and the consequences of these results on the

2000 presidential election. We conclude with an evaluation of the impact of the 1999–2000 federal elections on centre–periphery relations.

The formation of regional parties

The 1999–2000 electoral season was markedly different from the 1995–96 campaigns when the governors, the majority of whom had not yet been popularly elected, took their cues directly from President Yeltsin in the hope that the president would then return the favour and render his support for their own elections in the wave of gubernatorial elections in the autumn of 1996 and early 1997. Hoping to gain a greater voice at the federal level and to build a substantial base throughout the regions, Russian regional leaders began mobilising for the 1999–2000 elections at the end of 1998. Within a year four significant movements claiming to be regionally based had emerged, and fifteen governors occupied spots on party lists.

Moscow Mayor Yurii Luzhkov was the first regional leader to take decisive action, forming his Otechestvo (Fatherland) movement in December 1998. At that time Luzhkov's popularity was high and the mayor was considered one of the strongest candidates for the 2000 presidential race. Luzhkov envisioned Otechestvo as a new party for the regions. However, he had a major handicap in building such a party since many regional leaders resented Moscow's glittering success, believing that the capital's advantageous position had been earned at the regions' expense. Many governors were strongly sceptical of aligning with Luzhkov.

Nevertheless, Luzhkov had developed strong bilateral ties with several regional executives. Knowing that it is hard to be a successful governor in Russia without good ties to the president, some regional executives bet that Luzhkov would be elected Yeltsin's successor and jumped on his bandwagon early (see Table 4.1). In launching Otechestvo, Luzhkov sought to establish regional branches immediately with the goal of creating the party's foundations among regional activists rather than Moscow elites.[4] The movement set up seventy-three regional branches even before its official launch date.[5] Luzhkov hoped that this strategy would increase the party's appeal throughout the regions. However, the movement's success in establishing regional representations was less a result of Luzhkov's appeal to the masses and more a consequence of the political pragmatism of regional figures. Many influential and aspiring local politicians, including regional executives, hoped to use the Luzhkov alliance as a political springboard. Such factors were clearly the motivating impetus for the branches founded in Tver', Irkutsk and Volgograd. In some regions, local politicians sought to use Otechestvo as a vehicle to further ensconce their positions in opposition to the regional government. The attractiveness of representing Luzhkov's party for this purpose led to intense political competition among opposing local political factions as various groups fought for the right to establish and lead the official Otechestvo branch in their respective region. Such battles ensued in

Table 4.1 Political alliances of Russia's governors, October 1999

Region	Regional Executive	NDR	KPRF	Otechestvo	Golos Rossii	Vsya Rossiya	Announcement of Thirty-Nine	Yedinstvo	Other parties	Appeared on party list
Adygeya	Dzharimov	X				X				
Agin-Buryatiya	Zhamsuev	X								
Altai Krai	Surikov		X							
Amur	Belonogov		X							
Arkhangel'sk	Yefremov	X		X						
Astrakhan	Guzhvin	X			X	X	X			
Bashkortostan	Rakhimov	X				X	X			
Belgorod	Savchenko	X					X	X		
Bryansk	Lodkin		X							
Buryatiya	Potapov						X			
Chelyabinsk	Sumin				X	X	X	X		
Chita	Geniatulin						X			
Chukotka	Nazarov				X		X	X		
Chuvashiya	Fedorov					X	X			
Dagestan	Magomedov						X			
Evenkiya	Bokovikov		X				X			
Gorno-Altai	Zubakin						X		Gaidar	
Ingushetiya	Aushev					X				
Irkutsk	Govorin					X				
Ivanovo	Tikhomirov		X				X			
Jewish Autonomous Oblast	Volkov	X								
Kabardino-Balkariya	Kokov	X								
Kaliningrad	Gorbenko				X		X	X		
Kalmykiya	Ilyumzhinov							X		
Kaluga	Sudarenkov									

Region	Name								Affiliation
Kamchatka	Biryukov	X					X		OVR
Karachaevo-Cherkesiya	Khubiev[a]			X					KPRF
Kareliya	Katanandov			X			X		
Kemerovo	Tuleev	X			X		X		
Khabarovsk	Ishaev	X			X		X		
Khakasiya	Lebed'[e]				X		X		
Khanty-Mansi	Filipenko				X	X	X		OVR
Kirov	Sergeenkov	X			X		X		
Komi	Spiridonov		X				X		
Komi-Permyak	Poluyanov								
Koryak	Bronevich	X					X		
Kostroma	Shershunov			X	X				
Krasnodar	Kondratenko			X	X			Otechestvo[b]	
Krasnoyarsk	Lebed'[f]								
Kurgan	Bogomolov								
Kursk	Rutskoi						X	X	
Leningrad	Serdyukov								
Lipetsk	Korolev								
Magadan	Tsvetkov					X	X		
Marii El	Kislitsyn					X	X		
Mordoviya	Merkushkin		X						OVR
Moscow City	Luzhkov		X						OVR
Moscow Oblast	Tyazhlov[c]	X	X						OVR
Murmansk Oblast	Yevdokimov		X				X		
Nenets	Butov		X				X		
Nizhnii Novgorod	Sklyarov		X				X		
North Osetiya	Dzasokhov			X					
Novgorod	Prusak	X					X		NDR
Novosibirsk	Mukha[d]				X			X	
Omsk	Polezhaev	X		X			X	X	

Table 4.1 (*cont.*)

Region	Regional Executive	NDR	KPRF	Otechestvo	Golos Rossii	Vsya Rossiya	Announcement of Thirty-Nine	Yedinstvo	Other parties	Appeared on party list
Orel	Stroev									
Orenburg	Yelagin[e]	X								
Penza	Bochkarev				X	X	X			
Perm'	Igumnov	X			X	X	X			
Primorskii Krai	Nazdratenko				X		X	X		
Pskov	Mikhailov							X	Zhirinovsky	
Rostov	Chub	X			X	X	X	X		
Ryazan'	Lyubimov		X			X				
St. Petersburg	Yakovlev									OVR
Sakha (Yakutiya)	Nikolaev						X			
Sakhalin	Farkhutdinov	X					X			NDR
Samara	Titov	X			X					NDR
Saratov	Ayatskov	X								
Smolensk	Prokhorov		X				X			
Stavropol'	Chernogorov		X				X			
Sverdlovsk	Rossel						X		Transformation of Urals	
Taimyr	Nedelin						X			
Tambov	Ryabov[f]		X							
Tatarstan	Shaimiev					X				
Tomsk	Kress	X					X			NDR
Tula	Starodubtsev		X							KPRF
Tver'	Platov				X		X			Yedinstvo
Tyumen	Roketskii	X			X		X	X		
Tyva	Oorzhak	X					X			
Udmurtiya	Volkov			X						

			Union of Ulyanovsk Patriots	NDR
Ulyanovsk	Goryachev	X	X	
Ust'-Orda Buryatiya	Maleev	X		
Vladimir	Vinogradov	X		
Volgograd	Maksyuta	X		
Vologda	Pozgalev	X		X
Voronezh	Shabanov	X		
Yamal-Nenets	Neelov	X		
Yaroslavl'	Lisitsyn	X		

Source: Several sources were used in preparing this table, including the Carnegie Moscow Centre's *Regiony Rossii v 1998 g*, www.polit.ru, *Kommersant Daily*, *Golos Rossii regionalnyi zhurnal* and official candidate lists as published on the Central Electoral Commissions official website (www.fci.ru). We often encountered conflicting information so there may be some inaccuracies in the data.

Notes: X indicates affiliation at time of State Duma election in December.

[a] Khubiev was elected out of office in April 1999; Vladimir Semenov was elected to the post.

[b] Kondratenko had formed his own party called Otchestvo before Luzhkov adopted the name for his own political movement.

[c] Tyazhlov was elected out of office in December 1999; Boris Gromov was elected governor in January 2000.

[d] Mukha lost his reelection bid in December 1999; Novosibirsk Mayor Viktor Tolokonskii won election to the post in January 2000.

[e] Yelagin lost his seat to Aleksei Chernyshev in the second round of elections in December 1999.

[f] Ryabov was elected out of office in December 1999 in favour of his predecessor Oleg Betin. OVR = Fatherland – All Russia; KPRF = Communist Party of the Russian Federation; NDR = Our Home is Russia.

Voronezh, Smolensk and Primorskii Krai. The political battles within local Otechestvo branches greatly increased following the merger of Otechestvo (Fatherland) with Vsya Rossiya (All Russia) to form OVR (Fatherland – All Russia) in the summer of 1999, ultimately weakening the movement's authority in several regions.

With the majority of regional executives sceptical of Luzhkov's ability to lead a regionally focused movement, there was considerable room for other groups to take shape. At the end of January 1999 Samara Governor Konstantin Titov announced the creation of a new regional movement. Like Luzhkov, Titov was also clearly motivated by an interest to gather regional support for his own national political aspirations. In February 1999 he prepared a statement on the necessity of regional leaders' participation in the national elections, calling for the formation of a bloc that, 'could unite those who stand in favour of Russia's integrity, the strengthening of her economic and political sovereignty, and the development and prosperity of the regions.'[6] Thirty-three members of the Federation Council signed the appeal, including twenty regional executives. The signatories came from a wide range in the political spectrum, including vocal leftists – Kemerovo Governor Aman Tuleev and Chelyabinsk Governor Petr Sumin – and heavy-handed authoritarians – Primorskii Krai Governor Yevgenii Nazdratenko and Kaliningrad Governor Leonid Gorbenko (see Table 4.1). However, it seems that several of these signatories were unaware that the document was meant to serve as a basis for establishing a political party and was not intended to form a political alliance with Titov. Therefore, the number of governors and regional leaders backing Titov's party was significantly exaggerated.

Any significant regional backing of Golos Rossii (Voice of Russia) was short lived. It became clear relatively quickly that Golos Rossii would not operate as an organisation of regional interests, but as a platform for Titov to pursue his own political ambitions. Shortly after many governors defected to form the Vsya Rossiya (All Russia) party, Titov announced that Golos Rossii was a pro-presidential movement that did not accept Prime Minister Yevgenii Primakov's ideas of democracy.[7] Titov's interest in gaining presidential approval for his movement was likely related to the emergence of a more popular regional party, Vsya Rossiya. Golos Rossii quickly lost its regional base and eventually joined the right-wing coalition Union of Right Forces (SPS), a union of Sergei Kirienko's Novaya Sila group, Boris Nemtsov's Pravoe Delo, and Yegor Gaidar's Russia's Democratic Choice. Titov did not secure Yeltsin's approval at any point and evolved to become one of the few regional leaders to criticise Vladimir Putin vocally.

The second alternative to Luzhkov's Otechestvo (Fatherland), Vsya Rossiya, was formed in April 1999 by a group of republican presidents headed by Tatarstan President Mintimer Shaimiev, along with St. Petersburg Governor Vladimir Yakovlev, and the 'Russia's Regions' Duma faction. Vsya Rossiya's initial goal was to develop a regional electoral bloc strong enough to pass the 5 per cent barrier and elect regional representatives to the Duma. The founders of

Vsya Rossiya chose not to join Otechestvo for this purpose because they felt that representatives from Luzhkov's group would be primarily Muscovites. They rejected Golos Rossii as an option because they felt that the party was subordinate to one individual, and that many of the people in Titov's group were working simply to gain federal office.[8]

From the outset, however, Vsya Rossiya's founders expressed an interest in joining forces with either Otechestvo or Golos Rossii for the purpose of creating a more potent electoral bloc. Shaimiev felt that it was important that all of the different blocs and parties that had been created come together, otherwise many votes would be wasted and it would be impossible for any one group to form the Duma majority. The idea of an Otechestvo–Vsya Rossiya (Fatherland – All Russia; OVR) merger was met with scepticism by most analysts as the multiple conflicting interests of Luzhkov and the republican presidents seemed too numerous to make it possible for the two groups to work together. Nevertheless, in August 1999 the two groups announced their union, and shortly thereafter Primakov agreed to serve as the bloc's leader, taking on the role as the link bridging both sides. Primakov's addition essentially formalised the bloc's position as Kremlin opposition and provided the group with the figurehead it needed to improve its popular appeal.

As anticipated, Otechestvo and Vsya Rossiya encountered multiple problems in organising their union, with each party competing to take the leading role and contending with Primakov's sometimes divergent priorities as well as the interests of the Agrarian faction that had joined Otechestvo. These groups' distinctly different priorities were particularly apparent in selecting candidates to endorse. Vsya Rossiya complained that too many Muscovites appeared on the party list, and in several instances the regional representations of Otechestvo and Vsya Rossiya were on opposing sides of the local political scene and were thus unsuccessful at working together to present a united campaign for single member district candidates. The local level political infighting greatly inhibited the bloc's success on a variety of levels. One example was Primorskii Krai. When Primakov agreed to head the Fatherland – All Russia merger, he invited Primorskii Krai Governor Yevgenii Nazdratenko to participate in the group. However, Nazdratenko's top opponent in the region, Krai Duma Speaker Sergei Dudnik, had been heading the region's Otechestvo branch. Another notable conflict was for the single member seat in Kalmykiya, which Agrarian turned OVR member Gennadii Kulik had held for ten years. Luzhkov's wife, Yelena Baturina, announced that she was going to run from Kalmykiya as well. In the end, Kulik did not run, Baturina ran as an independent and Vitalii Daginov ran as OVR's candidate. Ultimately, Yedinstvo candidate Aleksandra Burataeva won the seat.

OVR's growing strength in late summer 1999 intimidated the Kremlin, which sought to counter the movement by establishing another regional bloc. In September thirty-nine members of the Federation Council signed an announcement to serve as the basis for founding the Yedinstvo movement. The regional leaders were Primorskii Krai Governor Yevgenii Nazdratenko, Belgorod

Governor Yevgenii Savchenko and Kursk Governor Aleksandr Rutskoi. However, just as many of the signatories to Titov's announcement that served as the foundation for Golos Rossii did not intend to form a political party, the same was true of several signatories of the 'Announcement of Thirty-Nine', and not all who signed the statement proceeded to give Yedinstvo their allegiance. Several of the signatories believed that they were signing a statement affirming their commitment to democratic elections in Russia, and many, such as Kemerovo Governor Aman Tuleev and Novgorod Governor Mikhail Prusak, were actively involved in other political parties.

The character of Yedinstvo's make-up demonstrated that its clear purpose was to steal support away from OVR. The only unifying quality of the governors backing the party was a clear desire to be on the Kremlin's good side. Some governors, such as Rostov Governor Vladimir Chub and Chelyabinsk Governor Petr Sumin, defected from OVR, which they had joined after abandoning Golos Rossii. Others, such as Rutskoi and Kostroma Governor Viktor Shershunov had previously been vocal critics of Yeltsin. Several Yedinstvo members represented heavily subsidised regions, such as Buryatiya and Kostroma, and others belonged to regions in need of the centre's influence to address difficult local issues, as in Sakhalin and Primorskii Krai. This paralleled the features of Our Home is Russia (NDR) in 1995–96, which attracted many governors who saw NDR membership as a way of lobbying the federal government.

With leader Viktor Chernomyrdin no longer in a position of federal power and having lost most of its regional leadership support to one of the four new movements, NDR's future in the State Duma looked bleak. It was clear already at the end of 1998 that the peak of NDR's success had passed and that the movement would have difficulty crossing the 5 per cent barrier in the 1999 State Duma elections if it did not align with another group. In the initial stages of Otechestvo's development, a large NDR faction led by Duma faction leader Aleksandr Shokhin wanted to align with the group, but this alliance never materialised.[9] As elections drew closer and Yedinstvo appeared on the scene, NDR negotiated the idea of merging with the group, but was unable to reach agreeable terms with the new party of power. NDR members submitted thirteen conditions for Yedinstvo to agree to for a merger to take place. Yedinstvo had to be willing to adopt NDR's programme and to support its list of single-mandate candidates. Additionally, NDR wanted its acronym in the name of a joint bloc and proposed that the leader of the NDR State Duma faction Vladimir Ryzhkov should have the second position on the federal party list. Yedinstvo did not want to comply with these arrangements, leaving NDR to enter the race on its own.[10]

Most governors who did not participate in one of the above parties or movements involved themselves in local-level movements. At about the same time as Luzhkov set up his Otechestvo movement, Saratov Governor Dmitrii Ayatskov announced that he was setting up his own new party called Moe Otechestvo (My Fatherland). However, Ayatskov ultimately abandoned this idea and returned to NDR. Kemerovo's Aman Tuleev and Altai Krai Governor Aleksandr Surikov were involved in a short-lived, leftist bloc called Za pobedu (For Victory) before committing to the Communists. Sverdlovsk Governor Eduard Rossel established his Transformation of the Urals party in 1993 and opted not to align with any of the new blocs. Ulyanovsk Governor Yurii Goryachev also had his own regional party and Orel Governor Yegor Stroev decided not to join any of the regional blocs.

Geographical distribution played an important and telling role in the development of regional political coalitions. Luzhkov's success at penetrating the regions and earning the support of regional executives was essentially limited to the north and central territories of European Russia, with only two regions, Udmurtiya and Novosibirsk, located a significant distance from the capital. Given these geographical limitations an alliance with Vsya Rossiya and its dominance in Russia's ethnically defined republics was clearly in Otechestvo's favour. Vsya Rossiya had been rather successful at attracting regional elites across the country, with significant support from regional executives in the North Caucasus, Volga area, Siberia and the Far East. Therefore, the Fatherland – All Russia alliance had the support of regional executives throughout the country. Yedinstvo was also well spread from the North Caucasus across central Russia to the Far East and Far North.

An interesting aspect of the various regional parties was the lack of regional representation on their party lists. While the primary reason given by the governors for starting their regional political initiatives was the desire to have regional issues better represented at the federal level, the level of regional representation on the party lists of these movements was no stronger than on the lists of the other parties and movements. On OVR's party list, only 54 per cent of the candidates came from the regions. Of the twenty-six parties and movements that participated in the State Duma elections, only three minor parties had poorer regional representation than OVR. Yedinstvo's regional representation was considerably better, at 73 per cent. However, of the major parties competing in the election, NDR had the best level of regional representation (87 per cent), and both Yabloko and the Communist Party of the Russian Federation (KPRF) had more candidates from the regions than either OVR or Yedinstvo. The lack of regional representation among the so-called regional parties only further demonstrates that the governors' real interest in forming and aligning with the new political movements was to put themselves in the best position for post-Yeltsin politics.

Ultimately, the activity of Russia's regional executives in forming regional parties did not advance the cause of party building in the Russian regions, but was simply the governors' latest tactic in trying to ensure future good relations with the Kremlin. Governors truly committed to any one political party or movement were few in number. As Table 4.1 demonstrates, many governors jumped from party to party over time, trying to align themselves with whichever group seemed to be the most powerful and influential at that moment. Sometimes, the governor himself did not join a party but assigned one of his deputies to each of the new parties so that he would have a stake in whichever party won. In Table 4.1 we have tried to identify the various alliances of the governors and to indicate, where possible, which party they were affiliated with during the State Duma elections in December 1999.

1999 State Duma elections

In the weeks leading up to the State Duma elections, the battle raged between OVR and Yedinstvo. Several governors pledged their support to the new Kremlin movement and Putin's victories in Chechnya successfully steered popular support in favour of the centre. OVR lagged behind, under heavy attack from the Kremlin, which used its control over national television broadcasters particularly effectively. At the end of October, Primakov, Luzhkov and Yakovlev issued an open letter to Russian President Boris Yeltsin accusing the presidential administration of meddling in the State Duma electoral process and violating the law and democratic standards. A few weeks later OVR Deputy Campaign Manager and former Yeltsin spokesman, Sergei Yastrezhembskii blasted the president's use of Russian Public Television as a campaign weapon and further criticised the Kremlin's role in the State Duma campaign.[11] At the beginning of December, Yeltsin dismissed Moscow Police Chief Nikolai Kulikov, greatly angering Luzhkov, who accused Yeltsin of acting arbitrarily with political motives.

In spite of what appeared to be an increased show of support in favour of Yedinstvo in the weeks leading up to the State Duma elections, the movement's ability to outdo OVR still seemed rather weak. The governors backing Yedinstvo generally came from relatively weak regions heavily dependent on federal subsidies. Several of the most active governors in the initial stages of the movement are unlikely to be re-elected and could face criminal charges once they leave office, including Kursk Oblast's Aleksandr Rutskoi, Kaliningrad Oblast's Leonid Gorbenko and Chukotka's Aleksandr Nazarov.[12] Yedinstvo was void of any charismatic regional leaders like those that had helped propagate OVR. Additionally, the governors and presidents backing Yedinstvo represented some of the country's smallest and least-populated regions. Yedinstvo's governors ruled over less than twenty million voters, or about 18.5 per cent of Russia's voting population, with only eight of the regions boasting over one million voters. OVR's supporting regional executives represented regions containing over 40.1 million voters, or 38.1 per cent of the electorate, including crucial regions such as Moscow City and St. Petersburg. Additionally, many of the regional executives backing OVR, such as Shaimiev and Bashkortostan's Murtaza Rakhimov, were known for their ability to command high support for their preferred candidates in elections.

OVR also had more professional candidates on its lists. OVR's party list comprised several high-level political figures, including regional executives and State Duma deputies, as well as many regional-level politicians, business people and academics. OVR had an organisational advantage over Yedinstvo in terms of

Table 4.2   State Duma election results, December 1999

Party	SMD	Party	Total (%)
Communists	55	67	124 (27%)
Yedinstvo	9	64	73 (16%)
OVR	32	36	68 (15%)
URF	5	24	29 (6%)
Yabloko	5	17	22 (5%)
Zhirinovsky	2	17	19 (4%)
NDR	8	0	8 (2%)
Agrarian	2	0	2
Nikolaev–Federov	2	0	2
In Support of Army	2	0	2
Pensioners	2	0	2
ROS	2	0	1
KRO–Boldyrev	1	0	1
Russian Socialist Party	1	0	1
Spiritual Heritage	1	0	1
Independents[a]	95	0	95 (21%)

Source: EWI, *Russian Regional Report* 4:48 (22 December 1999).
Notes: *SMD = single mandate list; OVR = Fatherland – All Russia; NDR = Our Home is Russia; ROS = Russian National Union; KRO = Congress of Russian Communities.
[a] When an officially independent winner had a clear alliance with a specific political party or movement, we placed the deputy with the respective party.

regional branches that gave it an edge in nominating and campaigning for single-seat races. Failing to merge with NDR and take advantage of the movement's established organisational structure, Yedinstvo had little time to coordinate its campaign, amassing a party list of mostly mid-level functionaries.

Given the various advantages OVR appeared to have over Yedinstvo, the Kremlin party's chances for success did not seem particularly high. As the elections drew closer, Yedinstvo's popularity increased in the polls, while OVR's decreased; however, no one predicted Yedinstvo's overwhelming performance. According to the preliminary results of the 19 December 2000 elections, the Communist Party led in both party-list and single seat voting, yet it failed to gather the same amount of representation that it held in the previous Duma. The Communists earned 24 per cent from party-list voting, plus fifty-five single seats, giving it control of 27 per cent of the Duma, down from the 35 per cent it previously held. The Communists were followed in the party-list voting by Yedinstvo with 23 per cent. OVR came in a distant third with 13 per cent, and SPS had a surprisingly strong showing of 8.5 per cent. Yabloko and Zhirinovsky's Bloc also passed the 5 per cent barrier, earning 5.93 per cent and 5.98 per cent, respectively. NDR failed to pass the 5 per cent mark, but managed to elect eight deputies in single member races. For results of State Duma elections, see Table 4.2.

The support that regional executives offered to political blocs and parties proved a highly influential tool on the electorate in their specific regions. Yedinstvo led in party-list voting in most of the regions in which the governor officially backed the pro-Kremlin movement. An interesting aspect of Yedinstvo's success in these specific regions is that their respective regional executives are generally not among the most powerful or influential. Most of the regional executives supporting OVR were not as successful at influencing the voters in their regions in party-list voting. In the twenty-two regions where OVR had the support of the regional executive, the bloc came in first only in six, including Moscow City and Tatarstan, which are home to two of the bloc's founders. OVR's highest showing was in Ingushetiya, where it earned 87.98 per cent of the vote. SPS had a strong showing in Titov's Samara Oblast, pulling in 22 per cent of the vote to come behind the Communists.

Even though Yedinstvo outdid OVR in the party-list voting, OVR's organisational superiority paid off in the single-member races, which elected thirty-two OVR deputies to Yedinstvo's nine. In sum, the two movements had each gained control of about 15–16 per cent of the new Duma (see Table 4.2). OVR's success in the single member districts was due in large part to the active support that specific influential regional executives gave to the movement. Moscow City provided OVR with ten seats (the city has fifteen districts overall). Tatarstan contributed three out of a possible five seats, and Bashkortostan delivered four of its six seats. Almost all of the OVR deputies elected in single-seat races came from regions in which the governor supported the movement. However, in general, governors were very successful in influencing the outcome of single-member districts. At least 43 per cent of the candidates elected in single-seat races had the support of the regional executive.[13] An almost direct correlation existed between the success of a governor's candidate and the strength of the governor in the region. Governor's candidates were particularly successful in Bashkortostan, Tatarstan, Krasnodar, Kemerovo, Kirov, Perm', Sverdlovsk, Tambov, Tula, Tyumen', Ulyanovsk and Moscow City. A governor's support was less important in regions where the executive is not as powerful.

The composition of the newly elected Duma, in which no one party was in possession of a clear majority, left OVR in a position possibly to command considerable clout. Yedinstvo had only a slight edge over OVR. Even if Yedinstvo managed to form a coalition with SPS (6 per cent) and the remainder of NDR (2 per cent), its collective strength would not reach that of the Communists. However, as anticipated, the deputies elected from OVR quickly broke down into several different groups, including the leftist forty-two member agro-industrial faction and the forty-one member Regions of Russia group, leaving OVR, the remainder of which is primarily Luzhkov supporters, with only forty-seven seats, or 10 per cent of the Duma. The handful of NDR deputies elected joined the Yedinstvo faction, as did many of the approximately 100 independents elected, giving the faction eighty-three seats or 18 per cent of the Duma. This is only slightly smaller than KPRF's eighty-eight seats, the largest Duma faction. For a breakdown of the State Duma factions, see Table 4.3.

Table 4.3   State Duma factions, May 2000

Party/group	No. of members
KPRF	88
Yedinstvo	83
People's Deputy Group	58
OVR	47
Agro-Industrial Group	42
Regions of Russia Group	41
SPS	32
Yabloko	21
LDPR (Zhirinovsky)	16
Independents	19

Source: State Duma Website (www.duma.ru), 9 May 2000.
Notes: KPRF = Communist Party of the Russian
Federation; OVR = Fatherland – All Russia; SPS = Union of
Right Forces; LDPR = Liberal Democratic Party of Russia

Even though the governors failed to establish a regional majority in the new Duma, the active role regional executives took in the electoral process, particularly in single-member district voting, has increased the dialogue between governors and Duma deputies. For the governors, the Duma is no longer an exclusively federal organ distanced from the affairs of the regions, but rather another venue through which the regions can influence policy. In March 2000 several State Duma deputies held a round table with the Siberian Accord inter-regional association to discuss methods for improving cooperation. The motive for this meeting was that Siberian initiatives often disappear in the Duma since deputies tend to work specifically for the interests of their particular district and a united approach is absent. The Duma members at the meeting adopted a decision to create an inter-factional group of Siberian deputies. The Siberian group may be the first in a subsequent series of regional lobbies and coalitions that could become a significant feature of the Duma.[14]

Governors have also sought out the aid of the new Duma deputies in conflict with the federal government. In May 2000 Irkutsk Governor Boris Govorin met with five of the region's seven State Duma deputies to ask them to coordinate efforts in protecting the region's interests in a dispute with the federal government over the ownership of the company Irkutskenergo.[15] The meeting between Govorin and the deputies was not the first, but it was the most representative since most of the State Duma members were present, and the deputies were not always in agreement on the oblast's best course of action.

While the governors were able to exert considerable influence over the State Duma elections, their impact was greatest in their ability to sway their constituents to vote for the candidates and parties they supported. The regional movements promoted by the governors – although succeeding in the goal of combining forces in order to curtail support for the Communists and to elect their own representatives to the Duma – failed to function as real political coalitions. OVR essentially dissipated after the elections and Yedinstvo stepped up as the Kremlin's new party of power. Following the movement's success in the State Duma elections and Yeltsin's subsequent resignation, governors quickly lined up to offer their support to the Kremlin's new party, and new leader, Vladimir Putin.

2000 presidential election

Yedinstvo's success in the State Duma elections clearly demonstrated that the Yeltsin Kremlin was not going to relinquish its hold without a fight. By resigning in favour of Putin and thus bringing presidential elections forwards by several months, Yeltsin ensured his prime minister's election leaving insufficient time for any possible opponents, including the long-expected Primakov–Luzhkov ticket, to campaign effectively. By employing this tactic, Yeltsin beat the governors at their own game. Over the course of 1999 many regional executives who had feared that their declining popularity would prevent them from winning re-election succeeded in moving up regional elections to prevent their opposition from gaining any real support.

Yeltsin's resignation sent a clear message to the governors that the height of their climb to power had been reached and that further challenges to the federal centre would meet with a strong rebuff. From the start of Putin's tenure as acting president it was apparent that he intended to restore central control over the regions. With the balance of power tipped back in favour of the centre, the governors quickly abandoned their opposition and immediately sought ways to rekindle warm relations with the federal centre. Rather than establish any sort of resistance to the centre's efforts to regain control, governors resorted to their traditional methods of pledging support to the centre in the hope that their support would translate into more favourable policy towards their respective region. Regional executives that had been aligned with Fatherland – All Russia (Otechestvo–Vsya Rossiya), such as Kareliya Prime Minister Sergei Katanandov and Udmurtiya Prime Minister Aleksandr Volkov – as well as governors who had stayed out of the pre-Duma political antics – such as Sverdlovsk Governor Eduard Rossel – were quick to congratulate Putin and offer their support.

Shaimiev and the other founding members of Vsya Rossiya found themselves with the greatest challenge to mend their ties with the Kremlin after having endorsed the Luzhkov–Primakov alliance. Immediately following the State Duma elections, Shaimiev, Yakovlev and Rakhimov sought a meeting with Putin and announced that Vsya Rossiya was separating from Otechestvo and would set up an independent faction in the State Duma. The governors announced that they would back Putin in the presidential campaign and quickly joined the initiative group to support his candidacy. Shaimiev also informed Tatarstan's voters that they should support Putin. Maintaining more autonomy from the centre than any other region, Tatarstan stood to lose the most if the region's relations with the centre went sour. However, Shaimiev refused to cave in entirely to Putin and continued both simultaneously to support the acting president and to argue in favour of Tatarstan's interests.

Several governors tried to impress Putin by supporting initiatives to strengthen the federal centre. In late February Novgorod Governor Prusak, Belgorod Governor Yevgenii Savchenko and Kurgan Governor Oleg Bogolmolov sent an open letter to Putin with suggestions to reform Russia's political institutions.[16] The suggestions included strengthening vertical power, giving the president the right to appoint governors and giving governors the right to appoint mayors. The governors also suggested extending the presidential term to seven years. The governors' strategy in issuing this letter was essentially to ensure their appointment as governors if Putin should try to reform the existing system to reestablish the appointment of governors. However, in spite of the multiple proposals and concepts for reorganising the federation that have entered into public debate, it is very unlikely that Putin would return to appointing governors, having spoken out strongly against revoking that right[17] (see Chapter 12). Regional executives are aware of this improbability and employed the tactic of volunteering appointment, without really meaning it, to further show their support for Putin.

Ultimately, even Luzhkov threw his support behind Putin. In February 2000 Luzhkov announced that Otechestvo's national leadership would decide which candidate to support in the presidential ballot by 10 March and allowed the party's regional branches to choose their own candidates independently, essentially allowing them to back Putin. Less than two weeks before the election, Luzhkov announced that Otechestvo would back Putin under rather vague conditions, such as maintaining democratic freedom in Russia, rejecting dictatorship by oligarchs, developing the economy and mobilising resources in support of the social sphere.[18]

Since there was no doubt that Putin would win the March election, the governors' goal became getting as good a showing in their regions as possible in order to secure friendly relations with the president. Regional executives with strong influence over the electorate, particularly presidents of ethnic republics, were successful at accomplishing this goal. Putin's strongest showing was in Ingushetiya, where he gained 85.42 per cent of the vote, the very same region that had given OVR its strongest support of 87.98 per cent only three months before in the State Duma elections. Putin's other top showings were in regions with reputations for shady practices where the regional executives heavily courted the acting president: Tatarstan (68.74 per cent), Bashkortostan (60.34 per cent) and Dagestan (76.69 per cent). The presidents of both Tatarstan and Bashkortostan had endorsed OVR in December 1999 and returned sizeable votes for the movement. Putin's success in these regions was also aided by his visit to the republics just days before the election. Nevertheless, in regions such as Tatarstan, the regional executive commands such control over the voters that he can essentially produce whatever electoral results are most expedient. In the period summer–autumn 1999, the person to back was Primakov, while in winter 2000 it was Putin, and these powerful regional executives were able to convince their constituents to vote accordingly.

Of the Kremlin's previous critics among regional executives, only Titov remained firm in his reproaches. The governor was quick to announce his candidacy against Putin in the March presidential elections, and his local opposition took on the leadership of the local Yedinstvo branch, further discrediting Titov in the centre's eyes. Although Titov had enjoyed considerable popularity in Samara, evidenced by the strong showing SPS had in the region in the Duma elections, local observers felt their governor was making a serious political mistake by joining the presidential race since he clearly stood no chance of winning and was unlikely to improve his national popularity by challenging Putin. As anticipated, Titov's sixth place finish with 1.5 per cent of the vote dented his popularity in the region, even though the governor had a rather respectable showing of 20.06 per cent in Samara. However, compared with Titov's 64 per cent victory in Samara's 1996 gubernatorial election, his 2000 presidential showing was weak. Days after the presidential elections, Titov resigned from his post as governor explaining that after his poor showing in the presidential election he had clearly lost the support of the people and could no longer serve as governor. It was obvious, however, that Titov was employing Yeltsin's tactic of resigning in order to facilitate early elections. Samara gubernatorial elections were set for July 2000 and Titov announced his candidacy within a month after his resignation.

Kemerovo Governor Aman Tuleev also chose to run in the presidential election, continuing the tradition he began when he first ran for the Russian presidency back in 1991. Tuleev campaigned in 1996 as well but ultimately withdrew in favour of Communist candidate Gennadii Zyuganov. In January 2000 Tuleev announced that he had little hope for Zyuganov as a candidate and would therefore run for the presidency himself. Tuleev showed little concern over the impact of his candidacy on his relations with the federal government. Tuleev is known for his rather erratic political behaviour. In the State Duma elections he simultaneously ran on the Communist Party list and supported the anti-Communist Yedinstvo, endorsing both Yedinstvo and Communist candidates in the single-member races. In the presidential race Tuleev outdid Putin in Kemerovo, pulling in 51.57 per cent to Putin's 25.01 per cent. Tuleev did not manage to gain more than 10 per cent of the vote in any of the other regions, yet he came in fourth overall with 3.02 per cent of the vote.

Once Putin's mandate was confirmed by popular election, governors were forced to wait and see how their various attempts to woo the president had paid off. Just three days after the presidential election Putin met with eighteen governors in the Kremlin. The meeting was kept highly secret and was not reported on the presidential administration's press website. The participating governors were apparently chosen for the strong support their regions had delivered for Putin's victory. Among those included in the secret meeting were Katanandov, Prusak,

Rossel, Ayatskov, Rakhimov, Shaimiev, Luzhkov, Vologda Governor Vyacheslav Pozgalev, Moscow Oblast Governor Boris Gromov and Irkutsk Governor Boris Govorin. The inclusion of Luzhkov and several of the other governors who had aligned with him in the 1999 State Duma race demonstrated that these governors are simply too significant for Putin to oppose directly and he therefore sought to bring them into his camp.

Consequences of federal elections for centre–periphery relations

The more aggressive role that governors played in the 1999–2000 federal elections was simply an attempt to expand their power at the federal and regional level. While Putin has made much of his new policy of re-imposing a vertical-power hierarchy, he now faces strong political actors in the form of the governors. Although Yeltsin was able to block the governors from gaining control of the presidency, they still have considerable clout. As a result of the 1999–2000 campaign season, the governors have increased their influence over the State Duma. They have also made clear to future presidential candidates that, as elected officials themselves, they play a crucial role in delivering the regional vote.

Even while he was serving as acting president, the governors taught Putin the limits of his powers. Putin's relationship with Vsya Rossiya founding member, St. Petersburg Governor Vladimir Yakovlev, dates back to when both were deputy mayors under former St. Petersburg Mayor Anatolii Sobchak. Yakovlev split with Sobchak and defeated him in 1996 while Putin remained on Sobchak's team. In the St Perersburg's 14 May 2000 gubernatorial election, Putin sought to unseat Yakovlev by backing Deputy Prime Minister Valentina Matvienko. The St. Petersburg gubernatorial race attracted considerable attention as observers watched to see if the new president could have his candidate elected to one of the most powerful regional posts. However, it soon was clear that Matvienko had no chance of winning and Putin called on her to withdraw her candidacy on the pretext that Putin needed her to help in the cabinet. Trying to put a good face on the loss, Putin then threw his support behind the incumbent.

The elections also demonstrated the effectiveness of the Kremlin's divide-and-rule policy over the governors. During the 1999–2000 electoral season the governors failed to build lasting horizontal coalitions which would give them substantial influence on federal policy making in the executive and legislative branches. While things looked bleak for the Kremlin in the summer of 1999, it was able to come roaring back in autumn of 1999 and winter 2000. Now instead of trying to build coalitions with each other, the governors are back to the old game of trying to secure their own power in their regions and then working to build the best possible relations with Moscow in order to win the best possible deal for themselves. Putin may not be able to name the governors of his choice, but he still has strong control over the country's purse strings allowing him to place considerable constraints over gubernatorial power.

Notes

1 This chapter is based on the research and analysis Robert Orttung and I prepared for the East–West Institute, *Russian Regional Report* (hereafter, EWI, *Russian Regional Report*). The chapter benefited tremendously from Robert Orttung's editorial and substantive assistance.
2 EWI, *Russian Regional Report*, 5:13 (5 April 2000).
3 In identifying which candidates the governors supported we relied heavily on information provided to us by the EWI Russian Regional Report network of correspondents on the ground.
4 EWI, *Russian Regional Report*, 3:45 (12 November 1998).
5 *Nezavisimaya gazeta* (15 December 1998).
6 'Obrashchenie k rossiiskoi obshchestvennosti', *Golos Rossii* (May 1999), pp. 32–34.
7 *Kommersant Daily* (21 April, 1999).
8 EWI, *Russian Regional Report*, 4:26 (8 July 1999).
9 *Kommersant Daily* (19 November 1998).
10 EWI, *Russian Regional Report*, 4:37 (7 October 1999).
11 EWI, *Russian Regional Report*, 4:44 (23 November 1999).
12 *Ekspert* (25 October 1999).
13 Following his inauguration, Putin announced that he was in favour of elections based on single member district voting rather than party list voting; see *RFE/RL Newsline* (9 May 2000). This is a strange approach for the president to support since it would conceivably give the governors greater influence in the State Duma elections.
14 EWI, *Russian Regional Report*, 5:13 (5 April 2000).
15 EWI, *Russian Regional Report*, 5:18 (10 May 2000).
16 EWI, *Russian Regional Report*, 5:8 (1 March 2000).
17 *Ibid.*
18 *Vedomosti* (16 March 2000).

High stakes, low chances: the failure of party politics in St. Petersburg

The rise of competitive electoral politics in post-communist Russia has brought about significant cross-regional differences both in voting patterns and in party development. Some of the regions display particularly unusual characteristics. One such 'deviant case' is Sverdlovsk Oblast, a region where political parties gradually emerged as important agencies of electoral mobilisation, even though the initial level of party development was rather modest.[1] In the majority of Russia's regions, the role of political parties continues to be negligible, which makes tracing the causal dynamics of party underdevelopment at the regional level quite a difficult task. In St. Petersburg, however, political parties that had flourished in the early 1990s became almost extinct by the end of the decade. There are therefore reasons to expect that an in-depth examination of the case of St. Petersburg can result in a better understanding of the causes of party underdevelopment in the regions of Russia. This is the major purpose of this chapter.

The lack of party strength in Russia's regions has been testified by recent studies which focused on candidate nomination strategies and electoral performance in the 1995 national legislative elections,[2] and in the 1995–97 gubernatorial elections.[3] It is not unusual to explain this situation with reference to a particularly unfavourable constellation of institutional and political factors in Russia as a whole.[4] Studies that have focused primarily on region-level factors of party development are few. In particular, it has been demonstrated that the electoral strength of administrative and economic managers impedes party development.[5] In a recent attempt to identify factors facilitating party development in Russia's regions, one of the authors of this chapter described and explained certain effects exerted upon the process by intra-elite conflicts on the regional level, electoral systems and several other institutional features.[6] The case of St. Petersburg calls a change in the research perspective from a focus on positive factors to a study of the negative influences upon party development, and from general to region-specific characteristics. At the same time, for the sake of making our findings compatible with the results of earlier research – and hopefully to build on this research – we have not changed the empirical base.

Therefore, our attention will be focused on regional legislative elections. However important, gubernatorial elections and national electoral contests held in
the city are of little concern to this chapter.

Political parties in St. Petersburg: cross-regional and historical perspectives

What is so specific about party politics in St. Petersburg? In order to answer this
question, we need to place the city in a wider cross-regional perspective by comparing it with the aggregate evidence on party development from the majority of
Russia's regions. While very little comprehensive information on the role of
parties in the regional legislative elections held in 1993–94 is available,[7] without
such information, any conclusions about the causal dynamics of party politics
in Russia are not sufficiently empirically substantiated. This led us to undertake
extensive library research aimed at extracting relevant data from the regional
newspapers of 1993–94, which allowed us to construct a database that covers
almost all regional elections held in Russia from December 1993 up to (but not
including) December 1999. The database does not include information on elections held in Chechnya, nor on the 1994 elections in the autonomous districts
(*okruga*) of Russia. We then divided the database into two parts. The first part
covers the regional elections held during the first electoral cycle in Russia, starting with those concurrent with the Duma elections of 12 December 1993, and
the second part includes those elections beginning on the same day as the second
Duma elections that were held on 17 December 1995. Given that the terms of the
regional assemblies elected in 1993–94 were normally limited to two years (even
though many of them managed to extend their lives), it is not surprising that the
numbers of cases in both data sets are almost the same: seventy-five elections in
seventy-five regions for the 1993–95 electoral cycle, and seventy-nine elections in
seventy-five regions for the 1995–99 electoral cycle. Table 5.1 provides data on
the comparative standing of St. Petersburg in relation to the national average of
party representation in regional legislative assemblies.

As follows from the table, the pattern of party development displayed by St.
Petersburg is, indeed, very unusual. The most striking dynamics can be observed
in respect of our principal indicator of party strength, the percentage of party
nominees in the assembly. As a result of the 1994 elections 55.1 per cent of party
nominees were elected to the St. Petersburg legislature, one of the highest levels
of party representation in Russia. This was considerably higher than the national
average of only 13.9 per cent. However, by 1998, the picture had dramatically
changed. While the national average increased by nearly 10 per cent, the level of
party representation in St. Petersburg fell to 28 per cent; this was still higher than
the national average, but almost half of that was obtained in 1994. A clue as to
why this happened can be derived from the second line of the table. The data
clearly suggest that the nationwide increase in party representation can largely
be explained by the improved performance of the Communist Party. In St.
Petersburg, however, the Communists failed to make any progress. Moreover,

Table 5.1   Political parties and electoral competitiveness (numbers of candidates per seat) in Russia's regional legislative elections, 1993–99

	Russia (national average)	St. Petersburg
Overall party representation in assemblies/assembly, per cent, 1993–95	13.9	55.1
Communist Party representation in assemblies/assembly, per cent, 1993–95	4.3	6.1
Electoral competitiveness, 1993–95	4.6	15.3
Overall party representation in the assemblies/assembly, per cent, 1995–99	23.2	28.0
Communist Party representation in assemblies/assembly, per cent, 1995–99	14.0	4.0
Electoral competitiveness, 1995–99	5.9	16.7

Source: Calculated by the authors on the basis of the official publications of the local and federal electoral authorities of Russia.

while on average non-communist formations were able to hold on to their electoral support, in St. Petersburg they suffered a massive set-back. One might expect that political parties lost their significance simply because local electoral politics in the city became less competitive than it used to be. However, data in Table 5.1 does not confirm this expectation. Both in 1994 and in 1998, the electoral arena in St. Petersburg remained more competitive than in any other region. Apparently, the stakes in the regional elections continued to be high, but something occurred in the city in 1994–98 that made political parties increasingly irrelevant, even within this highly competitive environment.

Many peculiarities of St. Petersburg's political development can be traced back to the very high levels of anti-Communist political mobilisation present in the city during the early phase of Mikhail Gorbachev's period of perestroika. An important factor in the development of political activism was the spread of what became known as 'informal groups'. The 'informal movement' in Leningrad (St. Petersburg's former name) was launched by several groups that expressed ecological concerns and protested against the demolition of buildings of historical importance.[8] Starting as early as 1988, these groups became increasingly politicised, and were soon supplemented by a number of explicitly political associations. In the view of their activists, who came to be referred to as 'democrats', the Communist regime had to be replaced by a democratic political order founded on human rights, civil liberties and economic freedom.[9] The city's populace became increasingly attentive to these demands.

As a testimony to this, the first relatively free elections to the USSR Congress of People's Deputies resulted in a decisive victory for the city's democrats. None of the communist bosses were elected, with the Leningrad delegation becoming one of the most radically reform-oriented in the Congress. This pattern was reiterated in the 1990 city elections that were won decisively by a coalition called 'Democratic Elections – 90', comprising a majority of democratic informal groups.[10] While the democrats managed to elect as many as 240 of their candidates to the city Soviet (Lensovet), the communist-supported candidates won in no more than sixty constituencies. This effectively left the democrats in charge. In May 1990, one of Russia's most prominent opponents of Communist rule, Anatolii Sobchak, was elected as the chairman of Lensovet. The democratic commitment of the Leningraders was reconfirmed in June 1991 when they voted overwhelmingly for Boris Yeltsin in Russia's presidential elections and for Sobchak in the mayoral elections. They also voted for the restoration of the city's historical name, St. Petersburg. By 1991, the city emerged as one of the strongholds of the pro-reform movement in the country.

The attempted coup of August 1991 changed the whole structure of opportunities available to Russia's major political forces. However, in contrast to the countries of East-Central Europe, this change was not very favourable for independent political actors, such as political parties. The major difference was that, in Russia, the advent of regime transformation did not coincide with 'founding elections'. Moreover, very few local elections had been held in the country between August 1991 to December 1993. Since parties are, by definition, electoral agencies, this left them without any significant role within the new political order. In the majority of regions, this lack of electoral competition resulted in the collapse of the democratic movement.[11] Later, the Communist Party regained its legal status and emerged as the largest and best organised national political party.[12] Similar trends in political developments were evident in St. Petersburg, but there were also quite visible differences from the mainstream. St. Petersburg was one of only a few regions where the local legislature (Lensovet), comprised a majority of newcomers with a background in the democratic movement. The Communist faction was only a minority group. Opposition to the political line pursued by the federal authorities and especially by the city mayor was most vocally articulated by several factions rooted in the democratic movement. One of them, initially called 'March', was particularly explicit in its criticisms of the authorities. In 1993 this 'moderate democratic' faction launched its own political party, the Regional Party of the Centre.[13]

Our analysis identifies two key factors that account for the very high levels of party development in St. Petersburg by the beginning of the first national electoral cycle. Both factors are related to theories of party system formation developed in the comparative literature on the subject. First, political parties come into being within the context of effective enfranchisement.[14] In contrast to formal enfranchisement that creates legal provisions for mass political participation, but often leaves the masses disinterested in and/or incapable of exerting any influence upon politics, effective enfranchisement requires a politically engaged citizenry. Arguably, the turbulent period of perestroika in Russia generally failed to produce the conditions consistent with such a requirement. St. Petersburg, with its unusually high level of anti-Communist political mobilisation, stands out as an exception in this respect. Political parties emerged because they were in demand. On the one hand, they were demanded by politically active citizens who viewed them as agencies of interest articulation. On the other hand, they were demanded by competitive political elites and counter-elites that, in the period 1989–91, used party organisation as an important communication channel with the masses. This, however, does not explain what facilitated party survival in the interlude of August 1991 to December 1993. Here, the second theory comes into play. Comparative research identifies the existence of internally divided legislatures, uncontrolled by the executive, as one of the most important factors of party development.[15] In contrast to many other regions of Russia, a legislature satisfying these requirements continued to function in St. Petersburg in the period 1991–93. By the very fact of its existence, it provided a natural niche for party survival. Moreover, within this 'permissive environment', political parties continued to crystallise and mature, as is shown by the activities of the Regional Party of the Centre. We therefore believe that it was the constellation of two factors – mass political mobilisation, and the creation of an independent partisan legislature – that crucially contributed to the unusually high level of party development in the city.

Party utility in the 1994–98 elections to the regional legislature

In the aftermath of the October 1993 events in Moscow, Boris Yeltsin issued a number of decrees that effectively abolished local soviets in the Russian Federation. In particular, the Lensovet was dissolved. In this period, Sobchak remained the sole power-holder in the city and he soon took advantage of his position to lay out a new set of rules governing legislative politics. Fresh elections were scheduled for March 1994.

The 1993 national legislative elections in Russia utilised a mixed electoral formula which combined elements of plurality and proportionality. But only a few regions followed the national example when drafting their own electoral laws. St. Petersburg, together with several national republics, adhered to the majority formula predominant in the perestroika era. Clearly, such an institutional choice made a lot of difference in terms of party development. Under plurality, or majority, rules it is individual candidates, and not political parties, who contest elections. In St. Petersburg, however, party-nominated candidates had a bonus in the sense that an electoral association (a party or a registered bloc of parties) was entitled to register a 'list' of up to fifty candidates by collecting at least 35,000 signatures. Another institutional characteristic that is worth mentioning in this context is the requirement of a minimum electoral turnout of 25 per cent (in a given constituency) for elections to be valid. Similar turnout requirements also existed in many other regions, and there were many instances when this provision prevented large numbers of deputies from being elected. St. Petersburg was not exceptional in this respect. The March 1994 elections returned only twenty-five of fifty deputies. The remaining deputies were elected in November 1994 after the turnout provision was dropped from the electoral law. During the interlude between March and November 1994, the St. Petersburg party scene changed quite drastically, so much so that we should consider these two contests as quite distinct.

In contrast with many other regional legislatures, the St. Petersburg Assembly was able to complete a full four-year term. The second Legislative Assembly was elected in December 1998, and the law which regulated this election was very similar to that employed in 1994.

A rough classification of political parties and blocs that contested the 1994–98 elections in St. Petersburg is presented in Table 5.2. As follows from the table, many political parties and movements did not survive more than one election. It is, however, possible to discern a number of patterns and continuities. The Regional Party of the Centre (RPC) formed the basis of the Beloved City coalition in 1994, while in 1998 it contested elections under the label of Yabloko. There is some organisational continuity between the major radical democratic groupings, i.e. between the Democratic Unity of St. Petersburg, Russia's Democratic Choice, and Accord – United Democrats of St. Petersburg. The 'Communists of Leningrad' bloc was created by two communist parties that contested the March 1994 elections separately from each other.

An interesting peculiarity of the 1998 elections was the participation of ten electoral associations, each of them nominating only one candidate. Clearly, such 'parties' were nothing more than the personal electoral vehicles of their leaders, and one may reasonably argue that such cases have to be considered as specific instances of independent candidate nomination. In this chapter, we have omitted specific references to these groups from our analysis.

In order to analyse the causal dynamics of party extinction in St. Petersburg, we have employed a theory developed by John Aldrich. The basic assumption of this theory is that 'politicians turn to their political party – that is, use its powers, resources, and institutional forms – when they believe doing so increases their prospects for winning desired outcomes, and they turn from it if does not.'[16] In other words, political parties survive only if they continue to be useful within the context of electoral competition. Is it possible to measure party utility? The simplest way to do that is, of course, to calculate the percentage of candidates nominated by a given party who win assembly seats. In this analysis, we use a slightly more complex measure. Since we are dealing with a specific process that apparently resulted in replacing party candidate nomination with independent candidate nomination, it is important to relate party utility to the utility of its major alternative. We achieve this by dividing the percentage of winners among all candidates nominated by a given party by the percentage of winners among all independent candidates. The larger the resulting Index of Party Utility (IPU), the more useful the given party. Values of IPU that are less than one indicate that the level of the given party's utility was lower than that of independent nomination.

Table 5.2 Political parties in the 1994–98 regional legislative elections in St. Petersburg, by political tendency, with indices of party utility (in parentheses, first-round utility/second-round utility)

Political tendency	March 1994	November 1994	December 1998
Radical democrats	All Petersburg (1.79/1.36) Democratic Unity of St Petersburg (5.21/0.90) New Initiative (0/0)	All Petersburg (0.14/0.24) Russia's Democratic Choice (0.80/0.69) New Initiative (0/0) Christian Democratic Union (0.13/0) The Movement for People's Consolidation (0.36/0.42)	Accord – United Democrats of St. Petersburg (3.28/1.18)
Moderate democrats	The Beloved City (0.99/1.52)	The Beloved City (0.97/0.72)	Yabloko (12.40/5.72)
'Centre' interest representation	Our City Is Our Home (0.47/0.39) Unity for Progress (0.39/0.33) Women of St. Petersburg (0.64/0) For the Life of Dignity (0.39/0) The Safe Home (0.38/0) Business Petersburg (0.34/0) Alternative (0/0)	The Public Association of Veterans (0.23/0)	Movement for People's Self-Government (0/0) North-Western Party of the Greens (0/0)
Nationalists	LDPR (0/0) Great Russia (0/0) Petrograd (0/0)	Peter the Great (0.45/0.38)	LDPR (0/0) Russian All-People's Union (0/0) Congress of Russian Communities (0/0)
Communists	Motherland (0/0) KPRF (0/0)	The Communists of Leningrad (0.89/0.58)	The Communists of Leningrad (5.33/1.54)
All parties	0.81/0.34	0.45/0.35	5.21/2.50

Sources: Calculated by the authors on the basis of data presented in A. Sungurov, *Etyudy Politicheskoi Zhizni Peterburga* (St. Petersburg: Strategiia, 1996); and in 'Vybory v Sankt-Peterburge', available on the internet at www.elections.spb.ru

Notes: LDPR = Liberal Democratic Party of Russia; KPRF = Communist Party of the Russian Federation.

In order to include more information in the analysis, we calculated the indices of party utility separately for the first and second rounds of the elections. When calculating IPU for the first rounds, we understand by 'winners' those candidates who either won by gaining an outright majority of the vote or made it through into the second round; this applies to those who came first or second in the race. When calculating IPU for the second round, we understand by 'winners' only those who finally won assembly seats. Table 5.2 reports the indices of party utility calculated for individual parties and for the aggregates of all parties that contested the given elections. The table omits specific information on the candidates nominated by the ten single candidate groups in 1998; however, their performance was taken into account when presenting the aggregate data for all parties.

As follows from Table 5.2, party utility in the March 1994 elections turned out to be rather low. However, the levels of utility achieved by individual electoral associations varied quite markedly. In the first round of the elections, two ideologically similar coalitions, Democratic Unity of St Petersburg and All Petersburg, proved to be instrumental in providing their nominees with electoral success, while the value of IPU obtained by Beloved City was almost equivalent to that of candidates of independent nomination. Other parties failed. Seven parties, including all three nationalist and both communist formations, did not manage to bring a single candidate into the second round, while six others – mostly interest representation groups – scored very modest levels of success. But, given the fact that three frontrunners performed much better, the overall IPU for all parties was rather high, at 0.81. This drastically changed in the second round. Only one party, Beloved City, managed to improve its IPU score. The utility of Democratic Unity of St. Petersburg fell to less than that of independent candidate nomination, plummeting from 5.21 to 0.90. Of all the other parties, only All Petersburg fared slightly better, so that the overall utility of all parties fell to a dismally low level, to 0.34. The striking difference between pictures emerging from the first and second round of the elections requires a theoretical explanation. Such an explanation can be developed by discussing certain specific characteristics of majority electoral systems.

Majority systems create different structures of voter incentives in the two rounds of the elections. The first round defines a 'Condorcet' winner, that is a contestant who beats every other individual contestant, and pushes himself or herself into the second round, along with the strongest of the remaining candidates. To achieve the position of a Condorcet winner, a candidate has to rely only upon a relatively small plurality of voters. By offering a point of attraction for the voters, a party label here may be instrumental in building such a plurality. The stronger the given party's appeal to its limited poll of voters, the more it is likely that its candidate will win in the first round. For candidates nominated by strong ideologically orientated parties, such as Democratic Unity of St Petersburg, a party label in the first round can be a very useful asset. In the second round, however, it is likely to become a liability. Once the poll of ideologically committed voters is exhausted in the first round, party labels may scare away those voters for whom such an ideology is not attractive. This prevents a Condorcet winner from building a coalition that would facilitate his or her own success in the second round. Under such conditions, the second round runner is at a natural advantage, provided that his or her ideological stance is less specific than that of the first-round winner. This explains, first, why independents defeated the radical democrats and, second, why Beloved City emerged as the most successful party. On the one hand, Beloved City was strong enough to get a number of its candidates into the second round. On the other hand, in the second round they were similar to independents in that they presented a 'moderate' alternative to the radical stance of Democratic Unity of St Petersburg.

What incentives were provided by the results of the March 1994 elections to the political actors of St. Petersburg? Most obviously sixteen parties proved to be of little or no utility for winning elections. Quite rationally, ten of them chose to abstain from further electoral participation, often by dissolving themselves altogether. Many individual candidates also chose not to run, which accounts for a visible decrease in electoral competitiveness. The communists came to understand that, as a strong ideological tendency enjoying a very modest level of support, they could only emerge as Condorcet winners if they acted as a single coalition. Hence the merger of 'Motherland' and the Communist Party of the Russian Federation (KPRF) into the 'Communists of Leningrad' bloc.

The leaders of Beloved City had reasons to view their strategy as quite successful, which created little incentive for change. The same point almost applies to All Petersburg. For the remainder of the radical democrats, however, the results of the March elections created a formidable challenge. Keeping Democratic Unity of St Petersburg alive clearly made little sense, since the utility of this label had already proved to be low. One way out was to obtain additional electoral resources by identifying themselves with the national 'party of power'; another was to attempt to enhance their electoral appeal by bringing in new, presumably more attractive, policies in order to bolster their ideological appeal. The first of these strategies was employed by Russia's Democratic Choice and the Christian Democratic Union, whilst the second was undertaken by the Movement for People's Consolidation. Apparently, it was assumed that reference to 'people's consolidation' in the latter party's name would indicate its ideological moderation, thus allowing it to invade the niche occupied in March by Beloved City. Since these strategies were mutually incompatible, the ultimate outcome of the democrats' soul-searching was the extreme fragmentation of the democratic camp, which did not prove to be an optimal strategy. Intriguingly, individual party candidates did not react to their very poor party performance in the March elections by choosing to run as independents in November. Apparently, party affiliation was deeply rooted in candidates' political consciousness. It took time for rational incentives to overcome such party affiliations.

As follows from Table 5.2, the November 1994 elections made these incentives particularly visible. This time, the values of IPU for all parties, both in the first and in the second rounds of voting, turned out to be lower than one. It is true that, the utility of being nominated by Beloved City was about the same as that of independent candidate nomination in the first round. In the second round, however, Beloved City was the strongest among the weak. Russia's Democratic Choice fared slightly worse, trailed by the communist coalition. All other parties simply failed. In a similar way to what happened in March, the performance of party candidates deteriorated from the first to the second rounds. Speaking of individual candidates, the lesson for the future was, of course, to avoid party nomination. As for political parties, the message was more complex. Three of them had, after all, proved to be of some utility: Beloved City, the communist party (parties) and Russia's Democratic Choice. One quality that was common for these otherwise very different entities deserves mention: all of the groups were ideologically distinct and were very well developed in organisational terms. Quite logically, a combination of these qualities facilitated party survival under the pressure of a majority electoral system. For parties that did not possess such qualities, the message was clear: wither away to be replaced by independent candidates. But when these parties departed from the city's electoral arena, they left a legacy in the form of an unusually populous (by Russian standards) 'political class'. Political activists who had contested elections but failed to win seats had little incentive to abandon politics altogether. Some of them were absorbed by city bureaucracy, but this was a limited niche, obviously unavailable to many aspiring public figures. For them, a seat in the Legislative Assembly remained the only feasible route to power. In contrast to many regional legislatures, the St. Petersburg Legislative Assembly retained its relative independence from the executive. This further increased the value of an assembly seat. The stakes continued to be high.

The most visible peculiarities of the 1998 elections in St. Petersburg were, first, the very limited scope of party involvement and, second, an extremely high level of competition among independent candidates.[17] This time, independents were in the majority. But, as follows from Table 5.2, those parties that managed to survive through the previous elections did better than the independents. Such parties included the heir of Beloved City, Yabloko; the Communist coalition; and Accord – United Democrats of St. Petersburg, the strongest figures of which came from Russia's Democratic Choice (DVR). In the first round of the 1998 elections, all three parties achieved very high levels of utility, with an unprecedented score of 12.40 for Yabloko. The overall value of IPU for all parties was as high as 5.21. In the second round, the utility of political parties markedly decreased in the same way as had happened in 1994. Still, it remained more than twice higher than that of independent nomination. At the same time, this relatively high level of success was obtained only by three 'old survivors'. None of the newcomers to the electoral arena managed to approach them in terms of party utility. Hence the phenomenon of party extinction in St. Petersburg. If the number of electorally useful parties is limited, so is, by implication, the number of successful party candidates. Other candidates run and win as independents, which naturally restricts the level of party representation in the assembly. In the final analysis, party extinction occurs as a rational reaction to the set of incentives provided by the institutional environments within which electoral competition takes place. But what enables independents to replace the extinct species? In order to answer this crucial question, let us examine the 1998 legislative elections more closely.

Factors of success in the 1998 legislative elections: a statistical inquiry

There are several widespread assumptions about what facilitates electoral success in Russia as a whole and in St. Petersburg in particular. One factor almost unanimously identified by political observers and analysts is money.[18] In particular, it stands to reason to believe that when parties fade away, high campaign spending becomes pivotal for winning elections. A more idealistic view, also widely advanced by political observers, is that personal reputations are very important. In the national Duma elections, the locally prominent 'notables' have the best chance of being elected.[19] A candidate who is well known by his or her constituents can beat a candidate with a lot of money available even without party support. The third factor that can be reasonably expected to facilitate electoral success is the support of the executive.[20] Undoubtedly, governors are by far the most powerful political actors in Russia's regions, and their support may matter a lot for anybody who chooses to cooperate. Fourth, it can be expected that incumbency provides a lot of electoral advantages. In particular, the advantage of incumbency in Russia can be related to the amount of state resources (mis)used by a candidate in the course of the campaign.[21] Fifth, as we have already seen, the support of three major political parties was not altogether irrelevant for electoral success. One more factor that can be meaningfully entered into the analysis is what we refer to as 'political consulting'. This requires more elaboration.

The failure of party politics in Russia as a whole, and in St. Petersburg in particular, did not coincide with the decline of competitive electoral politics. Quite the reverse, aspiring candidates grew in numbers. This facilitated the emergence of a new group of professional campaign organisers who call themselves, depending on the circumstances, 'political consultants', 'image-makers', 'political psychologists', etc. By choosing the term 'political consulting', we sought a compromise between a local tradition and substantive relevance. So far, little research has been done on this relatively new phenomenon,[22] and it is beyond the scope of this chapter to discuss it at length. Nonetheless, a number of the most important characteristics will be touched upon. First, many 'political consultants' have a personal background in politics. Many have participated in elections, often as early as 1989–90. Later, they employed their acquired skills to organise other people's campaigns. Second, political consulting started mostly as an individual activity but between 1995 and 1998, the political market in Russia witnessed the emergence of several 'oligopolies' claiming the lion's share of the profits. Most of them were based in Moscow. In many regions, Moscow-based firms were able to gain a near monopoly of the emerging markets in political consulting. St. Petersburg was an exeption in the sense that here Moscow political consultants had to compete with local firms. This naturally raised the price of the commodity they offered. Third, there is no strict separation between political parties and political consulting. Many political consultants not only originated from political parties but also continued to maintain links with political parties long after turning to their profit-oriented activities. For instance, members of local branches of the Liberal Democratic Party of Russia (LDPR) often take the job as campaign organisers for individuals who are not LDPR party members or even sympathisers, which does not prevent the LDPR from running its own candidates. The same can be said about youth organisations of some reform-oriented parties. Hence, political parties sometimes perform the function of political consulting. It is important to stress that this form of party support does not coexist with party nomination, which is a principal factor for distinguishing party candidates from independent candidates within the context of this analysis.

In order to establish which of the factors listed above led to electoral success in the 1998 legislative elections in St. Petersburg, we ran a series of linear multiple regressions. Our dependent variable is the percentage share of the vote obtained by the given candidate in the first round. Of independent variables, incumbency is a dummy that assumes the value of one if the candidate already held a seat in the legislature, and the value of zero if he or she did not. How can we assess the importance of party affiliation? One of the principle advantages provided by competing under a party label is that political parties are capable of transferring some of the support attracted by them in the previous national elections to their nominees in the regional elections. All six important parties that participated in the 1998 legislative campaign had direct predecessors in the 1995 Duma elections. Yabloko, the LDPR, and the Congress of Russian Communities participated in both campaigns under their own names. The KPRF, that participated in the national elections on its own, was a principal component of the 'Communists of Leningrad' bloc in the St. Petersburg elections. The principal components of another locally created bloc, Accord–United Democrats of St. Petersburg, ran in 1995 as part of a similarly labelled coalition, Russia's Democratic Choice–United Democrats. Russian All-People's Union participated in the 1995 national election in the 'Power to the People' coalition. Hence, in all cases we can register a continuity of participation at national-level and local-level electoral competition. Our second independent variable is the percentage of the vote received by the party that nominated the given candidate or by this party's direct predecessor in the 1995 Duma elections. For independent candidates, the value of the party affiliation variable was, of course, zero.

Other hypothetical factors of electoral support – money, candidate reputation, executive support and political consulting – are much more difficult to quantify on the basis of the officially published data. This led us to conduct a

Table 5.3　Multiple regression statistics (dependent variable is the percentage share of the vote received in the first round of the 1998 legislative elections in St. Petersburg)

	Unstandardised coefficients		Standardised beta-coefficients	t	Significance
	B	Standard error			
Party affiliation	0.771	0.123	0.466	6.280	0.000
Incumbency	10.996	2.713	0.301	4.053	0.000
Competitiveness	64.662	15.077	0.318	4.289	0.000
Intercept	−0.887	1.331		−0.667	0.507

Note: r^2 0.55

semi-standardised expert survey in St. Petersburg. We selected seven legislative election constituencies, each of them being representative in terms of their geographical location and the social composition of the electorate. Overall, as many as ninety-one candidates contested these seven seats in the 1998 regional legislative elections. Using a sliding scale, the experts, who were either candidates themselves or leading political consultants, were asked to estimate a value for the parameters listed above with respect to each of the candidate's campaigns. The minimal value for each of the factors was 1; the maximum values for money and personal reputations was 5; and the maximum values for political consulting and executive support was 4. The data derived both from the official sources and from the expert survey were built into a series of multiple regression models. Each of these models employed the percentage share of the vote received by the given candidate in the first round of the December 1998 elections as a dependent variable. One difficulty obviously stemming from such a procedure was that the expressed electoral outcomes were influenced by the varying levels of vote fragmentation in the different constituencies. To overcome this difficulty, we introduced an additional independent variable: the number of candidates who contested the elections in the given constituency. To neutralise the possible impact of outliers, we divided one by the numbers of candidates, thus employing a simple form of data standardisation. This operation yielded the values of the seventh independent variable employed in the multiple regression analysis, 'competitiveness'. It is important to stress that, in contrast to the other six variables, in this sense competitiveness does not reflect any substantial expectations concerning the factors of electoral success. This allows us to consider the value as a correction coefficient.

The values of three of the independent variables were established on the basis of 'hard evidence' not involving the expert survey. This allowed us to estimate their impact separately from the other estimated factors. As follows from the multiple regression statistics presented in Table 5.3, the joint influence of party affiliation, incumbency and competitiveness explains as much as nearly 55 per

Table 5.4 Multiple regression statistics excluding the variables 'executive support' and 'money' (dependent variable is the percentage share of the vote received in the first round of the 1998 legislative elections in St. Petersburg)

	Unstandardised coefficients		Standardised beta-coefficients	t	Significance
	B	Standard error			
Party affiliation	0.516	0.106	0.312	4.884	0.000
Incumbency	10.415	2.188	0.285	4.761	0.000
Competitiveness	64.852	12.149	0.318	5.338	0.000
Political consulting	6.295	0.909	0.432	6.927	0.000
Intercept	9.387	1.630		5.760	0.000

Note: r^2 0.71

cent of the variations in the dependent variable, with party affiliation emerging as the strongest individual factor of electoral success. This finding is consistent with the high levels of party utility registered for the first round of the 1998 elections in the previous section of this analysis. However, incumbency also turns out to be an important, albeit less significant, factor of electoral success.

We next proceeded to run multiple regressions employing data from our expert survey. Two of our hypothetical factors – executive support and money – did not survive such a procedure. When these variables were omitted for the lack of statistical significance, we produced the multiple regression model, statistics from which are shown in Table 5.4. In this case, the share of the explained variations in the dependent variable rose to 71 per cent. Party affiliation and incumbency retained their significance. The strongest single influence, however, turned out to be exerted by political consulting. Does this mean that money does not play a significant role in the electoral politics of St. Petersburg? In order to answer this question, it is important to take into account the fact that political consulting is paid for. In our data set, this factor correlates highly with money, which explains why campaign finance loses its significance in the resulting statistical model. This, however, implies that money may re-emerge as an important factor if we exclude political consulting. As is shown in Table 5.5, this is indeed the case. If political consulting is replaced with money, the percentage of the explained variations in the dependent variable falls by less than 3 per cent, while money emerges as one of the strongest factors of electoral success. The fact that it is not as strong as political consulting in the previous regression is understandable, given the fact that some parties were able to spend money on their own campaigns without hiring political consultants.

As we have seen, political parties tend to lose their significance as factors of electoral success in the second round. Is it possible to estimate this trend statistically? In order to achieve this, we ran an additional multiple regression that

Table 5.5 Multiple regression statistics excluding the variables 'executive support' and 'political consulting' (dependent variable is the percentage share of the vote received in the first round of the 1998 legislative elections in St. Petersburg)

	Unstandardised coefficients		Standardised beta-coefficients	t	Significance
	B	Standard error			
Party affiliation	0.634	0.106	0.383	5.980	0.000
Incumbency	10.430	2.291	0.285	4.553	0.000
Competitiveness	59.647	12.746	0.293	4.680	0.000
Money	2.666	0.443	0.378	6.020	0.000
Intercept	−6.099	1.418		−4.301	0.000

Note: r^2 0.68

Table 5.6 Multiple regression statistics (dependent variable is a dummy reflecting electoral success in the second round of the 1998 legislative elections in St. Petersburg)

	Unstandardised coefficients		Standardised beta-coefficients	t	Significance
	B	Standard error			
First-round	0.741	0.106	0.605	6.977	0.000
Performance	−0.301	0.115	−0.227	−2.613	0.011
Party affiliation	7.573	2.845	0.230	2.662	0.009
Gender	24.355	4.068		5.987	0.000
Intercept					

Note: r^2 0.40

relied exclusively on published data. In this analysis, we also extended the scope of inquiry to cover all forty-four constituencies in which the winners were not determined in the first round. Our dependent variable was a dummy that attributed the value of one to those candidates who won the elections and the value of zero to those who lost. The set of independent variables included first-round performance, measured as the percentage share of the vote received by the given candidate in the first round, and party affiliation and incumbency as previously measured in our tables above. In addition, we employed a gender variable. It is quite a common belief that female candidates are less successful in Russia's elections than their male counterparts, and there is certainly some empirical evidence to substantiate this claim.[23] In order to test whether this expectation holds in St. Petersburg, we introduced a dummy variable that attributed the value of one to male candidates and the value of zero to women. The resulting regression model is presented in Table 5.6. Incumbency is omitted because its impact upon second-round performance turned out to be insignificant. A relatively low share of the variations in the dependent variable explained by the model (40 per cent) is to be expected given the way this variable was constructed and the limited number of cases. The high level of significance assumed by one of the independent variables, first-round performance, is also not unexpected. Gender does influence electoral outcomes in St. Petersburg. The most important finding, however, pertains to the role of party affiliation which had a negative impact on electoral success in the second round. Hence, we may conclude that even in 1998 the utility of party affiliation was lower than what could be inferred from the data presented in Table 5.2. While the values of IPU reported for the three major parties remained rather high, this was mostly due to the fact that they were residually inflated by the positive role played by party affiliation in the first round. As demonstrated by multiple regression analysis, the second round actually reversed this pattern:

Conclusion

This analysis has allowed us to explicate the logic of party extinction in St. Petersburg. The important role played by political parties in St. Petersburg in the early reform period stemmed from the fact that (quite unusually by Russian standards) a very high level of mass anti-Communist mobilisation rose up at a period when the city legislature was particularly strong, during the 'interlude' of September 1991 to December 1993. Unlike in the majority of Russia's regions, political parties managed to survive, and the value of Legislative Assembly seats remained high. Hence, the multitude of party candidates in the March 1994 elections. However, the emerging pattern of electoral competition signalled that party affiliation was not of much utility for achieving electoral success. However, this message, strongly reinforced by the institutional environments within which legislative elections were held, and especially by the two-round majority electoral formula, took time to penetrate the consciousness of the candidates. In November 1994 party affiliation was still in demand, but its utility plummeted to an extremely low level. The rational response of the electoral candidates emerged only in the 1998 elections. The previously flourishing field of party politics in St. Petersburg shrank to the point where there were only three relatively successful parties whose candidates had to compete mostly against independents. While in the first round party affiliation for these three parties turned out to be instrumental in terms of electoral success, the second round rendered party affiliation counter-productive. No new incentives for party politics have materialised, and one may therefore expect that political parties in St. Petersburg are doomed to yet further decline.

As demonstrated in this chapter, the process of party extinction was accompanied by the emergence of political consulting. In effect, political consulting took the place of party affiliation in the electoral arena of St. Petersburg, which allows us to consider it as the functional equivalent of party organisation. In its turn, the rise of political consulting increased the role played by financial factors in determining electoral success. Party extinction is a process that contributes to the progressive deformation of Russia's nascent democracy in two closely inter-related ways. On the one hand, the demise of political parties discourages citizen activism. On the other hand, it encourages plutocratic and oligarchic trends by creating a power monopoly for economically privileged elites. Our examination of one case study, that of St. Petersburg, demonstrates that these trends prevailed even in those regions where the contextual factors inherited from the era of per-estroika could have been expected to counteract them.

Notes

1 V. Gel'man and G. V. Golosov, 'Regional party system formation in Russia: the deviant case of Sverdlovsk Oblast', *Journal of Communist Studies and Transition Politics*, 14:1–2 (1998), 31–53.
2 G. V. Golosov and I. Shevchenko, 'Political parties and independent candidates in single member constituencies', in V. Gel'man and G. V. Golosov (eds.), *Elections in Russia, 1993 1996: Analyses, Documents and Data* (Berlin: Edition Sigma, 1999), pp. 127–49.
3 S. L. Solnick, 'Gubernatorial elections in Russia, 1996–1997', *Post-Soviet Affairs*, 14:1 (1998), 48–80.
4 R. Sakwa, 'Parties and the multiparty system in Russia', *RFE/RL Research Report*, 2:31 (1993), 7–15; M. S. Fish, 'The advent of multipartism in Russia', *Post-Soviet Affairs*, 11:4 (1995), 340–83; G. V. Golosov, 'Who survives? Party origins, organisa-tional development, and electoral performance in post-Communist Russia', *Political Studies*, 46:3 (1998), 511–43.
5 D. Slider, 'Elections to Russia's regional assemblies', *Post-Soviet Affairs*, 12:3 (1996), 243–64; G. V. Golosov, 'Russian political parties and the 'bosses': evidence from the 1994 provincial elections in Western Siberia', *Party Politics*, 3:1 (1997), 5–21.
6 G. V. Golosov, 'From Adygeya to Yaroslavl: factors of party development in the regions of Russia, 1995–98', *Europe–Asia Studies*, 51:8 (1999), 1333–65.
7 See, however, N. Petrov, 'Vybory organov predstavitel'noi vlasti regionov', *Mirovaya Ekonomika i Mezhdunarodnye Otnosheniya*, 3:4 (1995).
8 E. A. Zdravomyslova, 'Mobilizatsiya resursov demokraticheskogo dvizheniya v Leningrade (1987–90)', in *Sotsiologiya Obshchestvennykh Dvizhenii: Empiricheskie Nablyudeniya Issledovaniya* (Moscow and St. Petersburg: Institut Sotsiologii RAN, 1993); R. W. Orttung, *From Leningrad to St. Petersburg: Democratisation in a Russian City* (New York: St. Martin's Press, 1995).
9 A. Sungurov, *Etyudy Politicheskoi Zhizni Peterburga* (St. Petersburg: Strategiya, 1996).
10 B. Kiernan, *The End of Soviet Power: Elections, Legislatures and the Demise of the Communist Party* (Boulder, CO: Westview Press, 1993).
11 See G. V. Golosov, 'New Russian political parties and the transition to democracy', *Government and Opposition*, 30:1 (1995), 110–19.
12 J. B. Barth and V. Solovei, *Russia's Communists at the Crossroads* (Boulder, CO: Westview Press, 1997).
13 A. Belkin, 'Lensovet: aprel' 1990 – iyun' 1991 gg.', *Vestnik Sankt-Peterburgskogo Universiteta*, Seriia 6:4 (1992); V. Ya. Gel'man, 'Vybory 1990 g. v Leningrade: pirrova

pobeda demokratii', in *Sotsiologiya Obshchestvennykh Dvizhenii: Empiricheskie Nablyudeniya i Issledovaniya* (Moscow and St. Petersburg: Institut sotsiologii RAN, 1993); M. Yu. Nesterov, 'Gorodskoi sovet Leningrada – Sankt-Peterburga v 1990–93 gg.', *Politicheskii Monitoring*, IGPI, 8:2 (1994).

14 S. Bartolini and P. Mair, *Identity, Competition and Electoral Availability: The Stabilisation of European Electorates, 1885–1985* (Cambridge: Cambridge University Press, 1990).

15 M. S. Shugart, 'The inverse relationship between party strength and executive strength: a theory of politicians' constitutional choices', *British Journal of Political Science*, 28:1 (1998), 1–29.

16 J. H. Aldrich, *Why Parties? The Origin and Transformation of Political Parties in America* (Chicago, IL: University of Chicago Press, 1995).

17 B. Vishnevsky, 'Peterburgskie vybory: turnir provokatorov', *Polis*, 2 (1999), 98–109.

18 V. Gel'man, 'The iceberg of Russian political finance', in P. Burnell and A. Ware (eds.), *Funding Democratisation* (Manchester: Manchester University Press, 1998).

19 L. Belin and R. Orttung, *The Russian Parliamentary Elections of 1995: The Battle for the Duma* (London: M. E. Sharpe, 1997).

20 O. Kudinov, S. Kolosova and N. Tochitskaya, *Kompleksnaya Tekhnologiya Provedeniya Effektivnoi Izbiratel'noi Kampanii v Rossiiskom Regione* (Moscow: Bankovskoe Delo, 1997).

21 D. Torkhov, 'Gruppy interesov kak aktory sovremennogo elektoral'nogo protsessa v Rossiiskoi Federatsii', in *Vybory v Rossiiskoi Federatsii: Federal'nyi i Regional'nyi Aspekty* (St. Petersburg: Strategiya, 1999).

22 V. Goncharov, 'Politicheskii konsalting v Rossii: konets epokhi vsemogushchestva', *Politiya*, 2 (1999), 40–55.

23 G. V. Golosov, 'Political parties, electoral systems, and women's representation in the regional legislative assemblies of Russia, 1995–98', *Party Politics*, 7:1 (1 January 2001).

The development of political institutions in three regions of the Russian Far East

Over a period of ten years beginning in 1990, the author of this chapter observed the evolution of political institutions in one central Russian province, Yaroslavl'.[1] Proceeding from the assumption that the prospects for democratisation nationally in Russia would be diminished if similar changes did not occur locally, the purpose of that exercise was to determine whether, in fact, political institutions in Yaroslavl' had become more democratic. The conclusions were, in many respects, discouraging. Although there was clear evidence that after ten years of transition from authoritarian rule the forms of democracy had been introduced, in many respects the norms and practices of democracy had not.[2] What had emerged, despite promising beginnings, was closer to what Giullermo O'Donnell calls 'delegative democracy'.[3] This chapter seeks to determine the extent to which the findings from Yaroslavl' are applicable elsewhere among the eighty-nine members of the Russian Federation. In particular, it focuses on three regions of the Russian Far East (RDV): Primorskii Krai, Khabarovsk Krai and Sakhalin Oblast. How comparable are the political institutions of these three regions to those that seem to have emerged in Yaroslavl'?

The question is important for several reasons. For one thing, there are implications for democratisation in Russia. If the political institutions of these regions bear the same earmarks of particularism and reliance on personal authority that we found in Yaroslavl', then the prospects for democracy may be dim. The future of Russia, to borrow a phrase from Robert Putnam, may be Palermo.[4] This is especially disconcerting given the similarity of authority patterns at the national level.[5] On the other hand, it may be that distance from the court intrigues of Moscow has encouraged more open, participant political systems to emerge, ones in which no single person can dominate politically and in which actors must play by democratic rules. Democratisation aside, answering the question may also be relevant to understanding the development of Russian federalism. The principle issue here is whether the Russian Federation will hold together in the face of centrifugal forces among its regional components.[6] Finally, as the burgeoning literature on Russia's regions has started to emerge from the publication pipelines, a fault line has begun to appear between those who find significant differences in regional political developments and those who stress commonalities. It is hoped that the material presented here will contribute positively to the literature.[7]

As already noted, the evolution of political institutions in Yaroslavl' demonstrated the tendency towards predominant executive power, so much so that it could best be regarded as a type of 'delegative democracy' albeit on the regional level. This conclusion is very similar to the findings of Andrei Tsygankov in his analysis of three very diverse Russian regions: Orlov, Bashkortostan and Krasnoyarsk.[8] In each case he examined the manner in which regional chief executives were elected, and, once chosen, the attitude of the executive towards political parties, the media and the legislatures in these regions. He concluded that while regions in Russia may have achieved 'vertical accountability' because executives are elected, they lack 'horizontal accountability' to other impendent political forces. Like the present author, Tsygankov finds this conclusion discouraging with respect to the prospects for democratisation. He argues that delegative democracy is dysfunctional for economic reform and may produce a 'trend toward authoritarianism' in the not too distant future by provoking a new economic depression.

Scope and methods

Because this chapter seeks to determine how similar the development of political institutions in regions of Russia's Far East is to what the author found in his study of Yaroslavl', the point of departure will be to ask whether these regions can also be best described as 'delegative democracies'. What is meant by the term and how do we propose to measure it? According to Guillermo O'Donnell, the progenitor of this concept, 'Delegative democracies rest on the premise that whoever wins the election to the presidency is thereby entitled to govern as he or she sees fit, constrained only by the hard facts of existing power relations and by a constitutionally limited term of office.'[9] Elected executives in such systems regard themselves as the embodiment of a national consensus, and therefore above particular parties or interests, and, for that matter, the people who elected them. 'After the election, voters/delegators are expected to become a passive, but cheering audience of what the president does.' Delegative democracies belong to the democratic tradition because 'vertical accountability' is ensured through the requirement of periodic election. However, they are a 'peculiar type of democracy', distinguished from true representative democracy by their lack of 'horizontal accountability'. By horizontal accountability, O'Donnell refers to 'a network of relatively autonomous powers (i.e. other institutions) that can call into question, and eventually punish, improper ways of discharging the responsibilities of a given official.'[10] Delegative democracies are characterised by weak insitutionalisation. 'The place of well-functioning institutions is taken by other nonformalised but strongly operative practices: clientelism, patrimonialism and corruption.' As a result, in O'Donnell's view, delegative democracies can 'hardly be less congenial to the building and strengthening of democratic institutions.'

This chapter uses several indicators to measure delegative democracy in the three regions of the RDV chosen for this study. First, there are the elections of the chief executives. According to O'Donnell, these are 'a very emotional and high stakes event' using electoral techniques such as run-offs to ensure that an absolute majority support is achieved.[11] We shall examine the elections of governors in the three regions under study as well as the political background of each individual in order, to better understand their base of political support. A second indicator is the nature of relations between the executive and legislative branches of government. To what extent is there a meaningful separation of powers? Part of the answer is to be found in the institutional arrangements set forth in the regional charters (*ustavy*). Can they be classified as presidential, presidential-parliamentary, premier-presidential or parliamentary? How autonomous or subordinate are the legislatures?[12] At the same time, the ability of a legislature to constrain the chief executive depends not only on their legal rights, but on the political composition of the elected deputies. We therefore also look at who the representatives to the regional assemblies are and how they were elected. This will necessarily also direct our attention to the existence of non-state political actors (political parties, interest groups, media) and whether they play a significant role in regional politics. To what extent are governors dependent on their support to gain power and to employ it effectively? Finally, we look at inter-governmental relations to determine whether there are constraints placed on regional executives from above (the national government) and from below (sub-regional elites). In the case of the former we focus on the role of presidential representatives[13] and relations between the governors and the Kremlin; for the latter, we seek evidence that governors are limited by the institutions of local self-government (*mestnoye samo-upravlenie*),[14] especially in the regional capitols.

The data on which this study is based come from several sources. Among official documents are the charters for each region, as well as election statistics and biographical information on the deputies of the regional assemblies and the governors. The regional press, much of it available from regional websites, was an important source. The author was also able to take advantage of a short grant from the International Research and Exchanges Board (IREX) to travel to Vladivostok and Khabarovsk in April 2000 where he interviewed some of the regional political elites discussed here as well as academic specialists. An invaluable source for background information and electoral statistics from the regions for national elections is the excellent compendium of information called *Politicheskii Almanakh Rossii 1997*, this was compiled under the editorship of Michael McFaul and Nikolai Petrov and published in 1997 by the Moscow Carnegie Centre. In order to keep up to date with current developments, the *Russian Regional Review* made available weekly via e-mail by the East–West Institute deserves special mention as does the Russian Federation Report produced by Radio Free Europe/Radio Liberty (RFE/RL). Beyond this, I made use of databases on regional elites collected at the Slavic Research Centre of

Hokkaido University which were made available by scholars there during a research fellowship at the SRC in Spring 2000.[15]

Primorskii Krai

At first glance, there would seem to be every reason to regard Primorskii Krai (PK) as a special case among Russia's regions. Political life in the region is notorious nationally, as well as regionally, for its scandals and corruption, so much so that one foreign observer was prompted to label it as a case study in 'warlordism'.[16] At the centre of much of this notoriety is the governor of the Krai, Evgenii Nazdratenko. Born in the Kurile islands in 1949, Nazdratenko rose from his initial occupation as an electrician to become, in 1991, the director of a mining company, Vostok, as well as a deputy to the Russian Congress of People's Deputies elected in 1990. In 1992 he co-founded an association of business executives called PAKT (*Primorskii aktsionernaya korporatsya tobaroproizvitelei*) several of whom were deputies in the Krai soviet.[17] The first governor of the region, Vladimir Kuznetsov, was appointed by Boris Yeltsin in 1991. He was considered a liberal reformer from academia and a political outsider whose removal by Yeltsin was eventually engineered by these deputies. In his place Nazdratenko's supporters in the Krai soviet sent his name to the President who agreed to the nomination on 24 May 1993. Soon after his appointment, the new governor replaced many of those in the previous administration with his supporters in the Krai soviet appointing them to leadership positions, including A. Pavlov, I. Lebedinets and V. Shkrabov.[18]

Nazdratenko is said to be a shrewd and pragmatic politician who rules with a strong hand, a '*khozyain*' (or 'boss') in the meld of Moscow mayor Yurii Luzhkov.[19] He does not come from a Party nomenklatura background and does not appear to have a well defined political ideology. Instead his politics appear to be largely opportunistic. For example, in May 1999 he announced he was supporting Otechestvo (Fatherland), the party of Luzhkov, and the candidacy of Yergenii Primakov for president. By the time elections occurred in December he had morphed into an equally enthusiastic supporter of Yedinstvo (Unity) and the presidential aspirations of Vladimir Putin. His ability to change direction when needed has enabled him to survive. Thus, before his appointment as governor in 1993, he often articulated views strongly favouring regional separatism, even speaking of a new 'Far Eastern Republic'. However, after 1993 when this rhetoric was no longer useful politically he abandoned it, and he now uses such language only sparingly to wring economic concessions from the Centre.[20] Also useful to the governor politically is his hard, one might say demagogic, stand on border issues. In 1995 he sought the annulment of the 1991 Russo-Chinese border treaty;[21] in 1994 he proposed annexing as Krai territory the four islands of the Kurile chain claimed by Japan;[22] he takes consistently populist views on the issue of illegal Chinese immigration. Clearly, the positions taken by Nazdratenko are consistent with a leader who portrays himself as protector of the region's interests, one standing above partisan politics.

Even the election of Nazdratenko as governor took place only after a confrontation with Moscow. Originally Nazdratenko proposed holding a gubernatorial election on 7 October 1994 to be followed by elections to a new Krai Duma on 23 October, despite the fact that only the Duma had the authority to schedule such elections. More importantly, such an election would challenge Yeltsin's continued control over the appointment of governors.[23]

When Yeltsin issued a decree on 4 October 1994 reaffirming his control of gubernatorial appointments, Nazdratenko was forced to back down and cancel the elections. Nevertheless, he continued to lobby for such an election and the PK along with a handful of other regions was granted an exception to do so at the time of the State Duma elections of 17 December 1995. In this election, Nazdratenko won 68.6 per cent of the vote among three candidates with slightly more than 62 per cent of the electorate participating. His closest competitor was his bitter enemy, Viktor Cherepkov, the mayor of the provincial capitol, who received only 17 per cent. Not only had Nazdratenko gained an overwhelmingly popular mandate, but he could now be removed by Yeltsin only through difficult legal proceedings, if at all.

In December 1999, at the end of his four-year term, Nazdratenko ran for re-election. Former Vladivostok Mayor Cherepkov withdrew as a candidate on 19 November 1999 citing harassment to his campaign by the governor whose administration had seized the Cherepkov campaign bank accounts. Cherepkov instead ran for a seat in the State Duma from district number fifty, only to find his name was removed from the ballot by the Krai election commission shortly before election day prompting 19 per cent of those voting to 'vote against all', thus invalidating the election altogether. Another potential competitor, State Duma deputy Svetlana Orlova was removed forty-eight hours before the election by the Krai Duma, leaving Aleksander Kirillichev, Director of the Primorkskii Shipping Company (PRISCO) as his chief rival among eight candidates. Using support from his contacts in the business community and among the municipal administrators, together with his dominance of local media, Nazdratenko won re-election with 65 per cent of the vote with slightly more than 50 per cent of the electorate turning out, thus avoiding a runoff election.[24] Kirillichev could muster only 20 per cent, with the rest at less than 3 per cent. Five months later, fearing that the Krai administration would retaliate against PRISCO, Kirillichev declined to run again as the company's Director; a Nazdratenko ally, Aleksander Lugovets, was chosen in his place.[25]

The history of the provincial legislature, the Krai Duma, has been similarly vexed. The Krai soviet had been abolished by Nazdratenko in accordance with Yeltsin's decree of October 1993, the governor's allies in it not withstanding. A new Krai Duma was to have been elected, as elsewhere in Russia, by March 1994. In the PK these elections were scheduled for 27 March. They were postponed until 23 October due to conflicts over the mayor of Vladivostok and because Nazdratenko hoped to hold a gubernatorial election beforehand. When that election was cancelled, the governor did his best to 'sabotage' elections to the

Krai Duma. His protege, Vladivostok mayor Konstantin Tolstoshein, asked contemptuously, 'Do we really need our own Duma these days?'[26] Elections took place in thirty-seven of the thirty-nine districts which comprise the Duma, but in only nineteen of them was the minimum required turnout of 25 per cent met, leaving the Duma six votes short of the quorum (two thirds of thirty-nine) needed to operate. Successful elections were held in eleven of the remaining twenty seats on 15 January 1995, with the remainder elected later in the year. The Krai legislature was off to a precarious start. The initial term of office was only two years because a provincial charter had yet to be adopted specifying a four-year term. A new Duma was therefore, supposed to be elected in January 1997. These elections were also postponed, until 7 December 1997. At least they were more successful. With 37 per cent of the electorate turning out to choose among 271 candidates, deputies were elected to all thirty-nine seats.

Legally, relations between the executive and legislative branches of government in the PK are defined by the regional charter, which was adopted on 6 October 1995. Essentially the charter creates a 'presidential' system in which the position of the legislature is 'subordinate'.[27]

This is to say that the governor is popularly elected and forms his own cabinet without approval by the legislature. The governor may veto legislation by the Duma, but this veto can be over-ridden by a two-thirds majority vote. The governor has the right to enact resolutions and executive orders (*rasporiazhenie*) as long as they are not unconstitutional. According to Article 51, the Duma may be dissolved under two conditions, one of which is self-dissolution (*samoraspuska*) by 50 per cent of the members. The second occurs if the Duma repeatedly passes legislation vetoed by the governor which has been found by the courts to contradict the federal constitution or the regional charter. In such a case, within two months after the court's decision the governor must hold a referendum on dissolving the Duma. The removal of an incumbent governor is contemplated in the charter, but is procedurally very difficult. It requires a two-thirds vote (out of thirty-nine) in the Duma after a court finding of constitutional (or charter) violations, a vote which must be confirmed by a Krai referendum. According to an unusual provision, if the governor is removed from office, or leaves due to illness or death, his place is taken by one of three people named in the governor's first speech to the Duma (Article 61).

The formal institutional relationship between the legislative and executive branches tells us only about the *pays legal*.[28] Even a strong parliament – and this is not the case here – will do little to check the power of an executive if it is composed of supporters. It seems clear that those elected to the first Krai Duma fell into this category. Of the thirty elected by January 1995, twelve were from administrative ranks and nine where heads of enterprises. Only one, a member of the Communist Party of the Russian Federation (KPRF), was elected representing a political party. Nazdratenko's partner from PAKT, Igor Lebedinets, became Duma Chair.[29] The Duma was said to be in Nazdratenko's 'pocket'.[30] The second Krai Duma elected in 7 December 1997 is less easily characterised in this fashion. For one thing only three incumbents were re-elected. For another, although the role of parties in PK politics is generally regarded as negligible,[31] three deputies are members of the KPRF, while another seven were supported by the National Patriotic Union of Russia (NPSR), and four more by the Liberal Democratic Party of Russia (LDPR). More significantly, at least eight of the deputies belong to a faction called Our City (*Nash Gorod*) allied with former mayor Cherepkov, while many of Nazdratenko's cronies in the first Duma left because they are members of the administration and are prohibited by the charter from holding public positions concurrently.[32] The faction proclaims its support for a rule of law over what they regard as the lawlessness of Nazdratenko's administration. On many issues they are joined by as many as ten other deputies creating a sizeable opposition block. The governor's supporters in the Duma, however, are well disciplined. On critical votes they are said to receive written instructions (*poiasnitel'nyi zapiski*) from Duma deputy and Krai vice governor, Vladimir Ignatenko, formerly the presidential representative to the PK.

Although the Chair elected by the second Krai Duma, Sergei Dudnik, was initially regarded as Nazdratenko's supporter, by 1999 he was considered to be the leader of a slim parliamentary majority opposed to the governor. After a concerted effort by Nazdratenko's supporters in the Duma during the summer of 1999 barely fell short of removing him, the struggle between them came to a head over the law on gubernatorial elections which Dudnik lost by a vote of twenty to eighteen in September. When Nazdratenko then easily won re-election in December, Dudnik could no longer hold on to his post and was replaced on 28 January 2000 by the acting speaker, Sergei Zhekov.[33] Zhekov, a former military officer with the nuclear fleet and currently a corporate head, had voted with Our City in 1998 before transferring his support to the governor. In April 2000 he was officially elected by a vote of twenty two to sixteen. With the removal of Dudnik, the last major opposition figure had been removed.

An independent mass media could constitute an important potential source of 'horizontal accountability', but in PK most are under the control of the Krai administration. In the first place this includes all the TV stations, which are the principal source of news for most people. Among the printed media, the two largest dailies, *Vladivostok* and *Novosti* (with a circulation of 53,000 and 43,000 respectively) are supported by the administration and clearly reflect the views of the governor. The other daily is *Utro Rossii* (circulation 15,000) which caries a lot of cultural news and is politically neutral. The dependence of the local media is largely financial. Advertising doesn't begin to pay for the costs of publication, and access to Dalpress, where these three papers are printed, is controlled by the administration. This is not to say that there are no opposition newspapers. Among them are the weeklies *Arsen'evskie vesti* (now funded by George Soros' Institute for an Open Society), *Zavtra Rossii iz Vladivostoka* (which supports Cherepkov) and *Dal'nevostochnye vedomosti*. There is also one Krai newspaper with national sponsorship, *Moskovkii komsomolets vo Vladivostoke*.[34] However, those papers that do voice criticism of the administration lead a precarious existence. *Zavtra*

Rossii was closed for a while and the editor of *Moskovskii komsomolets* was thrown out of its offices by the administration. The governor demanded his removal. In a different medium, the independent minded editor for Radio Lemma was beaten up in 1999 and his staff physically threatened.[35]

Local self-government as established in part six of the Russian Constitution of 1993 could become an important institutional check on the power of regional executives. Because it provides for considerable autonomy in the formation of municipal governance, it has become a thorn in the side of regional administrations, and, not coincidentally, a part of the Centre's strategy to rein in regional chiefs.[36] Of particular importance are the municipal governments of regional capitols because typically a large portion of the population is concentrated there. In the PK, nearly a third of the inhabitants live in the capitol, Vladivostok.

Nowhere in Russia have relations between the mayor and the governor been more acrimonious than in the PK. The first mayoral elections were held on 29 July 1993. The winner, retired military officer Viktor Cherepkov, beat eighteen other candidates including the one favoured by Nazdratenko, Boris Fadeev. Over the succeeding year, harassment of the mayor culminated in charges that he had taken bribes, charges that led to his arrest in February 1994 and his removal from office, forcibly, on 17 March 1994.[37] He was replaced by Konstantin Tolstoshein, a close ally of Nazdratenko who appointed him acting mayor. On 23 December 1994, a few days after Cherepkov was cleared of all charges, Yeltsin removed Cherepkov as mayor by presidential decree and Tolstoshein became permanent mayor. Cherepkov's suit against the President for acting unconstitutionally was upheld, however, and he was returned to his office as mayor by decree on 24 September 1996. In a bizarre turn of events, mayoral elections held on 27 September 1998 were invalidated when 54 per cent of the city's electorate voted against all candidates to protest against the removal of Cherepkov's name from the ballot by courts favourable to Nazdratenko the day before the election. Although that left Cherepkov in office, he was again removed by presidential decree on 11 December 1998, and again his office was forcibly occupied by a Nazdratenko appointee, this time a former Cherepkov ally, Yurii Kopylov. Kopylov remained in power as acting mayor because a new city Duma failed to be elected for the eighteenth time on 19 December 1999.[38] Mayoral elections were scheduled for 18 June 2000. Amid widespread accusations of fraud, Kopylov won these eletions, garnering 53 per cent of the vote against only 24 per cent for Cherepkov with 38 per cent of the electorate turning out. Vladivostok remains the only provincial capitol in Russia without a municipal council and Nazdratenko's man remains in control of the capitol city.

The one other institutional check on the power of regional executives is the Federal government, and especially the office of the President. This check was especially significant before the elections of governors, which took place in 1996–97 when chief executives still were largely appointed by Yeltsin and subject to removal by him.[39] Nevertheless, the Centre still has ways influencing the regions, including access to economic assistance and through the institutions of the presidential representatives. Relations between Nazdratenko and the Kremlin have been tempestuous and in 1997 there appeared to be a concerted effort on the part of Nazdratenko's enemies in the presidential administration, led by Anatolii Chubais, to oust the now elected governor. On 23 May 1997 Yeltsin appointed as his new presidential representative the chief of the Krai Federal Security Service (FSB), Viktor Kondratov, giving him special powers to solve the Krai's chronic energy crisis and to bring about some order to the political relations between the Krai and its capitol. Kondratov replaced Vladimir Ignatenko, an ally of Nazdratenko who had been appointed in January 1994 when *his* predecessor, Valerii Butov, was removed at the governor's request after Butov accused him of official misconduct. In June 1997 a visit by then First Deputy Prime Minister, Boris Nemtsov, led to speculation that new elections for both governor and mayor would be called.[40] In the end, however, it was Kondratov who was removed from both his posts in February and March 1999 and sent to head FSB operations in Moldova. His replacement in October 1999 was PK Vice Governor Valentin Kuzov, obviously more to the governor's liking.

How are we to explain the apparent inability or unwillingness of the Centre to deal more forcefully with Nazdratenko? For one thing, it is clear that an elected regional chief executive is harder to remove than one that is appointed, and since December 1995 Nazdratenko has held a popular mandate. One of the benefits of this position is that it confers *ex officio* a seat in the Federation Council, the upper house of the Russian Federal Assembly. While there is apparently little enthusiasm for Nazdratenko personally among the other regional leaders who make up that body, they have an institutional self-interest in resisting any attempts to remove or intimidate one of their own. It is doubtful they would have let his removal pass unchallenged. Moreover, as Minagawa and others have shown, Nazdratenko has cultivated friends in high places as well as enemies. In particular, Yevgenii Primakov, as Prime Minister, was said to have been responsible for ousting Cherepkov from his mayoral post in December 1998 following a Kremlin visit by Nazdratenko.[41] There is another possible explanation for Yeltsin's ambivalence towards Nazdratenko, and that is the political support for him shown by the governor and the Krai on repeated occasions. During the showdown with the Russian Congress of People's Deputies in October 1993, Nazdratenko took the side of the President. In the Krai, 72 per cent voted in favour of the constitutional referendum in December of that year. In 1996 he delivered the Krai vote for Yeltsin at almost exactly the same proportion as Yeltsin received nationally. In late autumn 1999, when it became clear that the 'party of power' nationally was Yedinstvo, Nazdratenko switched his allegiance to it despite earlier strong endorsements of Fatherland – All Russia (OVR) and Primakov. In return for delivering support in the national contest, Nazdratenko has enjoyed Kremlin support in local matters. This in turn is used by Nazdratenko to consolidate his position in the Krai. In short, it may be argued that in the case of the PK the relations between the Federal and regional authorities is more 'clientelistic' than adversarial.[42]

It is too early to predict how relations between Nazdratenko and the Putin administration will develop. Certainly Putin had to be disappointed with his showing in the March 2000 election for President. In PK he received an embarrassing 40 per cent of the vote to Genadii Zyuganov's 37 per cent, a remarkable result given the lack of support for Zyuganov against Yeltsin in 1996 and the fact that the large serviceman vote in PK could be expected to go for Putin. Speculation about the causes of this outcome varied during the author's visit to Vladivostok a week after the election, with some suggesting that Nazdratenko had joined some of the oligarchs in attempting to force a second round of voting which would have weakened Putin's mandate. Others noted that the governor did not actively campaign for Putin and that there had been little agitation on his behalf in the press which Nazdratenko controls. The new President's efforts in May 2000 to rein in wayward governors by threatening their removal in cases of non-compliance with federal legislation could leave Nazdratenko vulnerable. Nevertheless, in May 2000, the governor moved to mend fences, issuing a press release stating that 'I fully support the thoughts and ideas that the president has placed before the Russians. I completely agree with Vladimir Putin's opinion about strengthening vertical power'.[43] Not coincidentally perhaps, there are also rumours at about the same time suggesting that the Kremlin backs Nazdratenko's candidate for mayor of Vladivostok, acting mayor Yurii Kopylov.

Khabarovsk Krai

At first glance, political life in Khabarovsk Krai seems far different from that of its neighbour. Certainly the institutional chaos and capricious behaviour of elites characteristic of the PK is absent in Khabarovsk. Politics in Khabarovsk are as calm as those of the PK are turbulent; consensus and order prevail instead of conflict. Like the PK, however, the central place in the Krai's politics is occupied by its governor. Viktor Ishaev was born in Siberia in 1948 and, like Nazdratenko, he lacks a party nomenklatura background. After graduating from a Novosibirsk engineering institute, he spent twenty-four years in the Khabarovsk ship-building factory working his way from being a welder to a position as assistant director for commercial relations. From 1988–90 he was director of the Khabarovsk factory for aluminium construction materials. His first political post was that of first vice chair of the Krai soviet where from 1990–91 he was chief of the planning division. From this position he was appointed governor by Yeltsin on 24 October 1991. He appears to be quite popular in the Krai, having been elected to the Russian Federation Council in 1993 and then, convincingly, as governor on 8 December 1996.[44] With 49 per cent of those eligible to vote, Ishaev defeated four other candidates after receiving an overwhelming 77 per cent of the vote. His closest competitor was Russian State Duma deputy Valentin Tsoi who received only 7 per cent.

In addition to his impressive popular mandate, there other reasons why Ishaev fits the profile of the strong executive figure found in delegative democracies. For one thing, although both the Yeltsin administration and the KPRF supported him in 1996, he has always run for election independently of all parties and emphasises that he stands above them. His electoral campaign was conducted under the slogan: 'My party is Khabarovsk Krai!' In fulfilling this promise, Ishaev has often espoused populist policies. In particular, he strongly criticises the federal government for its putative indifference to regional interests. He has rejected the 1991 Russo-Chinese border treaty for giving back the Ussuriiski and Tarabarov islands to China and takes a predictably hard line on 'illegal' immigration into the Krai. He also uses his position as Chair of the Far Eastern Regional Association as a forum to attack Moscow for not giving more financial support to the region.[45] (In Federal Funds for Financial Support of the Regions, Khabarovsk ranks fifty-eighth out eighty-nine regions, while Primorskii Krai is ranked fifty-fifth and Sakhalin is thirty-fifth.)[46] In 1995 he called for creating a 'Far Eastern Republic', complaining that provinces were not being treated equally with republics. Perhaps for this reason, a year later in April 1996, Khabarovsk Krai became the first region in the RDV other than the Sakha Republic (Yakutiya) to sign a bilateral power-sharing treaty with the federal government.[47] Nor is Ishaev reluctant to use his authority to reward allies and punish opponents. In the December 1999 State Duma election for District 57, Ishaev's choice, Boris Reznik, overwhelmingly defeated incumbent Valentin Tsoi, Ishaev's gubernatorial opponent in 1996, under suspicious circumstances.[48]

The Khabarovsk Krai charter, which was adopted on 30 November 1995, like that of the PK establishes a political regime that is 'presidential' with respect to executive authority and places the legislature in a 'subordinate' position.[49] The directly elected governor (four-year term) chooses his administrative personnel without being obliged to gain parliamentary approval. The governor also has the right to adopt binding resolutions and administrative decrees. He may veto laws adopted by the Krai Duma, with two thirds of the sitting deputies needed to override this. There are, however, a number of distinctive provisions in the charter. For one thing, deputies to the Krai Duma may not concurrently hold any other state office nor can they be elected to another legislative seat. Full-time deputies may not receive a salary from another source. This provision (Article 26) excludes deputies to the Duma from the ranks of administrators. The Krai Duma can be dissolved, but only by a two-thirds majority of its twenty-five members (*samorospuska*), not by the governor (Article 33). Removal of the governor by the Duma, however, is contemplated, but only under the exceptional case of a finding by the federal Constitutional Court of unconstitutional acts, or for repeated violations of federal and Krai law, also confirmed by a court decision. If the governor dies in office, resigns, or is found to be incompetent by a court, the legislature chooses a replacement from among the administrators. One other unusual section (chapter 7) of the charter establishes procedures for working out differences between the branches of government. In particular, Articles 39 and 40 provide mechanisms for each branch to participate in the work of the other, including an opportunity for the governor to address the Duma with comments on draft legislation before a vote is taken. These provisions would seem to be an effort to promote consensus building between branches.

To date there have been two elections to the Krai Duma, the first having taken place on 13 March 1994 in accordance with Yeltsin's decree abolishing the soviets of October 1993. Because of low turnout (overall turnout was 33 per cent), or because a majority voted 'against all', seven of the twenty-five seats were not filled until the end of the year; however, at least the Duma had a quorum. Most of those elected were non partisan 'independents' from business backgrounds; two were local officials and two were from the military. Only four deputies were clearly identified with a political party, three of whom were members of the KPRF.[50] The initial term of office was two years so new elections were scheduled, and held, on 7 December 1997. With a turnout of 36 per cent, political participation in these elections barely increased, but deputies were chosen in all but two of twenty-five districts. The charter adopted in November 1995 established four-year terms. On the whole, it may be said that the development of political institutions in Khabarovsk has been far more orderly than that of the PK.

The composition of the new (current) Duma is somewhat different from its predecessor. In accordance with the 1995 charter, there are no deputies concurrently holding state posts or elected positions elsewhere. The one person occupying a government position (in the Ministry of Interior, or MVD) appears to have gone 'on reserve' during his tenure. Possibly because of the employment restrictions placed on deputies, eight of the twenty-five deputies are retired persons and presumably comprise a majority of the thirteen deputies who are full time. Eight more are professionals (teachers, lawyers, journalists) and five are directors of enterprises. The remainder appear to be full-time deputies (there are three vice chairpersons). More than a third of the deputies (nine) were re-elected from the previous session. The two women members won after repeat elections were held April 1997 in the two districts where turnout had initially been insufficient. The second session is more partisan than the first, with nine seats held by members of the KPRF. The chair of Yabloko also holds a seat.

Despite the growth in partisanship, the Duma does not seem ready to challenge the governor. For one thing parties generally are not strong in Khabarovsk; in 1996 the KPRF supported Ishaev as did the Yeltsin administration. For another, the Duma is chaired by the speaker from the previous session, Viktor Ozerov, a centrist from a military background who tends to defer to the governor. He was elected to a second term as speaker by four votes over the candidate of the KPRF, former raikom (district committee) first secretary Aleksander Gromov. Ozerov was instrumental in the December 1999 election of Ishaev's candidate to the State Duma, Boris Reznik. Despite the past history of cooperative relations between the governor and the Duma, on some issues the Duma has shown its willingness to vote against the governor.[51] Ishaev's proposal in March 1998 to scale back deputy privileges may lead to greater confrontation.

The relations between governor Ishaev and the Kremlin seem to be much smoother than is the case in Primorskii Krai, despite Ishaev's frequent criticism of the federal government's lack of support on regional issues. For one thing the conflicts that characterised Nazdratenko's relations with some of the Krai's presidential representatives has been absent in Khabarovsk. The first presidential representative, Vladimir Desyatov, a member of the Inter-regional group of deputies in the USSR Congress of People's Deputies, was replaced in November 1993 by Kondrat Yevtushenko, himself a former chief administrator in Amur province and someone said to avoid crossing Ishaev.[52] Beyond that the Krai has generally provided political support for Yeltsin, giving him a better than average vote of confidence in the April 1993 referendum and almost 60 per cent for President of Russia in 1996. Yeltsin, for his part, campaigned there in 1996 and signed the first power-sharing treaty with a far eastern province. At 27 per cent, Yedintsvo was the highest vote getter in the Krai for the December 1999 State Duma elections.[53] Ishaev was fulsome in his praise of Yeltsin when he resigned on 1 January 2000, and has joined other governors in jumping on the Putin bandwagon. In his statement on that occasion he called Putin 'a capable (*rabotosposobnyi*) man whose words are not divorced from deeds'.[54]

With respect to the media, it also seems clear that the governor is in control. Like in the PK, local television stations belong to the Krai administration and therefore this primary source of news for most reflects Ishaev's views. For the print media, each of the three dailies has it own official publisher. The largest, *Tikhookeanskaya Zvezda*, with a circulation around 70,000, receives most of its funding from the Krai administration. The other two are funded in large part by the city administration and by the Krai Duma respectively. There is an independent weekly, the *Khabarovsk Express*, which is supported by elements of the business community and which apparently voices some cautious criticism of the administration. An editor at one of these papers made the point that while there is no official external censorship as in the past, as a result of financial dependence, there is self-censorship. In his words, 'You don't go to the bathroom where you eat.' He also noted that the monthly salary of even his top journalists was less than one hundred dollars, a figure similar to what teachers get. Advertising covers only about 20 per cent of the costs of publication, and access to printing, paper and other materials is available only through the Krai administration. In one way or another 'all depends on the governor'.[55]

The one area of potential friction concerned the question of who would be mayor of the Krai capitol. It will be remembered that Viktor Cherepkov, the former mayor of Vladivostok, was the governor's leading rival for power in Primorskii Krai. Unlike in the PK, however, in Khabarovsk the issue was quickly resolved in the governor's favour. The process of choosing heads of municipalities had not been clearly established in 1994 because the law on local self-government had not yet been adopted. Although the election of mayors was contemplated, the nomination of the first mayor of the Krai capitol in the post-soviet era (40 per cent of the Krai's population live in Khabarovsk) was made by the Krai Duma in March 1994 at the insistence of Ishaev over protests from democratic factions that favoured direct elections. In this way Ishaev ensured that his man, Pavel Filippov would be chosen. Like Ishaev, Filippov followed a non-party career in industry (gas) and came to politics with Ishaev only in 1991 as a member of the Krai ispolkom (executive committee). From 1992–94 he was the vice governor under Ishaev in charge of state property in Khabarovsk. Relations between them are therefore highly cooperative. On 8 December 1996, also the date of Ishaev's election as governor, Filippov was elected mayor with 46 per cent of the vote, almost twice that of his nearest rival. In short, the governor faces no institutional limits that might be asserted either locally by the mayor of Khabarovsk or from above, by a presidential representative.

Sakhalin Oblast

Political life in Sakhalin Oblast is neither as quiescent as in Khabarovsk nor as turbulent as in Primorskii Krai. Smaller than the other two regions in population, this former island penal colony was home to Ainu and other aborigines before Russia and Japan shared possession of it from 1855–75.[56] Today the oblast administers the Southern Kurile Islands which were occupied by Russia after the Second World War and which the Japanese insist are part of its 'Northern Territories'. Although the position of chief executive in Sakhalin Oblast is pre-eminent in the political life of the province, it does appear to be not as dominant as in Khabarovsk and Primorskii Krais, nor does its incumbent, Igor Farkhutdinov, seem as secure. Also unlike them he is from a nomenklatura background. Born in Novosibirsk in 1950 and trained at the Krasnoyarsk Polytechnic Institute, Farkhutdinov worked as an engineer at an electric power station on Sakhalin until he entered party work, first in the Komsomol, and then by 1985 as an instructor in the Sakhalin Obkom (the oblast party committee). From 1985–95 he served as Ispolkom chair, first in the city of Nevel'sk and then in the provincial capitol, Yuzhno-Sakhalinsk, where he became mayor. It was not until 1995 that Yeltsin appointed him governor, the position to which he was elected in 1996.

An ethnic Tatar, Farkhutdinov was preceded as governor first by Valentin Fedorov and then by Yevgenii Krasnoyarov. Fedorov, an economics professor and liberal deputy to the Russian Congress of People's Deputies supported by Democratic Russia, had been appointed by Yeltsin in October 1991 and acquired favourable attention as the advocate of a special economic zone for Sakhalin. In spring 1993, however, he ran afoul of the oblast Duma which accused him of irregularities prompting his resignation. After serving briefly as a Deputy Minister of Economics in Moscow, he tried to get elected to the State Duma from Sakhalin in 1996, but lost and ended up as the chair of the government in Sakha (Yakutiya). In his place, the oblast Duma nominated, and Yeltsin agreed to appoint, Yevgenii Krasnoyarov, director of a Russian–Japanese fishing enterprise. Krasnoyarov was quite popular locally and in 1993 won the election to the Russian State Duma among six candidates, including Farkhutdinov who finished in sixth place. In April 1995, however, Krasnoyarov resigned 'of his own volition' and Yeltsin appointed Yuzhno-Sakhalinsk mayor, Igor Farkhutdinov, as governor.

Although Farkhutdinov won election to that post on 20 October 1996, it was not without controversy. Only 33 per cent of the eligible voters came out to choose among ten candidates. Running independently of any party support – although he chaired the local branch of Our Home is Russia (NDR) – Farkhutdinov took 40 per cent compared to his nearest rival, industrialist Anatolii Chernyi, who received 27 per cent. Although the election law specified that the winner needed an absolute majority, the oblast election commission still declared Farkhutdinov to have been elected governor. When this clearly illegal decision was challenged in the oblast courts, the oblast Duma hastily met before the court could render a decision and amended the law to require a simple majority.[57] This problem should not occur again, however. In March 2000 the Duma deputies voted narrowly that gubernatorial elections scheduled for later in the year would be decided by a simple majority.[58]

As established by the charter of Sakhalin Oblast adopted by the Duma on 26 December 1995, the institution of the chief executive is also less dominant relative to the legislature. Although the governor is directly elected (albeit by a simple majority) and independently appoints most of the members of his administration, he must submit the name of his first vice governor to the Duma for 'agreement' (*soglasie*). Like the governors of the PK and Khabarovsk, the governor of Sakhalin has the right to adopt binding resolutions and administrative decrees. Also, and unique among the regions examined here, the governor has the casting vote if the Duma is split. The governor may return laws to the Duma for reconsideration, but that body does not appear to need two thirds to over-ride. Perhaps most significantly, while the governor has no ability to dissolve the Duma (only the Duma can do so by a two-thirds vote of its full membership) it appears that the Duma can propose a governor's removal and submit that proposal to a popular referendum (Articles 20.n and 35:2).

As in the Khabarovsk charter there is a section intended to promote consensus between the branches of government in which members of each body are entitled to attend meetings of the other and make proposals. In case of disagreements, there is even a provision (Article 39:5) for setting up a sort of conference committee (*soglasitel'nyi komissii*) which has ten days to make a recommendation as to how matters may be settled before going to court. In short, while the regime in Sakhalin is 'presidential' the parliament is less 'subordinate' than in the other two regions of the RDV studied here.

The current composition of the Sakhalin Duma is said to be 'more aggressive' than in the other regions and to seek a bigger role in making laws.[59] If so, this would be a marked contrast with the first Duma elected on 27 March 1994 when elections were held in four multi-candidate districts each sending four deputies to the provincial parliament for a total of sixteen. Voter turnout was poor. Only 25 per cent of the electorate chose among fifty-two candidates with successful elections declared for twelve seats. Given the large number of votes cast 'against all' (17 per cent on average), the electoral base of the Duma was extremely low.[60] Even this twelve member Duma was so badly divided politically that it was unable to function effectively. The current Duma was elected concurrently with the governor on 20 October 1996. In accordance with the new charter, elections were held for twenty-seven deputies each to serve four-year terms. This time 34 per cent of the voters chose among 148 candidates running in nine three-member districts (three of which are in the oblast capitol, Yuzhno-Sakhalinsk) and all seats were filled. Three of the deputies from the previous session were re-elected.

While most of the current Duma deputies are from the ranks of industrial and business leaders (nine of whom are Directors) parties appear to have played a bigger role than in the Khabarovsk and Primore. Those supported by the KPRF, chaired by obkom first secretary Vladimir Paramoshkin, took six seats, while those of the liberal reform movement Civic Responsibility (*Grazdanskoi otvetstvennosti*) took four. Two more were elected by the Union of Women and two by the Association of Fisherman; one came from the ecological movement Cedar. Two groups emerged following the opening session; the Group of Industrialists (most of whom are also affiliated with NDR) counted eleven members and the KPRF claimed five. Five of the deputies are women while a sixth, Antonina Nachetkina, has an advisory vote as the elected representative of the Congress of Indigenous Peoples of the North. Boris Tretyak, the candidate for Chair supported by the industrialists, and by Farkhutdinov, won, along with the first vice chair from the previous session, Lyubov' Shubina.[61] Despite the more partisan composition of the deputies and the fact that they are institutionally more powerful than in their neighbouring regions, it would still appear that collectively they are unlikely to act as much of a constraint on the incumbent governor. The vote on amending the election law to accommodate his apparently dubious victory in October 1996 would seem to confirm this.

In his relations with the Kremlin, Farkhutdinov holds two major cards. The first of these concerns the territorial dispute with Japan. Because the disputed islands are under the oblast's administration (the four islands are part of the Southern Kuriles raion or region) Farkhutdinov has been vocal in his opposition to any settlement which would return them to Japan. After and Japanese Prime Minister Hashimoto agreed in November 1997 to sign a peace treaty by 2000, the governor signed an declaration reasserting the Russian status of the islands.[62] Like the other regional governors, however, his public rhetoric on the issue is not always matched in practice and, since 1993, Japanese have been able travel to these islands without visas. In a more recent expression of his patriotism, Farkhutdinov has called for closure of the Sea of Okhotsk to all but Russian fisherman.[63] Much of this seems designed more to get Moscow's attention than a non-negotiable demand.

The other card is the development of the substantial oil and gas reserves (350 million tons of oil; 425 billion cubic meters of gas) found on the island's eastern shelf. Three international consortiums (Sakhalin-1, 2 and 3) have invested large sums of money in extracting these resources. Despite the wealth that the sales of these products promises to bring to the region, the benefits up to the end of the twentieth century have been negligible, and problems have been numerous.[64] The governor can, with some justification, blame Moscow for this. For one thing, the Russian State Duma has been slow to pass legislation on production-sharing agreement that would provide guarantees to foreign investors.[65] Then, in August 1999, the company Exxon suspended production when an environmental impact study recommended against continuing with the Sakhalin-1 project. As a result of these delays, the standard of living in the oblast remains low and political alienation is high.[66] However, the first oil began to flow in July 1999, and Sakhalin may yet find itself in a commanding position among the regions of the RDV by virtue of its energy wealth.

Despite differences over these two issues, Farkhutdinov's relations with the Centre have been reasonably harmonious. The presidential representative in the oblast is Viktor Kamornik who was appointed in October 1993 replacing Vitalii Gulii, a former USSR Congress deputy and a journalist. Kamornik is a former member of the oblast administration and is not likely to oppose the governor. Along with the other regions discussed here, Sakhalin has largely delivered the vote. They favoured Yeltsin in the 1991 election, the 1993 referendum and in the 1996 presidential election by the same amount or better than he received nationally. In return, the Kremlin has given support to Farkhutdinov. Shortly before the 1996 presidential election, Yeltsin campaigned with the governor in Sakhalin, taking time to sign a bilateral power-sharing agreement with the region.[67] Farkhutdinov adroitly uses his trips to sessions of the Federation Council (where he is a member *ex officio*) to bring home the bacon, as he did in February 2000 when he announced that as a result of his meeting with the chair of the Russian Pension Fund, pensions in Sakhalin would be raised by more than average. Like his regional colleagues in PK and Khabarovsk, he was quick to jump on the Putin bandwagon on 8 December 1999, urging fellow governors to support him when he was still Prime Minister.[68]

While Farkhutdinov appears to faces few institutional limits from above, the situation locally has proven more troublesome. Local elections held for mayor in early 1997 resulted in victories for Farkhutdinov's opponents in a number of municipalities, including Kholmsk. Most significantly, in the oblast capitol of Yuzno-Sakhalinsk, where 30 per cent of the island's inhabitants live, the former Federal Security Service (FSB) chief for foreign currency control, Fedor Sidorenko, defeated industrialist Nikolai Kuznetsov, the governor's hand-picked candidate, to replace the previous mayor Vladimir Yagubov, an ally who Farkhutdinov had brought into the oblast administration.[69] The governor's inability to control the outcomes of local elections was also evident in the victory of the incumbent deputy to the Russian State Duma for territorial district 160, Ivan Zhdakaev. Zhdakaev is a member of the KPRF and had opposed the oblast administration on legislation dealing with the oil-production-sharing agreements on the grounds that it gave too much to foreign investors. The election commission of the oblast, and then the Central Election Commission, refused to register his candidacy, a decision upheld by the oblast court. The locally popular Zhdakaev was able to run, and win, only after that decision was voided by the

Russian Supreme Court. What these elections suggest is that Farkhutdinov is not able to take his electorate for granted and that he cannot act without taking into account the acts of other political players.

Conclusions

At the beginning of this chapter, we asked whether the political institutions which had evolved in the RDV during the ten years since reforms were first introduced in 1990 were significantly different from those of Yaroslavl' Oblast located in central Russia. The author's findings from research in that region led to the conclusion that while the forms of democracy had been introduced, the practices of democracy had been slower to take root. As a result of weak institutionalisation, governance was more personalistic and centred on the chief executive who, once elected, made decisions largely unconstrained by independent political actors. The system of government that emerged in Yaroslavl' by the end of the twentieth century could best be described as a 'declarative democracy', a term used by Guillermo O'Donnell to describe particularistic regimes that had emerged especially in recently democratised Latin countries. While chief executives in such regimes are accountable 'vertically' because they must be popularly chosen in periodic elections, the lack of well-developed formal and informal institutional constraints means that these executives are free to make decisions largely unchecked. Although O'Donnell had national executives in mind when writing about declarative democracy, research presented here and elsewhere suggests that the concept may be usefully applied to the rulers of Russia's regions.

First of all, the type of chief executives of the three regions of the RFE examined here seems to fit the model of delegative democracy. Each was chosen in elections that could be described, in O'Donnell's words, as 'emotional and high-stakes events'. As in Yaroslavl', the election law for each called for the winner to receive an absolute majority in order to ensure the broadest possible popular mandate and therefore the appearance of greater legitimacy. The only exception occurred in Sakhalin, but only because the governor's allies in the legislature hastily amended the law after the fact. However, whereas Sakhalin's Farkhutdinov could muster only 40 per cent against 27 per cent for his nearest rival, in the PK, Nazdratenko was re-elected in December 1999 by a margin of 65 per cent to 20 per cent, while on the same day, in Yaroslavl', incumbent governor Anatolii Lisityn won by the same per cent over his rival, oblast Duma chair Sergei Vakhrukov, who polled only 17 per cent. In Khabarovsk Krai in 1996, governor Ishaev achieved an even higher vote, polling 77 per cent against his nearest opponent's 7 per cent. In all three gubernatorial elections in the regions of RFE, the winning candidate portrayed himself as a regional saviour using populist rhetoric to attack the central government for failing to protect regional interests, including territorial demands from neighbouring countries. Characteristically, in all three regions, as in Yaroslavl', the winner also portrayed himself as standing above political partisanship. Finally, in all these three regions, with varying degrees of impropriety and varying degrees of success, each governor has shown himself willing to bend the rules in order to reward his friends and punish his enemies, politically as well as economically.

In institutionally developed democracies, one of the principle checks on executive authority is the parliamentary body, or legislature. Following the criteria used by Vladimir Gel'man to distinguish between ideal types of the separation of power and types of parliaments, we find that the terms 'presidential' and 'subordinate' best describe the balance of power between the executive and legislative branches in all three regions.[70] Again, Sakhalin is something of an exception because the governor requires Duma approval of his choice for first deputy and because there is provision for the Duma's role in removing a governor from office. Nevertheless the strong shift of the balance of power in favour of the executive branch following the dissolution of the soviets in 1993 is apparent institutionally in all four regions. Moreover, when it comes to the question of who in fact sits in the legislature, in Sakhalin – as in the PK, Khabarovsk and Yaroslavl' – the governors' allies predominate. In each of these regions in the RFE, the speaker is congenial to the governor if not an ally. One of the chief explanations for the weakness of regional parliaments, as Mary McAuley has argued, would appear to be absence of well-developed regional branches of political parties. In all the regions under study here, only a handful of deputies belong to a nationally identifiable party (mostly to the KPRF), and even then the candidates win regardless of party support. Most are members of the administration or are corporate heads who run as 'independents', preferring what McAuley calls the 'professional legislator' model to that of a constituency representative.[71]

Among other possible institutional constraints on regional executive authority examined here are the federal and local levels of government. On the federal level, one of the intended checks on regional chiefs was the office of the presidential representative. Yet, in the cases of Primorskii Krai and Yaroslavl', when the presidential representatives challenged the governors over issues of regional corruption, they instead found themselves removed from their offices by Yeltsin and replaced by someone more to the governor's liking.[72] In Khabarovsk Krai and Sakhalin Oblast, the representatives have avoided such confrontations. On the basis of the evidence, some of which has been presented here, it is possible to speculate that one of the reasons for weakness of the federal position is the clientelistic relationship that exists between regional elites who deliver political support to the Centre in return for which they are given a comparatively free rein within their regions. This relationship is also evident, at least in the cases of Primorskii Krai and Khabarovsk Krais, in the willingness of the Centre to allow regional chiefs to manipulate municipal elections in the regional capitols in their favour. In the PK, Yeltsin not once, but twice, removed by presidential decree the duly elected mayor of Vladivostok, Viktor Cherepkov, the governor's erstwhile opponent. Again, Sakhalin is an exception. The mayor of Yuzhno-Sakhalinsk, Fedor Sidorenko, among other municipal leaders in Sakhalin, opposes the governor and on 17 March 2000 announced that he would run against him in the autumn gubernatorial elections. In late October 2000 Farkhutdinov gained 56 per cent of the vote, easily defeating Sidorenko. The situation in Sakhalin, however, appears to be due more to Farkhutdinov's weak electoral base than to an unwillingness on the part of the Centre to go along with what he wants to do locally; this is evidenced by the blind eye turned on the governor's dubious victory in his October 1996 election.

Bringing together all the evidence regarding the development of political institutions of the three regions of the RDV examined here, it would seem that the similarities between them and those of Yaroslavl' are greater than the differences. Allowing for minor variation, they may best be described as delegative democracies at the regional level. While generalizing from a few cases certainly does not allow us to conclude that this model is applicable for all of Russia's regions, this conclusion does tend to support the findings of Mary McAuley and Andrei Tsygankov discussed earlier suggesting that the development of regional political institutions in Russia has resulted in rather similar regimes.

The implications of the findings presented here for the further development of democracy in Russia are not encouraging. As O'Donnell has argued, delegative democracies are not conducive to democratic consolidation.[73] However, if the species we are seeing is indeed delegative democracy, the genus is still democratic. There is nothing permanent or pre-ordained about the type of regime that seems to have emerged in Russia's regions. Indeed, it may be that such regime types are more characteristically found in periods of political transition. Given enough time and the right incentives, the forms of democracy may provide a frame for democratic attitudes and behaviour.

Notes

1 The findings of this research are to be published in a book by Jeffrey W. Hahn (ed.), *Regional Russia in Transition: Studies from Yaroslavl'* (Washington, DC: Woodrow Wilson Centre Press, forthcoming).

2 For more on this distinction, see Harry Eckstein, 'Congruence theory explained', in Harry Eckstein, *et al.*, *Can Democracy Take Root in Post-Soviet Russia? Explorations in State–Society Relations* (Lanham, MD: Rowman and Littlefield Publishers, 1998), p. 10.

3 Guillermo O'Donnell, 'Delegative democracy', *Journal of Democracy*, 5:1 (January 1994).

4 Robert D. Putnam, *Making Democracy Work: Civic Traditions in Modern Italy* (Princeton NJ: Princeton University Press, 1993), p. 183.

5 See, for example, Lilia Shevtsova, *Yeltsin's Russia: Myths and Reality* (Washington, DC: Carnegie Endowment for International Peace, 1999) and George Breslauer, 'Boris Yeltsin as patriarch', *Post-Soviet Affairs*, 15:2 (1999).

6 See, for example, the debate on this subject in 'Federalism in Russia: how is it working?' *Conference Report: 9–10 December 1998*, prepared by the National Intelligence Council, Washington, DC; Kathryn Stoner-Weiss, 'Central weakness and provincial autonomy: observations on the devolution process in Russia', *Post-Soviet*

Affairs, 15:1 (1999); Leonid Smirnyagin, 'Putin brain trust seeks to improve federal agencies in the Regions', East–West Institute, *Russian Regional Report*, 5:11 (22 March 2000) (hereafter, EWI, *Russian Regional Report*).

7 For a fairly comprehensive listing of sources and a literature review for 1998, see Michael J. Bradshaw and Philip Hanson, 'Understanding regional patterns of economic change in Russia: an introduction', *Communist Economics and Economic Transformation*, 10:3 (1998), 285–304. See also Joel C. Moses, 'Seratov and Volgograd 1990–92: a tale of two Russian provinces', in Theodore H. Friedgut and Jeffrey W. Hahn (eds.), *Local Power and Post-Soviet Politics* (Armonk, NY: M. E. Sharpe, 1994); Kimitaka Matzusato, 'Local elites in transition: county and city politics in Russia 1985–1996', *Europe–Asia Studies*, 51:8 (1999), 1367–400; Kimitaka Matsuzato, 'From ethno-Bonapartism to centralised caciquismo: features and genesis of the Tatarstan regime', paper presented at the Annual Meeting of the American Association for the Advancement of Slavic Studies, St Louis, MO, November, 1999; Darrell Slider, 'Pskov and the LDPR: elections and dysfunctional federalism in one region', *Europe–Asia Studies* 51:1 (1999); Nicolai Petro, 'The Novgorod region: a Russian success story', *Post-Soviet Affairs*, 15:3 (1999), 235–61; Vladimir Gel'man, 'Regime transition, uncertainty and the prospects for democratisation: the politics of Russia's regions in a comparative perspective', *Europe–Asia Studies*, 51:6 (1999), 939–56; Vladimir Gel'man, 'Regional'naya vlast' v sovremennoi Rossii: instituty, rezhimy, i praktiki', *Polis*, 1 (1998); Mary McAuley, *Russia's Politics of Uncertainty* (Cambridge: Cambridge University Press, 1997).

8 Andrei Tsygankov, 'Manifestations of delegative democracy in Russian local politics: what does it mean for the future of Russia?', *Communist and Post-Communist Studies*, 31:4 (1998), 329–44.

9 O'Donnell, 'Delegative democracy', 59. Unless otherwise noted, all the quotes in this paragraph come from pp. 59–62 of this article.

10 In related articles, O'Donnell seems to emphasise that horizontal accountability requires the existence of independent state agencies legally empowered to take actions ranging from 'routine oversight to criminal sanctions or impeachment'. Guillermo O'Donnell, 'Horizontal accountability in new democracies', *Journal of Democracy*, 9:3 (1998), 117. See also Guillermo O'Donnell, 'Illusions about consolidation', *Journal of Democracy*, 7:2 (1996), 44. However, it is not clear to this author why other non-state entities like parties, public interest groups and the media, or even individuals, for example, cannot perform the primary task of accountability, namely holding executives responsible for their actions in office and thereby constraining them from an abuse of authority. Indeed, O'Donnell names several of these institutions as means to 'enhancing' horizontal accountability (O'Donnell, 'Horizontal accountability', 122–3). It is for this reason that these other independent institutions will be considered in the present effort to determine what, if any, limits exist for regional chief executives, along with formal institutions such as legislatures and local and federal agencies.

11 O'Donnell, 'Delegative democracy', 60.

12 Here we will use a modified version of the classificatory scheme developed by Gel'man. See V. Gel'man, *Regional'naya vlast'*, 89–90.

13 For a good review of the development of this institution and how the sporadic nature of Yeltsin's attention to it undermined the effectiveness of his representatives, see Irina M. Busygina, 'Predstaviteli prezidenta', *Svobodnaya mysl'*, 4 (1996), 52–61.

14 The Russian Constitution adopted in 1993 devotes a section to the institutions of local
    self-government (*mestnoye samo-upravlenie*), which principally, although not exclu-
    sively, refers to the municipal subdivisions of the eighty-nine regions. These eighty-
    nine, by contrast, are considered part of the federal system of state power
    (*gosudarstvennaya vlast'*). The institutions of local self-government, at least on paper,
    have considerable autonomy in making policies on issues that effect the local popula-
    tion directly, and they are entitled to form their own political institutions and to elect
    their own officials independently of regional authorities. This has created the poten-
    tial for tensions between municipal and regional authorities, especially in regional
    capitols where the bulk of the regional population usually live; these are tensions
    which the Centre, on occasion, has encouraged in order to rein in regional heads. One
    of the most comprehensive discussions of these institutions is found in Kimitaka
    Matsuzato (ed.), 'Tret'e zveno gosudarstvennogo stroitel'stvo Rossii: podgotovka i
    realizatsiia zakona ob printsipakh organizatsii mestnogo samoupravleniya v
    Rossiiskkoi federatsii', *Occasional Papers on Changes in the Slavic-Eurasian World* 73
    (Sapporo: Slavic Research Centre, Hokkaido University, March 1998).
15 Since 1995, the Slavic Research Centre has been collecting biographical information
    and other data from regions in Russia and Ukraine. Much of this has been published
    in a series entitled *Regiony Rossii; khronika i rukovoditeli* (Sapporo: Slavic Research
    Centre, Hokkaido University) The most recent of these dealt with Nizhnii Novgorod
    and Ul'ianovsk and was published in May 1999. Two of the *Occasional Papers* series
    related to the regions under study here are Hugo Managua (ed.) 'Politicheskaya elita
    Primorskogo kraya', *Occasional Paper* 4 (1995) and, by the same author,
    'Politiciheskaya elita Khabarovskogo kraya', *Occasional Paper* 20 (December 1996).
16 Peter Kirkow, 'Regional warlordism in Russia: the case of Primorskii Krai',
    Europe–Asia Studies, 47:6 (1995), 923–47. A modified version of this article appears
    as a chapter in Peter Kirkow, *Russia's Provinces: Authoritarian Transformation versus
    Local Autonomy* (London: Macmillan, 1998).
17 Tamara Troyakova, 'Regional policy in the Russian far east and the rise of localism in
    Primorye', *The Journal of East Asian Affairs*, 9:2 (1995), 428–61.
18 Shugo Minagawa, 'Mode of political leadership in the transitional period: the case of
    Primorskii krai' (1999, unpublished manuscript made available to the author), pp.
    8–10; 'Primorskii Krai', *Politicheskii Almanakh Rossii 1997*, p. 383.
19 *Ibid.*
20 Mikhail A. Alekseev and Tamara Troyakova, 'A mirage of the 'Amur California':
    regional identity and economic incentives for political separatism in Primorskii Krai',
    in Mikhail A. Alekseev (ed.), *Centre–Periphery Conflict in Post-Soviet Russia: A
    Federalism Imperiled* (New York: St. Martin's Press, 1999), esp. pp. 222–8. At
    Nazdratenko's urging in July 1993, the Krai Duma considered a resolution declaring
    PK to be a 'republic'.
21 *Utro Rossii* (1 February 1995).
22 *Izvestiya* (22 March 1994), p. 1. See also, Kirkow, *Russia's provinces*, p. 129.
23 Yeltsin had been given the right to appoint and remove governors by the Fifth Congress
    of People's Deputies in autumn 1991, a right which he continued to exercise until he
    allowed the election of governors in 1996–97 *after* the June 1996 presidential election
    was over. A few exceptions to this practice were made in elections held in April 1993.
    See Jeffrey W. Hahn, 'Democratisation and political participation in Russia's regions',
    in Karen Dawisha and Bruce Parrott (eds.), *Democratic Changes and Authoritarian*

Reactions in Russia, Ukraine, Belarus and Moldova (Cambridge: Cambridge University Press, 1997).

24 *Vladivostok News* (20 December 1999); *Rezul'taty vyborov 19 Dekabrya 1999 goda: protokol izbiratel'noi komissii 25*. For information on election complaints, see Russian *Regional Report*, 4:48 (22 December 1999).

25 EWI, *Russian Regional Investor*, 2:21 (31 May 2000).

26 'Primosrkii Krai', *Politicheskii Almanakh Rossii 1997*, p. 386.

27 These terms follow the usage found in V. Gel'man, *Regional'naya vlast'*, 41, 89–90. All references to the Charter are from the *Ustav Primorskogo Kraya*, adopted by the Primorskii Krai Duma on 12 September 1995 and signed by Governor Nazdratenko on 6 October 1995.

28 For the distinction between *'pays reel'* and *'pays legal'*, see Guillermo O'Donnell, 'Illusions about consolidation', *Journal of Democracy*, 7:2 (1996) 43, as well his section on 'The importance of informal rules', 39–41.

29 Lebedinets later fell foul of Nazdratenko and was forced to resign as speaker in June 1995. See Kirkow, *Russia's Provinces*, p. 122.

30 'Primorskii Krai', *Politicheskii Almanakh Rossii 1997*, p. 386.

31 See Kirkow, *Russia's Provinces*, pp. 135–6; *Politicheskii Almanakh Rossii 1997* (p. 388) claims that 'political parties and movements have practically no weight in the Krai', although these observations predated the 1997 elections.

32 Minagawa, 'Mode of political leadership', 30.

33 *Russian Regional Report* 5:4 (2 February 2000); 4:37 (7 October 1999).

34 Information on the local media in PK was obtained during the author's visit to Vladivostok in April 2000. He is grateful to Tamara Troyakova for much of the data.

35 For details, see *Russian Regional Report* 4:34 (16 September); 4:41 (4 November 1999).

36 See, for example, Alfred B. Evans, 'Stress in the relationship between local and regional governments in Russia', paper presented to the Annual Meeting of the Rocky Mountain Association for Slavic Studies, Fort Worth, TX, April 1998.

37 'Primorskii Krai', *Politicheskii Almanakh Rossii 1997*, p. 385; see also Kirkow, *Russia's Provinces*, p. 134.

38 In September 1998 the Russian Federation Central Election Commission decided in a special hearing about Vladivostok that before a mayor could be elected, a new city Duma would have to be chosen and a city charter adopted. See, *Russian Regional Report* 4:1 (January 14, 1999). Failure to do so meant that acting mayor Kopylov would remain in power. Although voters passed a city charter in the 19 December 1999 municipal elections, only six seats of fourteen being contested were valid. Added to eight seats filled earlier, this still added up to only fourteen seats filled out of twenty-two and was therefore one short of the quorum needed (*Vladivostok News*, 24 December 1999).

39 McFaul and Petrov, 'Russian electoral politics after transition: regional and national assessments', *Post-Soviet Geography and Economics*, 38:9 (1997), 507–49; Steven L. Solnick, 'Gubernatorial elections in Russia 1996–1997', *Post-Soviet Affairs* 14:1 (1998), 48–80; Vladimir Kolosov and Rostislav Tuorvskii, '*Osenne-zimnie vybory glav ispolnitel'noi vlasti v regionakh: tsenarii peremen*', *Polis* 1 (1997), 97–108.

40 EWI *Russian Regional Review*, 2:21 (12 June 1997); 'Primorskii Krai', *Politicheskii Almanakh Rossii 1997*, pp. 387–8.

41 Shugo Minagawa, 'Mode of political leadership', 14. Among the 'friends', Minagawa mentions Sergei Filatov, Vladimir Shumeiko, Oleg Soskovets and Viktor

Chernomyrdin; among the 'enemies', Yegor Gaidar, Anatolii Chubais, Boris Federov and Grigorii Yavlinsky.

42 On clientelism, see O'Donnell, 'Illusions about consolidation', 40ff.

43 *Russian Regional Report*, 5:20 (24 May 2000).

44 He originally sought to have the election held at the time of the presidential election on 16 June 1996, but this bid was rejected by Yeltsin. See *Politicheskii Almanakh Rossii 1997*, p. 476.

45 *Russian Regional Report*, 3:47 (24 November 1998). The Far Eastern Regional Association has not been particularly successful in fostering inter-regional coopera-tion because the regional elites have more incentive to compete with one another than to cooperate. See *Russian Regional Report* 4:34 (16 September 1999).

46 This information was made available to the author by Shinichiro Tabata. See also his article, 'Transfers from federal to regional budgets in Russia: a statistical analysis', *Post-Soviet Geography and Economics*, 39:8 (1998), 447–60.

47 *Federal'noe sobranie; Gos. Duma, Sbornik dogovorov i soglashenie mezhdu organami gosudarstvennoi vlasti RF i organami vlasti sub'ektov RF* (Moscow: Izvestiya, 1997), pp. 356–97.

48 *Tikhookeanskaya zvezda*, 21 December 1999. See, *Russian Regional Report*, 5:2 (20 January 2000).

49 Gel'man, *Regional'naya vlast'*, 7–8. References in this paragraph are from the *Ustav Khabarovskogo Kraya*.

50 'Khabarovsk Krai', *Politicheskii Alamanakh Rossii 1997*, p. 417.

51 One such issue is; whether a law on housing norms should specify eighteen meters (Ishaev) or twenty meters (the Duma's position). This and other cases involving rela-tively minor differences was offered to the author as evidence that the support in the Duma for the governor's position is not automatic. Interview with deputy and vice speaker of the Khabarovsk Krai Duma, Zoya Sofrina, 6 April 2000.

52 *Ibid.*, p. 413.

53 *Tikhookeanskaya zvezda* (21 December 1999).

54 Ishaev's remarks were published on the krai website *Khabarovskii Krai novosti*.

55 The source for the interview cited here can be obtained by contacting the author.

56 John J. Stephan, *The Russian Far East:A History* (Stanford, CA: Stanford University Press, 1994), p. 45.

57 The author is grateful to Professor Nobuo Arai of Sapporo International University for this information.

58 *Sakhalinskie novosti* (22 March 2000). Of only twenty deputies voting, ten were for simply majority election, seven wanted an absolute majority and three abstained.

59 See EWI, *Russian Regional Report* 4:34 (16 September 1999).

60 'Sakhalinskaya oblast', *Politicheskii Almanakh Rossii 1997*, p. 858.

61 Some of this information comes from *ibid.* Some of it was from colleagues at the Slavic Research Centre of Hokkaido University.

62 EWI, *Russian Regional Report*, 3:18 (7 May 1998).

63 RFE/RL, *Newsline* (7 March 2000).

64 See Peter Rutland's report 'Sakhalin waits for oil and gas wealth', EWI, *Russian Regional Investor*, 1:29 (5 August 1999); EWI, *Russian Regional Report*, 5:11 (22 March 2000).

65 The production sharing agreement for Sakhalin was finally signed in May 1999. See EWI, *Russian Regional Report*, 4:18 (12 May 1999).

66 See Mikhail Alekseev, 'Sakhalin: the dying corner of the empire', *Russian Regional Report*, 4:39 (21 October 1999).

67 *Federal'noe sobranie; Gos. Duma, Sbornik dogovorov i soglashenie mezhdu organami gosudarstvennoi vlasti RF i organami vlasti sub'ektov RF* (Moscow: Izvestiya, 1997), pp. 623–46.

68 *Kommersant daily* (9 December 1999).

69 'Sakhalinskaya Oblast', *Politicheskii Almanakh Rossii 1997*, p. 855.

70 Gel'man, *'Regional'naya vlast'*, 89–90. According to Gel'man's classification, presidential systems are characterised by the 'popular election of the regional head who determines the composition of the cabinet and has broad norm-setting powers'. Subordinate parliaments 'have no means to control the cabinet, but are not completely subordinate to the executive power'.

71 McAuley, *Russia's Politics of Uncertainty*, pp. 265; 272. On the importance of the role parties play in Russia's regions and why they have been slow to develop, see Grigorii V. Golosov, 'From Adygeya to Yaroslavl': factors of party development in the regions of Russia', *Europe–Asia Studies*, 51:8 (1999), 1333–56. On the relevance of party development to the emergence federalism in Russia, see Peter C. Ordeshook, 'Russia's party system: is Russian federalism viable?', *Post-Soviet Affairs*, 12:3 (1996), 195–217.

72 For the events in Yaroslavl' see Kimitaka Matsuzato and Alexander B. Shatilov (eds) *'Regiony Rossii: khronika i rukovoditeli, Samarskaya i Yaroslavskaya oblasti'*, *Occasional Papers on the Slavic Eurasian World 35* (Sapporo: Hokkaido University, Slavic Research Centre, 1997), pp. 255–6.

73 O'Donnell, 'Illusions about consolidation', see esp. 40ff.

Regional democratisation in Russia: some lessons from Novgorod

The demise of the USSR has unsettled many traditional notions and transformed the entire region into a vast laboratory of political and economic experimentation. While the attention of most analysts has been focused on the Kremlin, even more dramatic shifts have been underway at the regional level where the weakening of Moscow's authority has given local authorities considerable leeway to forge their own destiny. As a result, a new field of study has emerged – regional Russian studies. This field has begun to look at the variations among regions in areas such as living standards and economic development.

But while acknowledging the growing socio-economic diversity among regions, most analysts have yet to find much variety among regions when it comes to democratic development. This seems especially odd since the modernisation theories, which analysts of democratisation draw upon, suggest that differences in economic and social conditions should be reflected in different levels of democratic development. Moreover, such political diversity is commonly acknowledged in the press.[1] Something is clearly missing from our theoretical approaches, and this is hindering proper appreciation of the diversity of Russian regional political development.

This chapter explores the limitations of current approaches to regional democratic development in Russia. It examines three popular explanations for regional diversity – structural explanations, elite explanations and single charismatic leader explanations – from the vantage point of the Russia region of Novgorod. Because Novgorod provides strong evidence of having proceeded quite far towards successful democratic consolidation, it provides what the late Harry Eckstein termed 'a crucial case study'.[2]

Novgorod: a region of economic success

The Novgorod region is situated in the north-western economic area of Russia, three hours south-east of St. Petersburg along the main highway to Moscow. The region has a population of approximately 740,000 and covers an area approximately the size of West Virginia. The largest city, Novgorod-the-Great, has about

230,000 inhabitants, followed by Borovichi with 61,000 and Staraya Russa with 40,000. The urban population constitutes about 71 per cent of the region's inhabitants, 96 per cent of whom are ethnic Russians.

Despite its lack of natural resources, extensive military-industrial infrastructure, and large rural population, the region has been a model of economic growth and social stability.[3] By the end of 1999, total foreign direct investment (FDI) in the region approached half a billion US dollars, and the region's per capita level of investment, both foreign and domestic, was second only to that of Moscow. This has allowed the administration greater discretion in setting budgetary priorities, including such items as funding the construction of a cancer care centre for the region, aiding the restoration of churches and monasteries, and redistributing resources to depressed districts.[4] As Michael Schmidt has put it, by allowing the region to raise additional capital for regional development, 'FDI directly assists the maintenance of social peace'.[5]

The link between economic development and democracy is considered to be one of the most reliable, and previous studies have shown a strong causal relationship between economic development and democracy.[6] But there are other indicators that provide more direct evidence of a high level of consensus on democratic procedures and values. Two of the most important are trust in local institutions and a high level of associational activity.

Trust in government

A high level of 'generalised trust' in society often results from participation in networks of civic engagement and, while generalised trust is not to be automatically equated with trust in government, some have argued that its very existence reflects a high level of social capital.[7] One tangible manifestation of the increased trust in government in Novgorod is the close interaction among the region's civic associations and the regional government in the *Obshchestvennaya palata*, or 'Social Chamber'.

The Social Chamber was set up by the Novgorod administration to allow representatives of registered social organisations to participate on a routine basis in the review of legislation pending before the Duma and to offer opinions and alternatives legislation as agreed by the Chamber. It meets on the last Thursday of each month and is chaired by either the head of the regional Duma or the governor.

To encourage public involvement and debate, the local law establishing the Social Chamber stipulates that all decisions of the Chamber must be conveyed to the media, along with any minority opinions supported by no fewer than one-fifth of those present.[8] The administration has also encouraged trade union participation, which has formed the basis for subsequent legislation on 'social partnership' between business, labour and government leadership.

The rapid introduction of local self-government seems to have had a positive impact on public trust in local government. Extensive surveys conducted in both

1995 and 1999 show that while confidence in the President, the national government and the State Duma has declined precipitously, public confidence in the region's governor, one's local mayor and the regional Duma have all doubled.[9] Not surprisingly, when Governor Mikhail Prusak campaigned for re-election in September 1999, he won outright, receiving over 91 per cent of the vote, with slightly more than half of the eligible electorate voting.

Associational activity in Novgorod

Another measure of democratic development commonly used by democratisation theorists is associational activity, and with local self-government on the rise it is not surprising to find civic associations in Novgorod thriving as well. What is surprising is the degree to which local government has encouraged civic activism. An examination of the number of registered civic organisations shows that, while the rate of growth in Russia as a whole has slowed considerably, and has been very nearly flat since 1996, the number of civic associations in Novgorod has continued to grow at a rapid pace.[10] By the end of 1999 there were some 615 officially registered civic organisations in the region.[11] As a result, Novgorod ranks among the top quarter of Russian regions in number of clubs and cultural associations per capita.[12]

Robert Putnam, who has studied the successes and failures of regions in Italy, has argued persuasively that 'participation in civic organisations inculcates skills of cooperation as well as a sense of shared responsibility for collective endeavours. Moreover, when individuals belong to "cross-cutting" groups with diverse goals and members, their attitudes will tend to moderate as a result of group interaction and cross-cutting pressures.'[13]

Comparing Novgorod to the regions of Italy reveals some interesting nuances. For example, almost three-quarters of all civic associations in Italy are sports clubs; all other groups have very low rates of participation. By contrast, in Novgorod sports associations form only about 10 per cent of the total. Most civic associations there are manifestly political or economic in nature.

Putnam calculates a 'high' participation rate in places where there is one club for every 1,000–2,000 inhabitants (in Trentino/Alto-Adige and Liguria). At the other extreme lies Sardinia, with a very 'low' participation rate of one club for every 13,100 inhabitants.[14] Applying his methodology to Novgorod today reveals an astonishingly high participation rate for the city of Novgorod-the-Great – one club for every 635 inhabitants – and a quite respectable (by Italian standards) rate of one club for every 4,000 inhabitants throughout the rest of the region.

Taken together these three factors – economic growth, trust in government and civic activism – provide solid evidence of a remarkable level of local democratic development. Not only has the region done much better than its neighbours at implementing economic and political reforms, but for many years now it has displayed an unusually high level of voter support for reform candidates, far higher than its level of wealth, urban concentration, ethnicity and age distribution would predict.[15] Given the widespread negative assessment of Russia's progress towards democracy and markets, explaining the Novgorod region's success poses an interesting challenge. How have contemporary analysts addressed it?

The structuralist view

According to the structuralist view, regions do not perform beyond the attributes they inherited from the Soviet past.[16] A classic example of the argument that structural changes in Novgorod still have very far to go is made by Zimine and Bradshaw.[17] In a nutshell, they contend that no serious structural economic or political transformations have taken place in Novgorod. The regional governor's policies represent 'a mix of populism and paternalism' reminiscent of the Soviet period, and the region's much vaunted stability has been purchased at the expense of true democratisation.[18]

There are several problems with this analysis. First, there is the authors' assumption that stability imposed from above has been a key reason behind Novgorod's success in attracting inward investment. If paternalism could lead to stability and stability in turn to foreign investment, then most Russian regions would be awash with foreign capital. While giving social stability its due, foreign investors more readily cite the administration's solicitous attitude towards potential foreign investors, willingness to negotiate on their behalf with Moscow ministries and, in particular, its willingness to offer long-term tax credits in exchange for large-scale investment and job guarantees.[19]

Second, Zimine and Bradshaw make no mention of the fact that Prusak and his advisors explicitly link economic reforms to political ones: specifically, the purpose of reducing the region's dependence on federal subsidies is to increase resources for local self-government, and hence increase the authority of municipalities, thus providing a virtuous circle of economic and political empowerment.[20]

As for the assertion that the governor's close relations with the government improved the region's ability to receive federal funding, it is worth noting that the decision to pursue a strategy of fiscal independence from Moscow was set up under Viktor Chernomyrdin.[21] The reason – the lack of reliability of Moscow funds. While Novgorod did receive transfers early, administration officials argue that this was the result of having paid into the fund earlier, rather than any special attention. This seems to be corroborated in part by the fact that before 1998 Prusak is not mentioned as an effective lobbyist in any of the many Moscow ratings.

Thus, it seems more logical to conclude that Prusak conducted his economic policies not because of federal support for them, but due to the centre's inability to continue to pay for old policies. Like the vast majority of regions, Novgorod is dependent on federal support but, unlike most, this led local officials to set fiscal independence as their goal. When federal policies coincided with this agenda, the regional government took advantage of them. When they did not, the government attempted to change them and to offset their impact in the region.

For this very reason, attracting FDI to the region has become the centrepiece of the region's economic strategy. Even Zimine and Bradshaw concede that Novgorod's success in attracting large-scale FDI has had 'positive multiplier effects', such as low unemployment and significantly higher real income growth that distinguish it from its neighbours. What they miss is that these multipliers include rationalisation of the government's role in the local economy, the devolution of fiscal responsibility and the empowerment of municipal governments.[22]

Finally, Zimine and Bradshaw suggest that, in the pursuit of regional stability that would attract foreign investors, Prusak has thwarted the development of democratic institutions. They cite an interview with the Deputy Head of the regional Duma, Lyubov' Andreyeva, to the effect that 'the purpose of deputies is not to create laws, but much simpler – to approve drafts presented by the Governor.'[23] This, along with the appointment of the Mayor of Novgorod to position of Deputy to the Governor, suggests to Zimine and Bradshaw that the Duma and municipal administration are little more than rubber stamps for the governor.

In her interview, however, Andreyeva does not say that the role of deputies is limited to approving the laws submitted to it by the Governor. Rather, she notes that in regions where, unlike Novgorod, deputies receive full-time salaries, they 'feel required to prepare draft legislation' to justify those salaries. This requires a large staff attached to individual legislators and she 'absolutely does not understand' the advantage to the region of paying for so many legislative personnel, whose basic function is to promote the careers of individual legislators.[24]

The Novgorod Duma has a large professional staff that reviews legislation, drafts amendments and sends proposed legislation back for review to the originating body. It is, however, attached to the Duma as a whole rather than individual deputies. In addition, the twelve Duma deputies who are simultaneously heads of districts, one-third of the total generally use their regional staff to provide additional legislative expertise.[25] In the interview cited by Zimine and Bradshaw, Andreyeva positively contrasts Novgorod's experience to that of St. Petersburg and Sverdlovsk where, she says, the proliferation of legislative staff has led to 'a lot of politicking' and much less actual legislative work.

Zimine and Bradshaw are simply wrong when they say that the Duma 'has not rejected a single draft law proposed by the Governor'.[26] It has never rejected final versions of legislation, but commonly returns draft laws to the administration for further work. This happens to nearly three out of four bills submitted by the administration.[27] Moreover, there is nothing preventing the Duma from initiating legislation and, according to its head, this happens about 30 per cent of the time.[28] Thus, the significance of the current Duma has not been reduced compared to the oblast soviet, as Zimine and Bradshaw state, but enhanced by the fact that it can now provide critical oversight on proposed legislation.

As for the argument that the appointment of the mayor of Novgorod is proof of subservience to the administration, the deputy chair of the city Duma of Novgorod-the-Great, Irina Kibina, sees it a bit differently. In a memo on the problems facing Russian federalism, she writes:

> Speaking of the real relations that have developed between regional governments [sub'ekt federetsii] and municipalities, we hasten to point out that, with a stable revenue base, municipalities can indeed conduct policies that are relatively independent of the policies of the regional government. This erupts into the political arena in the form of numerous conflicts between the governor and the mayor. The fact of the matter is that, even with all the economic, financial and political crises, it is specifically the municipal authorities that, in the majority of regions, have the greatest popular support, and the governor cannot ignore this, particularly until he is himself elected. In addition, it is the municipalities that know the daily life of the population best. Through systematic tax advantages offered to enterprises, and also through budgetary institutions and tailored social support, they can significantly influence the formation of public opinion. This, in turn, can be an invaluable help at election time, or it can simply affect how long this or that governor, mayor, and even bureaucrat holds office.[29]

The fact that the mayor has his own staff, an independent constituency in the city, an independent revenue stream that goes directly to the city coffers, by-passing the administration, and is in his own right highly regarded both locally and nationally, all give him considerable leverage in promoting the interests of the city. It is therefore more plausible to believe that the mayor's sympathy with the governor's reform course rests on a similarity of political beliefs, as well as the hope that, as a loyal ally of a popular governor, he will one day be in a position to succeed him.

Elite behaviour theories: the dismal science

While structuralists see local leaders as unable to effect significant changes because of circumstances beyond their control, elite theorists argue just the opposite. They point to examples where local arrangements among key players in the political and economic arena have allowed regions to overcome the limitations inherited from the Soviet era. Typically, such an elite compact is the result of an agreement among members of the former communist elite to divide up influence among themselves.

Kathryn Stoner-Weiss has proposed one of the most sophisticated versions of elite theory applied to Russia.[30] She argues that increased economic (sectoral) concentration in a region encourages cooperation between local political and economic elites. Regions with a high concentration of particular industries tend to be more successful at mitigating internal dissension and at presenting a united front in negotiations with Moscow. This results in better governance, as measured by greater public satisfaction with government. The close connection between political and industrial elites fosters a mutual dependence reminiscent of 'company towns' in the US experience.

The cooperation that arose form the concentration of the regional economy was such that the state included economic interests in the policy process, and economic interests gained material advantages from the state. In return, economic interests helped guarantee broad consensus on key issues and used their resources to promote government efficacy and legitimacy within society. These convergent interests therefore sustained consensus and higher government performance – at least in the short term.[31]

While this model has great deal of plausibility for many regions of the Russian Federation, it does not quite ring true for Novgorod. It is certainly not surprising to find that conflict between business and government lowers economic productivity, or that higher elite consensus leads to higher government performance. It is more problematical, however, to argue that such elite consensus is the result of a higher regional economic concentration. If this were so, one would expect to find better rates of economic success in regions with industrial concentrations related to sectors such as the defence industry (a point Stoner-Weiss in fact makes to explain Nizhnii Novgorod's economic success). In recent years, however, Nizhnii's economic situation has been far from stellar in recent years, and the difficulties of key regional enterprises even caused the region to default on a Eurobond payment in October 1999.[32]

In a shrinking economy, the federal government is certainly no guarantee of investment, those regional leaders who attempted to salvage their decrepit industrial base regardless of profitability, generally saw their resources dwindle faster than regions that did not. The contrast is greatest in those few regions where the political leadership chose to abandon its unprofitable industrial base because it could not be made globally competitive. In Novgorod the high level of sectoral concentration in electronics and machine building was quickly identified by the government as the root cause of the region's economic doldrums. Abandoning these traditional industries in favour of new ones that could attract foreign investors thus became the top priority and has fuelled the region's economic growth ever since.[33]

One of the most persistent flaws in elite theories is the assumption that actions undertaken by the elite must be self-serving in the narrowest possible sense. The higher the level of elite consensus, Stoner-Weiss warns, the more likely the elite is to consolidate into an oligarchy that excludes non-elites. Thus, the 'local heroes' of Russian politics today could very easily become the enemies of further economic and political development tomorrow.[34] Such a dismal view of elite motivations (shared by most Russian researchers) overlooks the fact that there are many individuals who, while serving their own interests, simultaneously try to serve interests of the broader community. It is thanks to just such 'an elite consensus around liberal economic policies' that Novgorod has achieved such impressive results.[35]

Why did most of the local elite support change rather than the status quo? When the regional Soviet disbanded itself in 1991, the business elite was split between new entrepreneurs, who had been pushing to establish a free-trade zone in the region, and traditional industries, now without the backing of the Communist Party. The newly appointed governor, Mikhail Prusak, chose to give something to each side. New entrepreneurs were encouraged to move into small businesses, and invited to participate in the formulation of new legislation that would encourage such businesses. At the same time, large-scale factories were not shut down, despite being a tremendous drain on the budget, but assisted in continuing to make their payments into the region's social fund. In addition, the administration set up a regional investment fund that it used to promote specific industries that it believed had a chance of becoming competitive.

In return for investment, the administration required that these industries accept large-scale foreign investment and even possible foreign ownership. While many local industries refused this offer, several others have been transformed into profitable enterprises that now compete in the global marketplace. Among them, the fire-resistant brick plant in Borovichi, the 'Jupiter' optics factory in Valdai and, in Novgorod-the-Great, the 'Kvant' television factory, 'Splav', which makes casings for nuclear energy plants, and 'Planeta', an electronic equipment manufacturer that was once the city's largest employer. All in all, small manufacturing increased by more than 80 per cent during the first quarter of 2000, compared to the first quarter of 1999.[36]

Constant interaction with foreign investors has also had a wide variety of coincidental benefits. It has increased the professionalism of the Novgorod administration, which prides itself on its ability to work successfully with foreigners. Foreign companies in Novgorod have their own Chamber of Commerce which, through membership in the region's Social Chamber, reviews and comments on all legislation pending before the regional Duma. Local officials admit that the Chamber's suggestions have improved the overall quality of local administration.

Foreign direct investment has also hastened the introduction of local self-government into the region. Unlike other regions that avoid the institutionalisation of legal constraints, the administration in Novgorod attracted foreign investment by preparing the necessary legal framework for it. Since foreign investors were looking for just such legal guarantees, it was essential that they be adopted by the local Duma as soon as possible.[37] In order to promulgate such laws, however, the Duma first needs to be elected, hence the incentive for regional authorities to work systematically towards the introduction of local self-government. As a result, in 1996, Novgorod became the first region in Russia to have elected representatives at all levels of government, from village elder to governor.

Rather than the dismal view driven by the excesses of 'new Russians', the Novgorod example suggests that it is more accurate to view elite behaviour in the regions as driven by the opportunity to extract wealth quickly. In resource-wealthy regions this opportunity shaped an aggressive policy by local magnates to control government institutions and exclude competitors. In such instances a few could profit handsomely at the expense of the majority.

However, in economically depressed regions like Novgorod, there were far fewer opportunities for profit. In such regions local elites and common people were in a similar situation: both were passengers of a sinking ship where all would drown unless they could find a way to support one another. In an environment of recurring competitive elections this has required elites to build a popular base of support, and to seek the advice of citizens' groups through institutions such as the Social Councils.

Of course, this begs the question of why elite consensus was successfully forged in Novgorod but failed in other poor regions. Elite behaviour theories, however, offer no satisfactory answers to this question, and we must look in other directions.

Authoritarian leadership

This approach to Russian regions privileges the role of the governor in shaping the political fortunes of the region. The continuing relevance of the 'great man' seems to be confirmed by the dominant role in Russian politics played by the President, first Boris Yeltsin and now Vladimir Putin. It is not a big leap from there to ascribing a decisive influence to governors at the regional level, particularly since the institutions at this level replicate those at the national level.

Among Russian analysts who stress the importance of authoritarian leaders, one of the most prolific and insightful is Vladimir Gel'man. As Gelman notes, there is widespread agreement among Russian political scientists on the characteristics that define the typical pattern of 'regional authoritarianism.' These include:

1 the domination of executive authority over legislative authority;
2 a strong personal loyalty between Moscow and the governor of the region;
3 indirect control over the mass media exerted by the executive branch;
4 neutralisation or suppression of potential opposition in the region; and
5 patronage of non-governmental organisations.[38]

At first glance these characteristics seems to fit Novgorod perfectly. Upon closer examination, however, the picture becomes more complex. First, while it is true that the executive tends to dominate the political process, there is also a clear division of responsibility and a give-and-take between the branches of government in Novgorod.[39]

Second, personal loyalty to Moscow is a rather ambiguous criterion. On the one hand, Prusak has been loyal to Yeltsin and had a very good relationship with Chernomyrdin. On the other hand, he had a notoriously bad relationship with Yevgenii Primakov. Moreover, at the same time that Prusak has been loyal to individuals, he has consistently pursued economic and political autonomy from Moscow, recently even suggesting that the regions of the north-west could form 'a counterweight to Moscow'.

The issue of press freedom is more serious. However, the openness of the local media to alternatives, the appearance of three independent local publications and an independent television studio, as well as the existence of programmes that are openly critical of the government (such as 'N-Buro 2000'), all suggest that it is the lack of commercial viability, rather than political pressure, that has constrained the number of alternative media outlets. While narrowly targeted publications – including trade publications, internet publications – and religious journals, have an easily definable target audience, mass publications no longer have the readership to be commercially viable without regional support. The regional administration has even subsidised the expansion of TV and radio programmes throughout the region in an effort to broaden the variety of information available to rural dwellers of the region.[40]

In this circumstance the local media has gone out of its way to invite visiting national political opposition leaders to participate in local talk shows. It conducts regular call-in shows on such 'hot topics' as sex education, skinheads and fascism in Russia, and regularly asks viewers to call in with their views. Local government officials appear on talk shows regularly (e.g. fortnightly) in order to talk about new developments.

There is certainly government patronage of local non-governmental organisations (NGOs), although whether government support of civic associations is more likely to benefit or harm civil society is still a matter of debate. While one school of thought holds that the government impedes the optimal functioning of both markets and social networks, and is therefore inherently inimical to the growth of civil society, another school finds that civil society needs formal state institutions in order to flourish.[41] As Michael Walzer has put it, 'civil society requires political agency. And the state is an indispensable agent – even if the associational networks also, always, resist the organising impulses of state bureaucrats.'[42]

Finally, there is the attitude of government towards political opposition. While the absence of an effective opposition is no doubt a hindrance to democratic consolidation, it is important to establish whether its absence is the result of government interference, or popular complacency. In Novgorod, the lack of interest in using political parties as a vehicle for opposition seems to be the result a general distrust of parties as ineffective and self-serving (this follows the pattern observed in other post-communist countries),[43] and a preference for NGOs over parties. NGOs are seen as more effective vehicles for addressing social needs precisely because they are well connected with policy-making structures.

Finally, the obvious popular support that Prusak enjoys has discouraged even prominent national figures from campaigning against him in the region. During the 1999 gubernatorial elections, for example, Prusak's margin of victory was no doubt inflated by the fact that the communists chose not to field a candidate. They chose to forfeit the contest not because they were in any way constrained, but because they did not believe that they would win. Thus, as a matter of strategy the local (KPRF Communist Party of the Russian Federation) chose to loose by default rather than be shown up as less popular in the electoral contest.

It should also be pointed out that the most popular party in the region, the (Liberal Democratic Party of Russia LDPR) fielded the head of its regional organisation. Since 1998, the LDPR has outstripped the KPRF both in total numbers of registered voters. Moreover, the only party that has an organisational base throughout the region is the LDPR, but this did not seem to make a great impression on the voters: only 3 per cent voted for it.

In the case of Novgorod, therefore, we see an elite consensus carefully buttressed by the proper legal framework. Contrary to Gel'man's description of local regimes that avoid the institutionalisation of legal constraints, the local administration has gone in exactly the opposite direction, pursuing a policy of attracting foreign investment by first preparing the necessary legal framework for it. As former vice governor Valery Trofimov explains, foreign investors were looking for just such legal guarantees, so they had to be put in place, and adopted by the regional Duma first.[44]

In order to promulgate such laws, however, the Duma first needs to be elected; hence the incentive for regional authorities to work systematically towards the introduction of local self-government. As a result, in 1996, as noted above, Novgorod became the first region in Russia to have elected representatives at all levels of government. In Novgorod elite consensus was carefully buttressed by a legal framework, setting it apart from the 'institutionalised arbitrariness' that analysts describe as the norm for other Russian regions.[45]

Conclusions

As we have seen, several of the most popular approaches to explaining regional differences in democratic development fail to describe political developments in Novgorod adequately. They thereby miss an important aspect of Russia's regional diversity. Part of the problem may lie in the persistent focus on national politics as the only key to democratic development throughout the country. This is clearly no longer sufficient to explain the variety of political regimes one finds in Russia today. Moreover, it obscures the impact that Russia's regions are having on the broader process of democratisation.[46]

Another sort of problem arises from the preference many comparativists have for broad comparisons over in-depth case studies. The advantage of large-scale comparisons is that, given a large enough pool, accidental variations tend to balance each other out, presumably revealing 'pure links' between structural determinants and the dependent variable being studied; in this case, democracy.[47] Because single case studies do not involve such systematic comparisons, it is claimed that they cannot adjudicate between rival hypotheses or control for confounding variables.[48]

Harry Eckstein, however, suggests that case studies are 'most valuable at that stage of theory building where least value is generally attached to them: the stage at which candidate theories are tested.'[49] Case studies have a very good track record in advancing theory because, unlike broad comparative studies, they permit more 'intensive analysis' not limited to a highly limited set of variables. This increases the probability that critical variables and relations will be found, and decreases the likelihood of 'superficiality in research.'[50]

Because case studies also allow one to examine the context of events, they make it possible to match analytic intent and empirical observation more precisely than in analyses covering a large number of cases with standardised indicators.[51] Finally, according to Dietrich Rueschemeyer, there is a tendency in large-scale comparisons to assume structural constraints as given, which exaggerates their role and imposes a structural bias in the research design of such studies.[52] While the distortion may not be serious for countries with stable institutions that have persisted for many years, it becomes a much more serious problem when looking at newly formed democracies where institutions have neither longevity nor stability.

To address these problems some scholars have proposed adopting a case-study method rooted in 'sophisticated historical explanation'. Similar to the appeal for more historically based research ('analytic narratives') made by rational choice analysts like Margaret Levi, they argue that by examining in detail a particular sequence of historical development, one can rule out a wide variety of non-essential theoretical explanations.[53] The adoption of such culturally and historically anchored approaches to Russian regions would provide a welcome reality check against the temptation to apply theoretical approaches that, 'however solid they may seem to a disembodied social scientist, . . . do not correspond with the people's own understanding of their predicament'.[54]

At present, democratisation theorists seem to have little use for Russian culture and history: they are simply not seen as contributing anything of value to the process of democratisation in Russia. It is argued that there is too little difference among local traditions to have any meaningful impact (a variant of the view that centralisation has dominated throughout Russian history). Moreover, the Russian cultural and historical tradition is often equated with nationalism and reaction. Given the scepticism regarding democratic culture in Russia generally, it seems even more unlikely that there should be signs of it at the local level.

All of this converges with the mistaken view that culture is a passive, received structure, rather than a vital tool of political transformation that political leaders can use to buttress social consensus. In fact, as Eric Hobsbawn has shown, new regimes routinely 'invent traditions' to suit their current needs.[55] The impressive results achieved in the Novgorod region should lead us to rethink the widespread assumption that Russian history is a burden to reform. Without reference to the past, no meaningful transition to the future is possible. The key lies in choosing the kind of past that provides the best model for the future.

Notes

1 R. Cottrell, 'Russia: an old-fashioned, modern look', *The Economist* (14–20 June 1997); V. Bennett, 'Restive regions wriggling under Moscow's thumb', *Los Angeles Times*, 14 September 1998.

2 H. Eckstein, 'Case study and theory in political science', in F. I. Greenstein and N. W. Polsby (eds.), *Strategies of Inquiry* (Reading, MA: Addison-Wesley, 1975), pp. 113–23.

3 N. N. Petro, 'The Novgorod region: a Russian success story', *Post-Soviet Affairs*, 15:3 (1999), 161–235; B. P. Ruble, N. Popson, 'The westernisation of a Russian province: the case of Novgorod', *Post-Soviet Geography and Economics*, 39:8 (1998), 433–46.

4 'O sotsial'no-ekonomicheskoi situatsii v Novgorodskoi oblasti (January–April, 2000)', available on the website of the Novgorod Regional Administration (http://niac.telecom.nov.ru).

5 M. Schmidt, 'Integrating Russia into the global economy: multinational corporations and regional government in Novgorod oblast' (MA thesis, University of Warwick, 1998), p. 29.

6 A. Przeworski, *Democracy and the Market: Political and Economic Reforms in Eastern Europe and Latin America* (New York: Cambridge University Press, 1991); S. Huntington, *The Third Wave: Democratisation in the Late Twentieth Century* (Norman, OK: University of Oklahoma Press, 1991), pp. 61–6; G. Marks and L. Diamond (eds.) *Reexamining Democracy: Essays in Honour of Seymour Martin Lipset* (Newbury Park, CA: Sage, 1992), chapter 6.

7 M. Foley and B. Edwards, 'Civil society and social capital beyond Putnam', *American Behavioral Scientist*, 42:1 (1998), 133; M. Levi, 'Social and unsocial capital: a review essay of Robert Putnam's making democracy work', *Politics and Society*, 24:1 (1996), 46; N. N. Petro, 'Creating social capital in Russia: the Novgorod model', *World Development*, 29:2 February 2001.

8 'Ob obrazovanii oblastnoi obshchestvennoi palaty', Decree 61-OD/236 of the Novgorod Regional Duma and the Administration of Novgorod Oblast, 29 August 1994). Personal copy.

9 For the 1995 survey, 100 participants were obtained from the city of Novgorod-the-Great and fifty from each of the region's twenty-two districts. 'Analiticheskaya zapiska ob itogakh sotsiologicheskog issledovaniya sotsial'no-ekonomicheskoi situatsii v Novgorodskoi oblasti.' (Veliki Novgorod: Dialog, August–September, 1998). For the 1999 survey, commissioned by Sberbank of Novgorod, 2,586 participants responded from all twenty-two districts of Novgorod and the city of Novgorod-the-Great, 'Monitoring: Novgorodskaya oblast' (Novgorod-the-Great: Dialog, July 1999).

10 S. P. Petrova, 'Tendentsii razvitiya 'tret'ego sektora' v regione na primere Novgorodskoi oblasti', *Upravlencheskoe konsul'tirovanie*, 3 (1999), 18–29; O. Alekseyeva, 'Tendentsii razvitiya nekommercheskogo sektora i budushchee resursnykh tsentrov.' Paper presented at the national meeting of NGOs in Moscow, 1998.

11 Petrova, 'Tendentsii', 18.

12 C. Marsh, 'Making Russian democracy work: social capital, economic development, and democratisation' (Doctoral dissertation: University of Connecticut, 1998), pp. 152–4. Data collected by Valeria S. Kalashnichenko (Special Order Department of Goskomstat: Moscow).

13 R. D. Putnam, 'Making democracy work' (Princeton, NJ: Princeton University Press, 1993), p. 89.

14 *Ibid.*, p. 92.

15 M. Wyman, S. White, I. McAllister and S. Oates, 'Regional voting patterns in post-communist Russia'. Paper presented at CREES Annual Conference, Cumberland Lodge, UK, 16–18 June 2000.

16 J. DeBardeleben and A. A. Galkin, 'Electoral behavior and attitudes in Russia: do Regions make a difference or do regions just differ?' in P. J. Stavrakis, J. DeBardeleben *et al.* (eds.), *Beyond the Monolith: The Emergence of Regionalism in Post-Soviet Russia* (Washington, DC and Baltimore, MD: Woodrow Wilson Center Press and Johns Hopkins University Press, 1997); B. van Selm, 'Economic performance in Russia's regions', *Europe–Asia Studies*, 50:4 (1998), 603–19.

17 D. A. Zimine and M. J. Bradshaw, 'Regional adaptation to economic crisis in Russia: the case of Novgorod Oblast', *Post-Soviet Geography and Economics*, 40:5 (1999), 335–53.

18 *Ibid.*, 343.

19 L. Koval', '"Cadbury" gotovit rossiyanam sladkuyu zhizn'', *Segodnya* (19 October 1998); 'Foreigners invest in Novgorod despite economic crisis', *Agence France Presse* (27 May 1999).

20 S. Y. Fabrichnyi, 'Razvitie mestnogo samoupravleniya na territorii Novgorodskoi oblasti', in V. I. Romashova (ed.), *Zemstvo i Vozrozhdenie ego Kul'turno-Khozyaistvennykh Traditsii* (Novgorod: Novgorod Regional Scientific Library, 1996), p. 39.

21 M. M. Prusak, *Reformy v Provintsii* (Moscow: Veche, 1999).

22 For more on this, see Petro, 'The Novgorod region', and Petro, 'Creating social capital'.

23 Zimine and Bradshaw, 'Regional adaptation', 341.

24 L. Mitrofanova, 'Davaite zhit' druzhno!' *Novgorodskie vedomosti* (8 December 1998).

25 Boitsev, A., Head of Novgorod Regional Duma, interviewed on 8 May 2000.

26 Zimine and Bradshaw, 'Regional adaptation', 341.

27 Boitsev interview.

28 *Ibid.*

29 I. Kibina, 'Rossiiskii federalizm: nekotorye voprosy teorii i praktiki'. Memo prepared for the law offices of Steptoe and Johnson (Washington, DC: 1999). Personal copy. My translation.

30 K. Stoner-Weiss, *Local Heroes: The Political Economy of Russian Regional Governance* (Princeton, NJ: Princeton University Press, 1997).

31 K. Stoner-Weiss, 'Why are some regions doing better than others?', East–West Institute, *Russian Regional Report*, 2:19 (29 May 1997) (hereafter, EWI, *Russian Regional Report*).

32 D. Lussier, '1999: year in review. Kremlin improves position over regions by year's end', EWI, *Russian Regional Report*, 5:12 (12 January 2000).

33 E. Tyshkevich and K. Bryuzgin, 'Novgorodskaya oblast'. A report prepared for the Russian Development Bank, Moscow (1998).

34 Stoner-Weiss, 'Why are some regions?'

35 Blair and Popson, 'Westernisation of a Russian province', 435.

36 'S nachala goda predpriyatiyami Novgorodskoi oblasti proizvedeno produktsii na 5 mlrd 994 mln rub', *FinMarket* (4 May 2000), available available on the website of the Novgorod Regional Administration (http://niac.telecom.nov.ru).

37 V. I. Trofimov, First Deputy Governor of the Novgorod Region, interviewed on 10 April 1997.

38 V. Gel'man, 'Regime transition, outcome of uncertainty and prospects for democratisation: the politics of Russia's regions in a comparative perspective'. Paper prepared for the conference 'On regime transition, outcome of uncertainty and prospects for

democratisation: the politics of Russia's regions in a comparative perspective.' Organised by BIOst, Cologne, Germany, 26–28 May 1999, p. 15.

39 L. A. Andreyeva, 'O realizatsii prava zakonodatel'noi initsiativy', *Upravlencheskoe konsultirovanie*, 2 (1999), 29–31; Mitrofanova, 'Davaite zhit' druzhno'.

40 Verkhodanov, Igor V., chief aide to the Head of the Novgorod Regional Duma, interviewed on 24 May 1999.

41 P. B. Lehning, 'Towards a multicultural civil society: the role of social capital and democratic citizenship', *Government and Opposition*, 33:2 (1998), 221–42.

42 M. Foley and B. Edwards, 'Beyond Tocqueville: civil society and social capital in comparative perspective', *American Behavioral Scientist*, 42:1 (1998), 9; C. J. Paraskevopoulos, 'Social capital and the public–private divide in Greek regions', *West European Politics*, 21:2 (1998), 159; L. Kenworthy, 'Civic engagement, social capital, and economic cooperation', *American Behavioral Scientist*, 40:5 (1997), 646; P. Evans, *Embedded Autonomy: States and Industrial Transformation* (Princeton, NJ: Princeton University Press, 1995); P. Evans, 'Government action, social capital and development: reviewing the evidence of synergy', *World Development*, 24 (1996), 1119–32.

43 G. Toka, 'Political parties in east central Europe', in L. Diamond *et al.* (eds.), *Consolidating the Third Wave Democracies* (Baltimore, MD: Johns Hopkins University Press, 1997), p. 116.

44 Trofimov interview.

45 V. Gel'man, 'Regime transition, uncertainty and prospects for democratisation: the politics of Russia's regions in a comparative perspective', *Europe–Asia Studies*, 51:6 (1999), 939–56; A. Tsygankov, 'Manifestations of delegative democracy in Russian local politics: what does it mean for the future of Russia?', *Communist and Post-Communist Studies*, 31:4 (1998), 329–44.

46 N. J. Melvin, 'Federalism and democracy in the Russian federation'. Unpublished manuscript (8 July 2000), p. 4.

47 D. Rueschemeyer, E. H. Stephens and J. D. Stephens, *Capitalist Development and Democracy* (Chicago, IL: University of Chicago Press, 1992), p. 35.

48 M. Steven Fish, 'Democratisation's requisites: the post-communist experience', *Post-Soviet Affairs*, 14:3 (1998), 212.

49 Eckstein, 'Case study and theory', 113–23.

50 *Ibid.*

51 Rueschemeyer *et al.*, 'Capitalist development', 35.

52 *Ibid.*

53 M. Levi, 'A model, a method, and a map: rational choice in comparative and historical analysis', in M. I. Lichbach and A. S. Zuckerman (eds.) *Comparative Politics: Rationality, Culture, and Structure* (Cambridge: Cambridge University Press, 1997), pp. 19–41.

54 L. Whitehead, 'The drama of democratisation', *Journal of Democracy*, 10:4 (1999), 95.

55 E. Hobsbawm and T. Ranger, *The Invention of Tradition* (Cambridge: Cambridge University Press, 1983).

Problems of democratisation in the Komi Republic[1]

The processes of democratisation are tenuous and multifaceted. This is recognised by the many scholars investigating this phenomenon across the world. It is not often the case, however, that those studying political transitions examine sub-national government. Instead, many focus on national elites and national institutions, while others study mass opinion with broad surveys. This leaves a gap of examination at the intermediate level that misses the real meat of political processes at mid- to lower-levels of government and society. Transitologists seem to expect elite democratisation will 'trickle down' to lower government levels. Thus, one needs only study the top in a transition to know the direction of a political system. In many cases, however, this argument is unfounded. This is particularly the case in federal systems and most especially so in large federal systems such as the Russian Federation. Understanding a system through its parts may be more important to understanding a society's transformative future than the larger whole.

The Russian political system is divided into eighty-nine regions. These include twenty-one ethnically identified republics and sixty-eight other 'lower' regions. That this division provides the regions de jure and de facto differences in political standing vis-à-vis the centre is unusual for functioning federal systems, and has raised fears for Russia's integrity.[2] A process of bilateral treaties between approximately half of the regions and the centre has led scholars to describe the divergent status among regions as 'asymmetrical federalism'.[3] Given the differences in status, it becomes even clearer that Russia's developmental possibilities cannot be solely gathered from a 'top-down' analysis. Additionally, most of the post-Soviet period has seen a weak Russian central government forced to cede varying levels of autonomy to the regions.[4] While theory predicts that devolution of authority from central powers to regional entities signifies a rise in regional democratic practices,[5] the opposite is the case for much of Russia. That is, democracy has not been developing in the regions despite central weakness.[6]

This chapter focuses on the political transformation of the Komi Republic; as for its eighty-eight counterparts in Russia, Komi's adaptation to nationwide reform has been tumultuous. After a decade of development, the question to be analysed here is: Is the Komi Republic a democracy? I employ the theoretical models of Juan Linz and Alfred Stepan to answer this question,[7] and I have found that Komi meets their criteria for completion of a democratic transition, but has not yet consolidated its democracy. I begin by presenting Linz and Stepan's model of transition and consolidation. I do not present the entire model, but those parts particularly relevant to Russia. I then briefly describe the Komi Republic before examining the liberalisation, transition and consolidation phases of the region's political development.

Theory of democratisation

There has been much debate as to whether the political transition models employed in Latin America and Southern Europe are applicable to the post-communist region.[8] After all, the transformation occurring in former communist states is much more complicated. It has been described as a triple transition, or one that includes the political changes found in other world regions, but adds the re-making of formerly command economies and the re-shaping of personal and social identity.[9] Further criticism of transitology has targeted an apparent teleology in the theory that deterministically leads to democracy, with little possibility for another outcome.[10]

For much of the literature on transitology, these criticisms are quite valid. The models are not always applicable to post-communist transitions. Nevertheless, although Linz and Stepan's scholarship has been a mainstay of the transitology school, their recent work offers a potential solution for investigating post-communist transformations. Their wide-ranging book takes a risky stab at conceptualising a variety of transitions under a multifaceted rubric. While at times unwieldy, Linz and Stepan's path-breaking creation places the post-communist transitions alongside the other regional transitions, while recognising the differences between the systems and, to some degree, accounting for the complexity of the East European transitions.

The democratisation process has various stages, with each successive stage influenced by the stages that come before. To understand which one of the varying paths a particular society might take in its political transformation, one must know the prior regime type of the society under consideration. For the majority of Eastern European states, including the USSR, Linz and Stepan characterise the prior regimes as: 'post-totalitarian'. Implicit in this category, they claim that communist states of the late 1980s no longer met the strict guidelines to be classified as 'totalitarian'. They differentiate between the two 'communist' regimes as shown in Table 8.1.

I continue by briefly applying the theory to the Soviet society and to the Russian regime that follows, before looking at the Komi Republic, where I concentrate my investigation on Komi development during the period of liberalisation and beyond.

Table 8.1 Characteristics of totalitarian and post-totalitarian ideal regime types

Characteristics	Totalitarian	Post-totalitarian
Pluralism	No significant political, social or economic pluralism	Limited, but not responsible social, economic and institutional pluralism. Almost no political pluralism.
Ideology	Developed, guiding ideology that provides a reachable utopia	Guiding ideology officially exists but is weakening along with faith in utopia
Mobilisation	Widely mobilised population into numerous regime-created organisations	Declining interest in leaders and population in organising mobilisation
Leadership	Undefined boundaries and unpredictability. Successful party members.	Rising concern for personal security among political elite. More technocratic success.

Source: J. Linz and A. Stepan, *Problems of Democratic Transition and Consolidation: Southern Europe, South America, and Post-Communist Europe* (Baltimore: Johns Hopkins University Press, 1996), pp. 44–5.

A totalitarian regime is best exemplified by the USSR under Stalin's rule (1928–53). These twenty-five years were characterised by extreme party control under a strict, utopian ideology, a non-existent civil society and the absence of political competition. The population was widely mobilised into party organisations, school clubs, and state-created community groups, among others. Leadership roles were concentrated on Stalin and local-party bosses. With Stalin's death, the majority of the remaining Soviet leadership was neither willing nor able to continue such harsh conditions. Thus, the period of post-totalitarianism begins, although the process is quite gradual. With the accession of Nikita Khrushchev as the Soviet leader in 1956, society moved away from the strict controls of the party leadership, but many aspects of the regime continued. This would change under Leonid Brezhnev (1964–82) as Soviet society lost its dynamism, entering a period of *zastoi* (stagnation) in the 1970s.

As its leaders aged, the Party became ossified as members sought to maintain their privileged positions. While communist ideology ostensibly guided society, its recognition as the basis of the USSR became more an act of lip service for personal advancement and no longer elicited past enthusiasm. Citizens lost interest in the Soviet future and popular mobilisation ceased to carry much importance. As society became more corrupt, a black market developed alongside the state-controlled command economy and initiated underground economic and social pluralism. While there was rising political dissent, political pluralism was not permitted by the leadership. Dissident ideas appeared in *samizdat* (self-publication), but were restricted by authorities, with many dissidents either imprisoned or sent to internal exile. While the USSR had become post-totalitarian, it was not through elite-policy initiation but more through processes of decay.[11]

According to many transition models, if a non-democratic society is to develop into a fully fledged democracy, there are three basic stages: liberalisation, transition and consolidation. The process of liberalisation often includes the relaxation of media censorship, greater state allowance for independent groups, legal safeguards and the toleration of limited opposition.[12] This typically describes the Michael Gorbachev period (1986–91), particularly after 1986, as the consequences, whether intended or not, of *perestroika* (restructuring) and *glasnost'* (openness). During this period, the Soviet people witnessed, an expanded opportunity to speak out, more economic and (eventually) political opportunities, the removal of the Communist Party monopoly, and relatively free and fair elections spread across the fifteen republics.[13]

The liberalisation process spawned two simultaneous reactions across the USSR. One reaction exposed the conservative substrata among the Soviet political elite, a portion of which ultimately challenged the liberalisation process in the August 1991 coup. While the failure of the coup doomed the integrity of the USSR, its purpose had been in part to halt the other reaction breaking down the bonds among the fifteen republics: the rising independence activities in most of the All-Union Republics. While not the first to secede from the USSR, Russia became an opposition force under its democratically elected president, Boris Yeltsin, who not only resisted Soviet directives, but called for the Russian regions to push for greater sovereignty.[14]

While 'preparing the ground' for a transition, liberalisation does not ensure democratisation. Much depends on the characteristics of the prior regime. Linz and Stepan's model provides a series of vague if not particularly definite developmental possibilities for varying regime types. What paths towards democracy, then, can be taken by a post-totalitarian state? As in any transition, the unique characteristics of a particular state come into play, and the fact that Russia was a unit of the larger Soviet whole complicates matters.

Yeltsin's 1991 election raises some of the difficulties for identifying the dividing line between a period of liberalisation and the start of a democratic transition. The very fact of that election was a result of the liberalisation process taking place in Soviet society. However, liberalisation need not be followed by democratisation. For example, the Khrushchev period has been characterised as a process of liberalisation, but it by no means signified the democratisation of the USSR. Democratisation goes further than liberalisation to include national, free competitive elections to determine who governs, and requires the solidification of those rights acquired with liberalisation.[15] When, therefore, did the democratic transition in Russia begin? Did it occur with the collapse of the USSR, and Russia's independence, with the New Year of 1992? Or, did it begin with Yeltsin's election in 1991? A difficulty is that Linz and Stepan argue that democracy cannot exist in the regions of a state that is overall non-democratic.[16] Yet, while this may apply to the consolidation of democracy, the process of demo-cratic transition would seem exempt, as the seeds for democracy may first grow in a region. Thus, it is fair to say that Russia's democratic transition begins with Yeltsin's election (some claim that 1990 Russian regional elections mark democ-racy's founding moment[17]), yet becomes a fully fledged transition only after the Soviet collapse.

The next step of democratisation is the completion of the transition. Linz and Stepan tell us that a democratic transition is complete when:

- sufficient agreement has been reached about political procedures to produce an elected government;
- a government comes to power that is the direct result of a free and popular vote;
- this government de facto has the authority to generate new policies; and
- the executive, legislative and judicial power generated by the new democracy does not have to share power with other bodies de jure.[18]

Whether the Russian Federation meets these standards is difficult to judge. Certainly, the transition was not completed before 13 December, 1993, when a new Russian constitution was approved by the people simultaneously with the election of a parliament. The period prior to this date saw a government para-lysed by a patchwork of amendments to the Soviet-era constitution and an unworkable relationship between a communist-era parliament, the Supreme Soviet and President Yeltsin. Beyond mentioning the autocratic fashion in which Yeltsin overcame his opposition, and question of whether the 1993 electoral turnout was sufficient to meet the required 50 per cent threshold,[19] one could rea-sonably claim that the transition was complete with the seating of the new par-liament in early 1994: the institutions of democratic society were in place.

The completion of the transition brings on questions of the consolidation of the democratic regime: At what point does democracy become established within the society so that it becomes the 'only game in town'? To make this deter-mination, Linz and Stepan provide two overlapping measures. First, there need to be three clear signs of regime acceptance in society:

1 behavioural acceptance of democracy or no significant groups pushing for a non-democratic regime or secession;
2 attitudinal acceptance of democratic procedures and institutions among a majority of the population; and
3 constitutional acceptance or recognition of, and behavioural habituation to, the laws and procedures established in the new regime.[20]

Second, Linz and Stepan argue that certain conditions must be met in 'the five arenas of democracy' shown in Table 8.2.[21]

Without directly examining Russia's relative degree of democratic consolida-tion, it is clear that the Russian Federation continues to face significant chal-lenges in trying to achieve the three components and five arenas of democracy.

Table 8.2 Five arenas of consolidated democracy

Arena	Conditions
Civil society	There are self-organising groups, movements and individuals that are relatively autonomous from the state. They act to articulate values and advance interests
Political society	Institutions that develop to arrange for the legitimate contestation for public power and the state. The core institutions include political parties, elections, electoral rules, leadership and more
Rule of law	Constitutionally guided governance, self-binding procedure, high threshold to change, strong judicial system and legal culture
State bureaucracy	A usable bureaucracy that reflects the wishes of democratically elected leaders and implements the basic police, tax and service functions effectively and efficiently
Economic society	A recognised set of norms, institutions and regulations that mediate between state and market

Source: J. Linz and A. Stepan, *Problems of Democratic Transition and Consolidation: Southern Europe, South America, and Post-Communist Europe* (Baltimore, MD: Johns Hopkins University Press, 1996), pp. 7–15.

Chechnya's violent attempt to secede is an obvious sign that the regime has not been accepted behaviourally. While attitudinal acceptance of the regime is questionable,[22] the lack of consistent acceptance of the centre's constitutional authority is exhibited in the frequent refusal of the eighty-nine federal subjects to implement federal legislation and directives.[23] Furthermore, it is quite clear that the country is seriously lagging behind in all five arenas. Thus, while the institutions appear to exist, they are not functioning democratically. This is the effect of Yeltsin's strategy to re-make economic institutions prior to reforming political institutions. If significant political reform had come first, the economic reform would have come more easily. As it is, poor strategising on the part of post-Soviet Russian elites initiated the troubled transformation that continues to afflict Russian society.[24]

   In terms of democratisation, the situation for the regions is frequently more straightforward. Rather than having to govern eighty-nine regions spread over a vast territory with woefully inadequate resources, regional leaders often face more compliant local districts with almost non-existent economic or political resources of their own. Even lacking their own resources, regional elites have frequently managed to develop regimes similar to pacts or political fiefdoms focusing authority on a single individual.[25] The result has often been a more stable and consistent political regime that frequently 'looks' more democratic than Russia as a whole. Such is the case for the Komi Republic. While Linz and Stepan's model was not developed for sub-national analysis, it is broadly applicable in this case given Russia's diversity and weak federal structure.

Komi Republic

Komi is a multi-ethnic region bordering the western side of the northern Ural mountain range. Russians comprise over half of the population, while ethnic Komi make up less than 25 per cent. Although ethnic issues are important, they do not threaten to destabilise the republic. Furthermore, unlike the case for other regions that must constantly confront ethnic issues, beyond certain superficial accommodations such issues do not currently have a major impact on political decision making. During the late 1980s and early 1990s, however, Komi nationalist movements actively pursued regional autonomy. Current groups like Komi Kotyr (Komi band/gang) and Zashchitim Sebe Sami (We Defend Ourselves) have advocated evicting Russians to create a Komi state.

Komi seems to have a bright economic future. Extraction of fossil fuels (oil, coal and gas) is the largest industry in the region, making up approximately 50 per cent of Komi's GDP. Oil is the main export, providing 63 per cent of total export revenue, followed by timber-related products (16 per cent) and coal (11 per cent). Komi has trade relations with more than forty foreign countries and has been actively expanding its ties with other regions in Russia.[26]

Playing a role in Komi's governability, however, is the geographic split of the republic's economic resources into three overlapping areas:

- In the south, where the capital Syktyvkar is located, timber and other agricultural industries are most evident.
- In the middle of the republic, around Ukhta and stretching up to Pechora, gas and oil are the prevalent industries.
- From Pechora to the north, coal is the dominant industry.

As coal becomes less economically viable to produce, particularly in the harsh climate of the main coal-mining area in the arctic circle region Vorkuta, it will markedly decline as part of Komi's GDP. Facing pay shortages and closing mines, many inhabitants of northern Komi have migrated to other parts of Komi and Russia. This helps explain an already declining population of 1,163,000 that is expected to decline further to 1,034,00 by 2015.[27]

Liberalisation

Komi's political change began under Gorbachev, albeit more slowly than in Moscow. The defining moments of Komi's political reform are:

1 In spring 1990 the popular election of regional legislators in the first truly free election in the region under Soviet rule took place.
2 In August 1990 Komi became one of the first Autonomous Soviet Socialist Republics to declare sovereignty.[28]

The time was full of hope among local political officials in the Syktyvkar City 'Council'.[29] The national movement Democratic Russia was an active force in local politics. There were several independent newspapers that were frequently critical of political authorities without significant repercussions. In all, this met the general tenor of Linz and Stepan's liberalisation processes: media restrictions were being relaxed and there was some room for political groups to form and compete.

Indications emerging from the liberalisation period were (imperfectly) akin to the reforma-pactada, ruptura-pactada transitional path. In a post-totalitarian society, this path involves the development of a collective leadership around democratic processes as a means of protecting the interest of leadership and certain opposition in a closed partnership. Members of the pact work together to ensure that all are winners in the next elections. Eventually, the pact breaks apart, but not until democratic institutions become established in the political culture of leaders and citizens alike.[30] In Komi, the first aspect of the pact existed, but the second did not emerge as in other democratic transitions.[31]

During the reforma-pactada period, the power structure revolved around the Komi Supreme Soviet, headed by Yurii Spiridonov, and the Council of Ministers (the government), headed by Vyacheslav Khudyaev. They loosely meet Linz and Stepan's standards as the transition initiators. This resembled a regime-initiated transition, in which the last First Secretary of the Communist Party, Spiridonov, in Komi had been elected along with Khudyaev to the Supreme Soviet in spring 1990. Spiridonov would soon be elected as chairman of the legislature. Part of the balance existed along ethnic lines as well, recognising the Soviet policy of dividing authority in the ethnic republics (Spiridonov is Russian, while Khudyaev is Komi). The simple alliance between these institutions and the leaders of the enterprises producing Komi's natural resources signified basic peace in the republic and a unified stance towards federal authorities. In this vein, Komi signed the short-lived 1992 Federation Treaty, which recognised national republics as state entities, providing the republics with complete legislative and executive authority over their territories.[32] In many ways, an underlying obstacle to democratisation lay in the Komi leadership's struggle for sovereignty from the USSR and Russia.[33]

While it may be difficult to determine whether these regional leaders were intent on transforming Komi into a functioning democratic polity, such a determination is now moot. With the violent confrontation between President Yeltsin and the Supreme Soviet in October 1993, the Komi alliance was broken by Yeltsin's decree dissolving all regional soviets (including the Komi Supreme Soviet). With his position of power threatened, Spiridonov began a drive to become the sole leader within Komi. Furthermore, the release of the draft Russian Constitution in November 1993 pushed Spiridonov towards a more aggressive assertion of Komi sovereignty, as the text did not carry the same degree of regional independence found in the Federation Treaty. Together, these two events were the catalysts for Spiridonov's drive for sole leadership in Komi and his spirited resistance to federal authority. Ultimately, 'international' pressures (as represented by the federal government) redirected the transition towards a semi-democratic path under the direction of one leader.

An ordered transition?

Yeltsin's response to the lack of support from the regional soviets during the confrontation with national Supreme Soviet broke the balance between the Spiridonov camp and the Khudyaev camp. The transition path had to change as Yeltsin's directive to dissolve the soviets ruptured the pact before the democratic institutions and attitudes had sufficient opportunity to develop. The seventeen-month period from October 1993, after Yeltsin's directive, until February 1995, when the new legislature was elected, saw the completion of a 'new' transition. The pact was ruptured in November when Spiridonov used the legislature to place a referendum item, creating the post of Komi president, on the 12 December 1993 election ballot. Prospects for a presidential post directly challenged Khudyaev's position in the Council of Ministers. Knowing that he would probably lose a future presidential race, Khudyaev and his supporters were temporarily relieved by the referendum's defeat. Not deterred, Spiridonov turned to 'his' legislature to write a new Komi constitution that included the presidential post in the form of the 'Head of Republic'.[34]

Linz and Stepan discuss the importance of the constitution-making environment for the completion of the transition process. They describe six 'contexts and formulas that present the most confining conditions for democratic consolidation . . . to those that present the least'.[35] The route that best describes constitution-making in Komi is the fourth in that list, or the third least confining environment. This process describes the use of a constitution created under highly constraining circumstances reflecting the de facto power of nondemocratic institutions and forces. Such a constitution may be formally democratic and thus consistent with a transition being completed, but democratic consolidation may be hampered because a constrained constituent assembly, while believing that other institutional arrangements are more appropriate for the creation and consolidation of democratic politics, may be de facto prevented from selecting them.[36]

In February 1994 the Spiridonov constitution was adopted, creating the position of chief executive and eliminating the Council of Ministers. Apart from leading the legislature, Spiridonov was also seen as the most competent leader in the region, with Khudyaev occupying a distant second.[37] With the aura of victory surrounding Spiridonov, those deputies who hoped to align themselves with Komi's future had constrained choices. Whether they believed other institutional arrangements were more appropriate would be speculation, although individual political success was probably the driving factor for most supporters of the Spiridonov constitution.

In May 1994 Spiridonov defeated Khudyaev convincingly in elections for the post of Head of the Republic. He would use the constitution and the continued existence of the Supreme Soviet to develop an administrative and legislative structure that benefited the head's position. With the election of the new legislature, the State Council, in January 1995 and its installation in February, the transition process for Komi was complete: a constitution had been adopted, elections to the executive and the legislative bodies had taken place, and they were each functioning along constitutional guidelines.

For Russia scholars, labelling the process above as a 'completed democratic transition' seems nonsensical, because the process leading to this end had so many irregularities that seemingly undermine its legitimacy. For example, the wishes of the population, as expressed in the defeat of the December 1993 referendum to create the presidency, were ignored less than two months later when the equivalent post was created legislatively. Yet, this is where the 'grey areas' of democratisation become most apparent. Where were the people when their decision was ignored? In fact, they were trying to survive in difficult economic conditions. Ultimately, for the process of transition, the popular role is not vital as so much depends on the elite establishment of new institutions. Furthermore, it cannot be forgotten that the people did (albeit with low turnout) participate as voters to executive and legislative posts. Yet, their absence (in terms of protest) exemplified the distance between the political elite and the people that greatly limits the prospects for consolidation.

Consolidation: the impossible dream?

The Komi Republic has a long way to go in order to consolidate its democracy. Interestingly, its development in the three components of a consolidated democracy (attitudinal, behavioural, constitutional) show a system that is 'surprisingly' stable and indicative of near consolidation. On the behavioural level, there are no significant economic, political or social forces pushing to create a non-democratic regime or to secede from the region.[38] Although there are some rather insignificant 'radical' nationalist forces, the more mainstream representative of the Komi people, the Committee for the Renaissance of the Komi Nation, has not advocated drastic measures. Their leader, Valerii Markov, is aligned with Head Spiridonov, an alliance that aided the former's December 1999 election to the State Duma.

Attitudinal acceptance of democratic mores and institutions is less evident. In 1994, residents of Komi expressed uncertainty about the meaning of democracy and significant apathy in even considering their positions vis-à-vis the political institutions. This is where the issues of economic concern become most important. Over the past decade, the people of this region have faced high inflation, significant wage arrears and rising unemployment. Such conditions have removed public attention from the form of government towards the elusive arrival of a stable system, irrespective of the type of political system, be it authoritarian or democratic. The fact that people crave a certain end over all potential processes speaks to the difficulty of identifying true attitudes. It shows a 'subject', even authoritarian, approach to government: People look for a leader to take them to stability. Therefore, it is the end, some sort of *svetlee budushee* (the radiant future, prophesised by communist leadership), not the institutional means of getting there, that matters.[39]

From a constitutional perspective, Komi shows signs of moving towards consolidation. Interestingly, one has to think of the national constitution, as well, almost as an international influence on domestic processes.[40] In this area, Komi has frequently avoided complying with the Russian Constitution, the Russian Supreme Court and Russian Constitutional Court rulings. The prime example has been the struggle over the implementation of the 1995 federal law on local self-government.[41] Locally, the Komi Constitution has been employed as intended by Spiridonov to govern the republic as he pleases. While there has been some resistance in several districts to implementing regional constitutional guidelines concerning local government, the use of the constitution as the institution guiding Komi politics has been relatively straightforward.

While the record is mixed when examining Komi's consolidation alongside the three components, there are fewer signs of solidifying democratic practices in the five arenas (Table 8.2), although the 'components' and 'arenas' have significant overlaps. In going through each of the arenas one by one, this overlap is evident. Linz and Stepan further demonstrate that the five arenas are interdependent. Thus, there is a great deal of blurring at the edges of institutional development. Overall, it becomes particularly clear how far Komi must travel to reach a democratic 'end'.

As an autonomous force for the advancement of particular interests, civil society in Komi is weak. The signs of weakness became evident beginning in 1992 as personal economic concerns led to diminishing interest in popular participation in social life. More recently, however, there has been a revival of citizen-based organisations, with 412 organisations registered with the republic in summer 1999. While about twenty-five of these organisations were political parties, about 90 per cent of the groups have no political agenda.[42] The difficulty for many of these organisations to remain autonomous rests in their generally perilous financial status. As I have shown in the past, groups such as Women of Russia are provided with much needed office space, a secretary and a telephone by the regional authorities in Syktyvkar. As these resources can easily be taken away, the agenda of the organisation is circumscribed.[43]

The quandary for civil society in Komi is probably best exemplified by the media, a body that is vital for communicating the interests and concerns of societal groups as a way of pressuring political society. In 1993–94 there were several independent newspapers in Komi that were willing to oppose the policies of the regional authorities. The recourse for governing authorities displeased with press coverage was limited.[44] Since the economic crash in 1998, however, local newspapers have not been able to afford (especially) paper and have had to receive a subsidy from the regional authorities. As a result, newspapers have been forced to bend to the will of those authorities if they hope to continue printing.[45]

Additionally Komi television has long been controlled by regional authorities. To ensure the 'proper' message is presented, disagreeable reporters are removed from their posts.[46]

Ultimately, it is not in the interest of the political authorities for an independent, influential civil society to exist. One official argued that civil society is fundamental to the existence of democracy. Yet, its development as an effective force must be slow and controlled; development into that effective body is five or ten years in the future. For now, the administration will provide financial and other resources to organisations willing to work in a 'consensual' fashion with that administration.[47]

The current situation in the development of political society can be presented through the contrast of two organisations: Preobrazhenie Severa (Transformation of the North) National Patriotic Union of Russia (NPSR)). Transformation of the North was originally formed out of seven politically oriented organisations in 1998 (it comprised thirteen organisations by summer 1999) to defend the interests of the Komi Republic.[48] Formed on the suggestion of the erstwhile Spiridonov detractor Igor Bobrakov (with the Head's blessing) his organisation has flourished with the support of the then 'party of power', Our Home is Russia (NDR), an organisation of which Spiridonov was then described as being the informal leader.[49] In addition to acting as an 'ombudsman' for citizens dissatisfied with government services, the organisation sought to ensure the election of a 'democrat' to the State Duma in 1999 elections, as previous deputies had been 'communists'. While succeeding on this front, their union of political organisations also succeeded in having twenty-four of thirty-eight candidates elected to the fifty-seat State Council in February 1999 elections.[50] Just as the State Council has been described as being in Spiridonov's pocket, Transformation of the North has been so labelled by opposition groups.[51] It has received significant and positive local press coverage (an almost sure sign of its 'collaborative' relationship), its leader (Bobrakov) is employed at *Respublika*, the official newspaper of the republic, and it has held public meetings with Spiridonov in attendance.

This organisation is contrasted with NPSR, an alliance of socialist and nationalist political organisations, which is probably the most independent group in the Komi Republic. It has almost no funding, meagre (self-funded) office facilities and no access to the mainstream media.[52] It is also the group most similar to Socrates' gadfly in pushing the lazy horse of Komi government to react. Through the frequent use of the regional and federal courts, this organisation has gradually forced Komi authorities to address regional laws that contradict the 1995 federal law on local self-government.[53] That numerous rulings in NPSR's favour have not yet produced a system of local self-government in concert with the federal law only stresses the weakness of political movements outside the 'inner circle' of Komi politics.

Ironically, it has been at the level of local self-government where the most significant developments in political society have occurred concerning party development. Both NPSR and Yabloko have been pleased with elections to local soviets in some of the twenty districts of the republic where small pockets of party-based candidates were elected in February 1999. Albeit a slow development, Komi Yabloko Party Chairman Moiseev and NPSR Chairman Musinov are optimistic.[54] Unfortunately, the fact that many deputies in the local soviets are budgeted workers (under the direction and pay of the Spiridonov administration) reduces their independence on all issues that are important to regional authorities.[55]

The quandary of evaluating the rule of law in Komi arises as a result of the relative lack of permanency of some of the more important laws and constitutional guidelines. What appears clear is that individual rights are more consistently recognised in the Komi Constitution and in practice than in Soviet times, but that political officials and the law-enforcement bureaucracy are having difficulty controlling many types of crime. The most significant problems concerning the rule of law take on an 'international' character in that Komi laws frequently violate federal laws. A June 2000 announcement from the federal prosecutor in Syktyvkar identified twenty-four violations of the Russian Constitution in the Komi Constitution.[56] If the reaction of Komi authorities to contradictions in laws on local self-government is predictive, these violations will only be addressed over the course of the next several years. Furthermore, the Komi administration is not averse to interpreting legal guidelines so as to give the Komi Constitution priority over the federal constitution.[57]

Most evident, however, is the way in which the laws have been adapted to the whims of top political leadership. An appropriate example concerns opposition in the Syktyvkar City Council to Spiridonov's candidate for Head of Administration. Knowing they could not defeat the candidate outright, a group of deputies purposely missed sessions of the council to ensure there would be no quorum. Recognising the stalemate could not be overcome without one side backing down, the 'pocket' State Council simply lowered the requirements for a quorum, and the Head's candidate was approved.[58] The legislature has been even more accommodating in amending the Komi Constitution to help Spiridonov be re-elected, while also changing laws to ensure the continued existence of the administrative hierarchy in the republic.[59] That Article 106 of the Constitution requires a super-majority (two thirds) to amend the constitution has been no obstacle to Spiridonov as it is readily achievable.

The issue of legal consistency in the Komi Republic is not so much one of whether the laws are followed or not. In fact, Deputy Speaker of the State Council Ivan Kulakov claims the laws are scrupulously followed: As intended a system with a strong executive was created alongside a weak legislature. Kulakov argues that those who criticise the parliament do not understand the Constitution.[60] Again, the real test of the laws will be with the election of a more independent legislature or a strengthened central government.

The usefulness of the state bureaucracy focuses on its effectiveness both as a body providing community services and as a policy tool for elected leadership. In Russia there have been problems within the national bureaucracy in terms of collecting taxes and distributing revenues and services. There have also been widespread claims of corruption among bureaucrats. Moreover, budgeted workers such as teachers and doctors often wait months for salaries, while federal and regional authorities balance tax and revenue accounts on paper without exchanging funds. Many of the same difficulties afflict the Komi Republic, where taxes have been difficult to collect and, moreover, many former state services, such as health care and education, have declined in quality. Given the high oil prices in 2000, however, significant rises in planned expenditures were predicted.[61]

However, not all of this increased money appears to be directed towards the provision of services. It is said that old party workers continue to control the bureaucracy,[62] and the Komi administration spends far more on running the bureaucracy than neighbouring regions through a system of reserve funds controlled by the Head of the Republic.[63] Moreover, as opposition figures in the State Council have complained, there is no legislative committee to monitor budgetary expenditures.[64] That Komi also invests heavily in a civil service academy suggests that bureaucrats, whether former Party members or not, receive extensive benefits.[65]

The institutionalisation of a market under the regulation of the political society and state bureaucracy has been one of the great difficulties facing all regions of Russia. Despite its apparent natural resource wealth, Komi has not escaped these problems. In part, as explained above, Komi is roughly divided geographically into three economic zones. The coal region in the north is a dying area with little profit and little incentive for Syktyvkar's involvement, other than to mollify potentially striking workers.[66] The oil and gas industry of the middle carries much of the potential for Komi wealth in the long term. Spreading across these two regions is significant mineral wealth, a fact that has spurred Komi authorities to explore a law in violation of federal guidelines to begin charging fees for mining rents that are variable, rather than fixed as currently, in order to take advantage of revenues from productive mines. Finally, the timber region of the south also promises wealth, but difficulties in privatisation processes prior to recent restructuring of the production enterprises in the region, have resulted in mixed results after a period of quiescence.[67]

Fundamental to the economic system in Komi is a corporatist relationship between the 'generals' (managers) of industry and the political authorities in Syktyvkar. Since 1995, industry leaders, who have worked in concert with Spiridonov, have occupied 25 per cent of the seats in the fifty-member State Council. While this relationship is difficult to identify because many negotiations are secretive, recent announcements of petroleum giant Lukoil's support for Spiridonov's run for a third term underline the close relationship between Komi government and industry. It is, of course, the case that the government is in a position to either reward companies through subsidies or tax 'breaks' or to punish those companies through enforcing tax laws.[68] Furthermore, in 1998 the State Council solidified the corporatist link by amending the Komi Constitution

Table 8.3 Characteristics of authoritarian and democratic ideal regime types

Characteristic	Authoritarian	Democracy
Pluralism	Political system with limited, not responsible political pluralism, but often extensive social and economic pluralism	Responsible political pluralism that is reinforced by autonomy in society
Ideology	No elaborate, guiding ideology, but there is a distinctive mentality	Intellectual commitment to citizenship and procedures of contestation. Value individual.
Mobilisation	Little extensive or intensive political mobilisation	Participation through autonomously developed civil society and competing political parties. Low regime mobilisation.
Leadership	Leader or small group exercises power within ill-defined, but predictable norms	Freely elected leadership within constitutional limits and periodic free elections

Source: From J. Linz and A. Stepan, *Problems of Democratic Transition and Consolidation: Southern Europe, South America, and Post-Communist Europe* (Baltimore, MD: Johns Hopkins University Press, 1996), pp. 44–5.

to allow the Head and his deputies to hold positions in commercial and civic organisations.[69]

Conclusions

In using the Linz and Stepan model, it is evident that the Komi political system has shown little development towards consolidation since the end of its transition in winter 1995. While it is true that the society has lost many of the facets of post-totalitarianism, it is far from arriving at a functioning democracy. In looking at Table 8.3, it should be evident on the basis of the above examination that the characteristics of Komi politics most resemble the authoritarian regime.

This raises a question of whether Linz and Stepan's theory accurately represents the developments in this post-communist region. For, can a political entity have completed its democratic transition and still be largely authoritarian in nature? If one remembers that the creation of democratic institutions does not necessarily signify that they function democratically, then there is no contradiction. As I have argued elsewhere, democratic institutions do not necessarily make democrats. Cultural attitudes and behaviour do not change quickly. Thus, non-democratic behaviour will frequently continue within democratic institutions if such is the cultural baggage of that polity as it is for Komi.[70]

Despite the fact that Linz and Stepan were theorising with a national state in mind, the application of their model provided a detailed sketch of the political evolution of the Komi Republic and could do so for any number of regions in Russia. While I am still troubled by the elite orientation of the model, it is flexible enough to accommodate an in-depth analysis of the components of consolidated democracy if the scholar applying the model so chooses. The breadth of the model further allows it to encompass post-communist politics without losing sight of the complexities of such a society. In this respect, those arguing that 'Russia is unique' are still able to develop a productive analysis, even if many of the historical and cultural factors that *are* Russian are missing.

In truth, the chronic problem of a teleological leaning towards democracy, that plagues much of the transition literature, is apparent here. Although the model measures a society's relative democratic development against a particular standard, the possibility for regime 'backslippage', although recognised, is not sufficiently developed. Despite a certain circularity, the notion of an 'open-ended' transition carries a lot of promise in this research.[71] Nevertheless, we need to consider more carefully the characteristics and forces that drive political change, no matter the direction of that change.

What then is the political future for the Komi Republic? As Komi officials are quite willing to admit, democracy does not currently exist in the region. In fact, they believe that neither the people nor the conditions are right, nor are they likely to be right in the next ten years.[72] The 'wild' card for the future is in the hands of the centre and Russia's new president, Vladimir Putin. If the central government is able to bring the regions into conformity with federal rules and regulations, Komi may well be forced to adapt to a new set of 'international' factors. Whether this is towards regional democracy or a stronger, more centralised state focused on Moscow is as yet unclear.

Notes

1 Research for this publication was supported by a grant from the International Research and Exchanges Board, with funds provided by the US Department of State (Title VIII programme) and the National Endowment for the Humanities. None of these organisations is responsible for the views expressed. Support for this project was also received from the Faculty Research Committee, Northeastern State University, Tahlequah, OK 74464.

2 G. Lapidus, 'Asymmetrical federalism and state breakdown in Russia', *Post-Soviet Affairs*, 15:1 (1999), 74–82.

3 S. Solnick, 'Is the centre too weak or too strong in the Russian federation?', in V. Sperling (ed.), *Building the Russian State: Institutional Crisis and the Quest for Democratic Governance* (Boulder: CO, Westview Press, 2000), pp. 137–56.

4 K. Stoner-Weiss, 'Central weakness and provincial autonomy: observations on the devolution process in Russia', *Post-Soviet Affairs*, 15:1 (1999), 87–106.

5 B. Weingast, 'Constitutions as governance structures: the political foundations of secure markets', *Journal of Institutional and Theoretical Economics*, 149:1 (1995), 286–320.

6 J. Alexander, A. Degtyarev and V. Gel'man, 'Democratisation challenged: elite games of transition', in B. Ruble, J. Koehn and N. Popson (eds.), *Fragmented Space:*

Centre–Region–Local in the Russian Federation (Washington, DC and Baltimore, MD: Woodrow Wilson Press and Johns Hopkins University Press, 2001).

7 J. Linz and A. Stepan, *Problems of Democratic Transition and Consolidation: Southern Europe, South America, and Post-Communist Europe* (Baltimore, MD: Johns Hopkins University Press, 1996).

8 V. Bunce, 'Should transitologists be grounded?', *Slavic Review*, 54:1 (1995), 111–27; T. L. Karl and P. C. Schmitter, 'From an iron curtain to a paper curtain', *Slavic Review*, 54:4 (1995), 965–78; V. Bunce, 'Paper curtains and paper tigers', *Slavic Review*, 54:4 (1995), 979–87.

9 C. Offe, 'Capitalism by democratic design? Democratic theory facing the triple transition in East Central Europe', *Social Research*, 58:4 (1991), 865–92; J. Alexander, 'Uncertain conditions in the Russian transition: the popular drive toward stability in a 'Stateless' Environment', *Europe–Asia Studies*, 50:3 (1998), 415–43.

10 V. Gel'man, 'Regime transition, uncertainty and prospects for democratisation: the politics of Russia's regions in a comparative perspective', *Europe–Asia Studies*, 51:6 (1999), 939–56; Alexander, Degtyarev and Gel'man, 'Democratisation challenged'.

11 *Ibid.*, p. 376.

12 *Ibid.*, p. 3.

13 *Ibid.*, pp. 378–9. Linz and Stepan show that the Gorbachev regime did not advance beyond the stage of liberalisation. National elections to form a government at the centre never occurred.

14 J. Kahn, 'The parade of sovereignties: establishing the vocabulary of the new Russian federalism', *Post-Soviet Affairs*, 16:1 (2000), 64.

15 Linz and Stepan, *Problems*, p. 3.

16 *Ibid.*, p. 19.

17 S. H. Barnes and J. Simon, *The Post Communist Citizen* (Budapest: Erasmus Foundation, 1998).

18 Linz and Stepan, *Problems*, p. 3.

19 V. Vyzhutovich, 'Tsentrizberkom prevrashchaetsia v politicheskoe vedomstvo', *Izvestiya* (May 4, 1994), p. 4.

20 Linz and Stepan, *Problems*, p. 5.

21 *Ibid.*, pp. 5–7.

22 J. Alexander, *Political Culture in Post-communist Russia: Formlessness and Recreation in a Traumatic Transition* (London: Macmillan Press, 2000).

23 Stoner-Weiss, 'Central weakness', 94.

24 Linz and Stepan, *Problems*, pp. 390–7.

25 Gel'man, 'Regime transition'.

26 Much of this information is from 'Regional profile: Komi Republic', East–West Institute, *Russian Regional Report* (executive edition, 2 April 1998) (hereafter, EWI, *Russian Regional Report*).

27 '2015 gody respublika "postareet' na vosem" protsentov', *Molodesh severa* (9 July 1998), 2.

28 Kahn, 'Parade of sovereignties', 60.

29 As told the author on several occasions by Y. Shabaev, former Deputy Syktyvkar City Executive Committee, Syktyvkar.

30 Linz and Stepan, *Problems*, pp. 55–65.

31 *Ibid.* p. 90. See discussion of the Moncloa Pact in Spain.

32 V. Shalapentokh, *From Submission to Rebellion* (Boulder, CO: Westview Press, 1997), pp. 99–100.
33 Linz and Stepan, *Problems*, p. 377. They describe 'how *independence* came to be privileged over *democratisation*' for the all-union republics.
34 Spiridonov used the pretext that the referendum turnout had not reached the 50 per cent threshold required by Komi law to be considered valid. Thus, he could legally 'ignore' the wishes of the population. See Alexander, *Political culture*.
35 Linz and Stepan, *Problems*, pp. 81–2.
36 *Ibid.*, pp. 82–3.
37 Alexander, *Political culture*.
38 Linz and Stepan, *Problems*, p. 6.
39 For a full discussion of attitudes in the Komi and Kirov regions, see Alexander, *Political culture*.
40 Linz and Stepan, *Problems*, pp. 72–6. They do consider the influences of foreign policies, 'spirit of the times' and diffusion on domestic politics.
41 See Alexander, Degtyarev and Gel'man, 'Democratisation challenged'; see also J. Alexander, 'Pluralism in the Komi Republic? Overcoming executive resistance', *Demokratizatsiya*, 7:3 (1999), 370–82.
42 Interview with O. Azarov, head of the Department for Public Relations, Administration of the Head of the Komi Republic (22 July 1999), Syktyvkar.
43 Alexander, 'Pluralism'.
44 *Ibid.*
45 Interview with B. Kolesnikov, Correspondent for *Krasnoe Znamya* (14 July, 1999), Syktyvkar.
46 Interview with N. Moiseev, Deputy to the State Council and the Syktyvkar City Council (16 July 1999), Syktyvkar. He had long been a television personality in the region until forced out, as he claims, by Spiridonov.
47 Azarov interview.
48 Alexander, 'Pluralism'. The organisation includes local branches of Russia's Democratic Choice, Our Home is Russia (NDR), Fatherland and others.
49 Article 84 of the Komi Constitution bans the Head of the Republic from membership in a political party. It was reported that Spiridonov ultimately placed his support behind the Fatherland party list.
50 Interview with I. Bobrakov, Chairman, Transformation of the North (20 July 1999), Syktyvkar.
51 Interview with L. Musinov, Head of the Komi Department of NPSR (14 July 1999), Syktyvkar and Moiseev interview.
52 Musinov interview.
53 For more on Komi local self-government, see Alexander, Degtyarev and Gel'man, 'Democratisation challenged'.
54 Musinov and Moiseev interviews.
55 Moiseev interview.
56 Shabaev, 'Komi constitution demands serious revisions', EWI *Russian Regional Report*, 5:24 (21 June 2000).
57 Azarov interview.
58 Moiseev interview.
59 Alexander, Degtyarev and Gel'man, 'Democratisation challenged'.

60 Interview with I. Kulakov, Deputy Speaker of the Komi State Council (27 July 1999), Syktyvkar.
61 Y. Shabaev, 'Komi benefiting form high oil prices', EWI, *Russian Regional Report*, 5:4 (2 February 2000).
62 Interview with L. Zavialova, Deputy to the Komi State Council (13 July 1999), Syktyvkar.
63 Shabaev, 'Komi benefiting'.
64 Interviews with V. Kuznetsov, former Director of the Committee for the Budget, Taxes and Economic Policy in the Komi State Council, Deputy in the Komi State Council (14 July 1997 and 21 July 1999), Syktyvkar.
65 Shabaev, 'Komi benefiting'.
66 Y. Shabaev, 'Komi: no success in reforming state-owned coal industry', EWI, *Russian Regional Report*, 4:47 (1999).
67 Y. Shabaev, 'Komi: one forestry enterprise succeeds . . . while another fails', EWI, *Russian Regional Report*, 4:45 (1999).
68 Kolesnikov interview.
69 Alexander, Degtyarev, and Gel'man, 'Democratisation challenged'.
70 Alexander, 'Political culture'.
71 Gel'man, 'Regime transition'.
72 Kulakov and Azarov interviews.

Democratisation, structural pluralism and fragile bi-centrism: the case of Volgograd Oblast

The diversity of political developments in Russia's regions has provided scholars with new opportunities to engage in broad comparative research.[2] The combination of two empirical dimensions of comparative studies – cross-national and cross-regional – is the best way forward to provide a theoretical explanation of contemporary Russian politics.[3] However, the insufficient theoretical basis of post-Soviet politics (pending new empirical studies of politics in Russia's regions) remains the major obstacle for such an explanatory research perspective.[4] Thus, the next stage in the development of Russian regional politics must be the formulation of 'hypotheses-generating' case studies[5] that promote theory building.

A major aim of this chapter is to further the theoretical literature on democratisation through a comparative study of regional politics in Russia. Methodologically this problem is very close to what Dankwart Rustow in his seminal article called the 'genesis' of democracy.[6] Rustow based his theory-building analysis not on the testing of well-developed models (such as socio-economic or cultural variables), but on an original empirical conceptualisation of two cases of the regime transition process in Sweden and Turkey. Rustow's dynamic model of democratisation made a significant contribution to the literature on transitions.

Although not such an ambitious project, this article uses a similar methodological approach. The case of regime transition in Volgograd Oblast in 1986–99 serves as the empirical basis for a more general analysis of regional democratisation. During this period, the regional political regime was transformed from a late-Soviet monocentric regime with a predominance of informal institutions to a fragile bi-centric regime with a significant role for formal institutions. Thus, the region has shown clear signs of a shift towards the creation of formal democratic institutions which operate according to clearly defined rules. However, the outcome of the transition process was not a consequence of the deliberative choice of competitive actors. The effects on the regional political regime depended upon the conditions of the ancien regime as well as upon peculiarities of the transition process:

1 the breakdown of the Communist regime in the course of the so-called 'February revolution' of 1990; and
2 the dynamics of institutional engineering, imposed upon the region by external actors (in particular, the installation of electoral practices and the devolution of significant self-governing powers granted to the region from the Russian Federal government in Moscow).

The transformation process of the political regime in Volgograd Oblast included the following stages, according to the transition model that I have outlined elsewhere:[7]

1 the decline of the ancien regime (1986 to February 1990);
2 the breakdown of the ancien regime (February to March 1990);
3 uncertainty and unsuccessful efforts to achieve regime stability (March 1990 to December 1996);
4 exit from uncertainty (December 1996); and
5 formation of the new regime (although not yet consolidated) (since December 1996).

In sum, it is possible to discern a positive move towards democratisation in Volgograd's transition. The very fact that all actors have agreed to political contestation within the framework of formal institutions may be considered as a 'contingent institutional compromise', which has led to a balance of forces among the major political actors[8]; in other words, the formation of a democratic regime. This conclusion is not weakened by the fact that, as a product of the regime transition, there was a considerable degree of elite continuity from the previous Soviet regime. However, it would be incorrect to conclude on these grounds that the old Communist nomenklatura was simply brought back to power.[9] On the contrary, these circumstances only underline the significance of the three most important political innovations which have appeared during the regime transition process:

1 the transformation of political competition among actors, which was previously conducted in secrecy, to more transparent forms;
2 the institutionalisation of political competition through the creation of formal norms and rules;
3 contestation between actors is now transferred to the field of mass electoral politics.

This chapter consists of three parts. The first is devoted to an analysis of the influence of the modernisation processes on the formation of political actors, as well as on the dynamics of Volgograd Oblast's political development during the decline and breakdown of the Communist regime. In the second part there is a detailed study of political actors and their interactions during the period of uncertainty are discussed. The third part examines the role of institutional transformations in the process of exit from uncertainty. In the conclusions the characteristics of the new regional political regime and its prospects are analysed.

The decline and breakdown of the Communist regime

It is widely recognised that the conflicts which emerge in the course of modernisation play an important role in the formation of political systems. Since the publication of Lipset and Rokkan's seminal study on the origins of parties, it has generally been accepted that, once developed, there was a 'freezing' of the structure of party competition formed out of the social cleavages which developed during the period of the industrial revolution and the creation of the nation state in Western Europe.[10] Lipset and Rokkan sought to uncover consistent patterns in the social cleavages which emerged from societal conflicts in democratic political regimes. However, as correctly noted by Giovanni Sartori, this approach fails to explain why some cleavages translated into a basis for party competition while others did not.[11] Sartori concluded that cleavages are not only a reflection of the political system, but are also formed by it through 'translators', primarily by political elites. The model was further developed by Rokkan, who attributed a key role in the process of party formation to alliances of political entrepreneurs and to their choice of strategies for resource mobilisation.[12] Finally, Angelo Panebianco added the further dimension of intra-elite conflict as an explanatory factor for a party's organisational structures and the institutionalisation of party systems.[13]

Thus, studying the causes and consequences of conflicts among political actors together with an analysis of cleavages at the societal level produces an important framework for the analysis of regime transition. Indeed, elite cleavages which emerged during transition and were transferred into the field of electoral politics may serve as the basis for a new party system.[14] In a broader sense, the main dimensions of the political regime – competition between actors and the predominant type of institutions – are determined to a significant extent by the structure of social cleavages. Elite divisions formed under the ancien regime acted as the basic structural pre-conditions for the rise of intra-elite conflicts at the initial stage of transition i.e. decline and breakdown of the ancien regime.[15] In turn, as the regime collapses, these intra-elite conflicts may be accompanied by mass mobilisation organised by competing actors (along with the mobilisation of societal cleavages). At the final stage of transformation the 'freezing' of the cleavages among political actors is the most important element of the consolidation of the new regime. But what about the dynamics of the formation and mobilisation of these cleavages, and what is their impact on the transition process?

In the study of contemporary Russian politics the problems of cleavage structures has been addressed primarily through an analyses of mass electoral behaviour in national elections.[16] At the same time, the territorial effects of cleavages were approached using the concept of the 'spatial diffusion of political innovations'.[17] This concept corresponds to the opposition between 'centre' and 'periphery' as discussed in modernisation theory.[18] However, these analyses were limited to studies of electoral behaviour, and no attempt was made to ascertain the causes of these cleavages.

Cleavages – both at the societal and the elite levels – became visible in Russia only during the course of elections. But they arose not from the process of the regime transition in 1980–90, but primarily as a by-product of the modernisation of Russia during the Soviet period. Industrialisation, urbanisation and mass migration in the USSR created a cleavage between a highly modernised 'centre' and poorly modernised 'peripheries'. Big cities – regional capitals with their agglomerations of population and industry – were the main centres of social, economic and cultural modernisation,[19] while the rest of the regions were (with some exceptions) semi-peripheral or even peripheral zones. This cleavage during the late-Soviet period was further complicated by the existence of two different administrative systems, one for industry and one for agriculture. At the regional level, industrial administration was characterised by a significant degree of decentralisation whilst, in contrast, agriculture (primarily grain production) was the principle resource base of the central authorities, with strong local ties forged between agricultural managers and the regional party apparatus. These two administrative systems brought forth the phenomena of 'localism' and 'departmentalism'. Regional party bodies as represented by members of the party apparatus played a mediating role in regulating conflicts and integrating the regional governance as a whole (although in pursuit of their own interests).[20]

One of the consequences of the modernisation process was the increasing differentiation and complexity of the regional administration of big cities, which accumulated an even greater significant share of regional resources. This led to urban administrations increasing their autonomy in relation to regional (to a greater extent to 'rural' than 'urban') administrations, especially in the sectors of building, infrastructure (transport, communications), supply and services (not to mention higher education, science and culture). This, in turn, formed the foundation for 'city versus region' conflicts, which were, however, not entirely the same as conflicts between the industrial and agrarian administrative systems (large enterprises in cities were even more independent from urban administrations). Thus, the structural preconditions for a differentiation of actors and for the growth of conflicts of interest between them entered the agenda in the late-Soviet years, although the political regime was non-competitive, and conflicts of interests emerged only in a latent form.

In addition, the late-Soviet period also shaped and consolidated the system of regional territorial-industrial organisations, which created a basic mass clientelism at both the enterprise and regional levels.[21] Thus, both the basis of societal cleavages and the mechanisms of their mobilisation by actors were created prior to the beginning of the transition, although at this time they existed only in a latent form. Intra-elite conflicts – moving from a latent to a more explicit form during the early stage of the transformation of regional political regimes – was provoked not only and not so much by ideological divisions between 'hard-liners' and 'soft-liners', but by changes in the balance of forces. Under the influence of the federal centre's policy the following events occurred:

1 the weakening of party apparatchiks;
2 the growth of the autonomy of industrial enterprise directors;
3 the growth of the autonomy of urban administrations;
4 the reduction in the inflow of resources from the Centre to regions in general and to the agrarian sector in particular.

This entailed open demarcation of actors' spheres of influence, but in essence the key lines of conflicts depended on regional resources. In highly urbanised industrial regions with a comparatively small agrarian sector, the lines of cleavage were drawn between different segments of industrial management and/or urban administrations. In less urbanised industrial-agricultural regions with a large agrarian sector, the cleavage fell between industrial and agrarian managers. Whether temporary alliances or more stable coalitions of actors were formed during those conflicts depended on the concrete conditions of transformation in various regions. In a number of cases mass social movements (mostly comprising democrats) were drawn into regional politics in the wake of these intra-elite conflicts.[22] On the one hand, competitive actors (primarily, urban managers) tried to use public rallies and protests as a weapon in their struggle for power. On the other hand, the divisions between elite groups created a broader range of political opportunities for public movements, which strengthened the efficiency of protesting forces.[23] However, this mobilisation did not lead to the transfer of competition based on social cleavages into the field of electoral politics. On the contrary, the conflict developed as a zero-sum game, resulting in the collapse of the ancien regime and the instigation of the period of uncertainty.

Political actors and their interactions during the period of uncertainty

Volgograd Oblast, 1986–90

The transition process in Volgograd Oblast clearly illustrates the importance of intra-elite conflict and cleavage structures in the breakdown of the ancien regime. The formation of the late-Soviet political regime in this region and its subsequent transformation were the consequence of several decades of modernisation. Newly reconstructed after the Second World War, Volgograd (named Stalingrad between 1925 and 1961) was transformed into a large city in the late-Soviet period. It soon became a centre of machine-building, metallurgy and the defence industry. Up to 40 per cent of the economic potential of the oblast was concentrated in Volgograd. The latent opposition between the city and the oblast arising from their different resource bases became explicit during late 1980s. This regional resource profile and the governance structure led in the Soviet period to the emergence of two relatively autonomous city-based elite groups, which can be called industrial and urban (according to resources under their control). A third, agrarian group, in coalition with member of the obkom (the oblast party committee) apparatus, constituted a monolithic unity until 1986. The most important factors, contributing to the relative autonomy of these groups, were:

1 the powerful influence of the regional centre – the city of Volgograd;
2 the independence of the directors of the giant factories from regional authorities; and
3 the agrarian 'specialisation' of the obkom.

The major industrial enterprises in the region were subordinate first and foremost to ministries in Moscow rather than the regional administration. Indeed, the two districts of Volgograd where most of the enterprises were situated constituted a kind of a 'city within a city' dominated by the enterprises. The city itself was divided into two parts. In one of them the heavy industrial companies of national importance were located, while in the other part, run by the city council, there were all the medium-sized and small companies and businesses. The region itself (without Volgograd) was almost exclusively agrarian, with agriculture as its main economic resource developing in rather risky conditions. The links between the obkom leaders and the extraterritorial industrial group (which itself has a lack of unity) were weak, and did not lead to the formation of deep informal ties or relationships.

Thus, the emergence of cleavages among the elite followed the lines of those government structures that had developed over the past forty years. The shift of these cleavages from latent to open form began at the very beginning of perestroika. This period was marked by an attempt of the agrarian group to strengthen its position by extending its control of resource inflows from outside. The new First Secretary of the Obkom, Vladimir Kalashnikov, appointed to this post in January 1984, had previously served as Russian Soviet Federative Socialist Republic (RSFSR) Minister of Land Reclamation and Water. On taking up his new regional post he actively began promoting the idea of a new irrigation project, the 'Volga-Don-2' canal, to divert water from the Volga basin and to create a land reclamation system in the area between the Volga and the Don.[24] Implementation of this plan would have fundamentally changed the system of regional agricultural governance and significantly strengthened the position of the obkom and Kalashnikov himself. This project would have given the regional party leadership a monopolistic control over resource redistribution. In essence, it would have created a new 'centre' in the region and restructured the 'periphery', i.e. the agrarian enterprises. This move provoked conflict within the agrarian group. In 1986 the vice chairman of the Regional Executive Committee in charge for the regional agrarian affairs, Ivan Shabunin, having been simultaneously the informal leader of the regional agrarian group, opposed the agricultural policies of Kalashnikov and was subsequently removed. The agrarian group had to accept a new formal leader. However, at the first opportunity provided by the Centre, the agrarian group escaped the control of the obkom. This opportunity was presented by the establishment of Agroprom (the administration of management of the agro-industrial complex) in the region and throughout the country, which was not subordinate to the regional authorities. In 1989 the ousted Shabunin was elected as its chairman. At the same time, the agrarians began to criticise the national media of the 'Volga-Don-2' project and of Kalashnikov personally. Thus, although re-elected in 1988 for a new term in office, Kalashnikov lost support of the agrarian group.

Simultaneously Kalashnikov lost his control over the city of Volgograd. In 1988 a new conflict emerged between Kalashnikov and the obkom secretary in charge of ideology, Alexander Anipkin, following further divisions within the party elite between 'hardliners' and 'softliners'. Anipkin was removed and formally demoted to the post of first secretary of the City of Volgograd. This led to rivalry between the obkom and the city committees, adding to the latent 'city versus oblast' conflict. During the same period, despite tight controls over the regional mass media (TV, radio and three local newspapers), the obkom gradually lost control of its political base: public opinion turned against it.

In this period also, control over some economic resources was transferred to Agroprom. The economic crisis in the country in general and in the region in particular was deepening, causing a considerable decline in the standard of living for the bulk of the population. Supplies of staple foodstuffs and quality of life were also declining. In 1988–89 the first independent 'informal associations' emerged. At the start of 1990 these organisations, having acquired extensive public support and the general label of 'democrats', played a key role as organisers of mass anti-obkom demonstrations.[25] In light of the upcoming regional and local elections, as well as the general weakening of Communist power, the Centre was not ready or able to intervene into regional political processes. Also representatives of the industrial directorate played no role during this process or in the period of mass demonstration, considering these problems intra-regional and basically of no concern to them.

Thus, by the start of the spring 1990 election campaign for the regional and local Soviets (which stimulated political protest activity on the part of social movements throughout the country), the leadership of the obkom found that it was isolated. They:

1 did not have support from the Centre;
2 lost the support of the agrarian group which managed to distance itself and chose to take a neutral position during mass demonstrations;
3 did not have any influence over the industrial directorate;
4 lost its control over the population.

As a result, two conflicting political groups formed, one consisting of the First Secretary of the Regional Committee and its apparatchiks, and the other consisting of the leadership of the Volgograd City Committee of the Communist Party of the Soviet Union (KPSS) and the 'democrats' supported by the region's population. The obkom leaders tried to use strategies of force; however, their loss of the control over the political and administrative resources at the city level made those strategies ineffective. At the end of 1989 and the beginning of 1990, as part of a series of demonstrations against corruption, an alliance was formed between the leaders of the 'democrats', who led the anti-Communist protests, and the city authorities, led by Anipkin. In a situation where the Centre and the main economic interest groups (the industrial directorate and the agrarians) chose non-intervention, this coalition was victorious. Eventually after a series of rallies and further public demonstrations (the 'February Revolution'), the entire membership of the obkom was forced to resign. The election of Anipkin as Obkom First Secretary just before the regional and local council elections in Volgograd however, did not, lead to his victory or to a strengthening of the city administration. Anipkin failed to gain the support of either the agrarians or the industrial group, having also lost his influence over the 'democrats'. The latter, having converted their influence into votes, lost interest in further mass mobilisation campaigns. However, the democrats' influence in the regional assembly (the Oblast Soviet) was not strong enough to make up a majority, let alone a 'veto group'. After achieving their goal, the anti-obkom coalition broke up and none of its representatives attempted to take the post of the Oblast Soviet chairman, which, given the weakness of the obkom, was now the most powerful post in the region.

These events produced uncertainty in both the composition of actors and the set of political institutions in the region. Although the uncertainty as to who would become the key actor was rather short term, the institutional uncertainty was, in contrast, systemic: the formal institutions of the ancien regime almost completely disappeared, while new institutions either did not appear at all or were rather fragile. Thus, after February–March 1990, the strategies of regional actors developed in an institution-free environment. The breakdown of the previous regime[26] resulted not only in an institutional vacuum, but also in large-scale and long-term uncertainty, which lasted in the Volgograd Oblast for more than six years.

Uncertainty
The breakdown of the ancien regime was accompanied by a new set of social cleavages which arose from the post-communist economic and political reforms. At the regional level this entailed significant consequences such as:

1 the decline of social-economic development and a narrowing of the resource of the majority of regions, their 'peripherisation' vis-à-vis the Centre;
2 a relative rise in the influence of cities – i.e. regional capitals and urban managerial groups – due to the development of economic sectors connected to resource redistribution (trade, services, finances);
3 a considerable weakening of the influence of most industrial managers (especially the directors of large defence enterprises), apart from infrastructure sectors (energy supply, transport, telecommunications);
4 a partial reduction in the influence of the agrarians caused by the reduction in their resource base.

As a result of such developments, the reconfiguration of actors' positions and resources was determined by a combination of 'old' and 'new' cleavages, while their strategies were developed in accordance with the specific opportunities open to them in a particular region, this in turn depended mainly on the nature of institutional reforms. Thus, although uncertainty of both actors and institutions emerged as a result of the former regime's breakdown, its regional variations depended upon each region's structural characteristics.

The 'peripheralisation' of the regions was caused by the refusal of the federal centre to implement any kind of sensible regional policy during the general economic crisis. Under these conditions, regional actors attempting to secure resources for the region from outside turned out to be restrained both by the shortage of resource bases and by the dominance of informal institutions in the distribution of resources by the Centre. This resource crisis also limited the actors' choice of strategies. After 1991, regional leaders, whether old or new, were faced with two major problems:

1 most of them did not have sufficient political resources (particularly electoral legitimacy);
2 the economic (and in a number of cases, the administrative) resources of the actors were also limited.

In regions with one dominant group (mainly, agrarians), this crisis led to a redistribution of the remaining resources in favour of that group in a manner of a 'zero-sum game'; however, in regions with a more pluralistic structure, changes in resource redistribution depended on the balance of power between these groups.

First of all, city actors experienced a short-term boom during privatisation and the establishment of a free-market infrastructure. Despite the general 'peripheralisation' of the regions, the concentration of resources in cities continued to increase from 1991. This contributed to the independence of urban political actors vis-à-vis regional ones and to the development of an 'urban–rural' cleavage. But the relative strengthening of urban 'centres' was undermined by the emergence of a new urban 'periphery' in the course of economic de-industrialisation. Thus, cities were split into new: profitable and more or less promising 'centres' and new hopeless 'peripheries'. In these conditions the position of urban administrators (especially in cities with a large concentration of defence enterprises) has been rather ambivalent. At the same time, agrarians whose resources diminished (although not as much as those of industrial directorate), also failed to achieve a dominant position under the new conditions of structural pluralism. The conflicts and alliances between these elite groups reflecting new cleavages and coalitions shaped the reconfiguration of actors' positions, and determined whether or not a dominant actor appeared during this period of uncertainty.

At the societal level the cleavages that were mobilised during the breakdown of the former regime lost their significance for a time, especially due to the moratorium on gubernatorial and mayoral elections imposed by the federal centre in Autumn 1991. This process of mass demobilisation was also followed by the collapse of clientelism, especially amongst industrial groups. With their resource base shrinking, enterprise directors were unable to maintain an effective resource exchange within a system of patron–client relations. Subordinated mass clienteles now faced the problem of 'exit, voice and loyalty'[27]: either to join other mass sectoral clientele, or to remain loyal with their former patrons, or to participate in some form of protest. The latter choice was most likely to occur when societal cleavages were mobilised during the breakdown of the Ancien regime, and the ability of the governments (both regional and city) to offer mass patronage in exchange for political loyalty were restricted. However, those cleavages were not transferred to the field of regional electoral politics, and their importance for the regional political regime remained relatively marginal.

Thus, along with a shrinking resource base and the 'peripheralisation' of the regions, the main problems for actors seeking a dominant position under structural pluralism were:

1 to provide mediation between the resource-rich centres and the needs of the resource-scarce periphery; and
2 to maintain balance of political influence among actors.

Thus, the dominant actor was forced to pursue compromise strategies through the channels of informal institutions. But the effectiveness of these strategies depended to a large degree upon the dominant actor's ability:

1 to satisfy demands of other actors and their mass clienteles (i.e. to form an effective system of resource exchange); and
2 to prevent the rise of alternative centre(s) with their own mass clienteles and systems of resource redistribution.

In some regions where both these conditions were met, 'elite settlements' were achieved on the basis of compromise between dominant and subordinated actors.[28] However, if actors were unable to meet one or both of these conditions, patron–client interactions were undermined and open competition and struggle between actors was the name of the game.

Volgograd Oblast, 1990–95

The dynamics of the political development of the region progressed according to the terms described in the section above. The reconfiguration of actors, together with the shrinking regional resource base undermined the patronage system (both at the actor and mass clientele levels), leading to a high degree of uncertainty under which the dominant actor's strategies became ineffective.

As a result of the breakdown of the ancien regime in spring 1990, the regional Communist Party elite was forced out and subsequently eliminated from the political process. Running for the position of Chairman of the Oblast Soviet, the representative of the obkom failed to obtain the support of the main groups represented in the legislature, while the 'democrats' did not even offer a candidate. After much bargaining and backstage discussions, a compromise candidate was chosen, Valerii Makharadze, the director of a small enterprise in the town of Kamyshin. He was proposed by the industrial directors and accepted by the agrarians. In exchange for this the leader of the agrarians, Ivan Shabunin, was elected unopposed to the post of chairman of the Oblast Executive Committee.

For the Oblast Soviet (where a significant proportion of the members were elected from rural districts) informal institutions are of decisive importance for deputies. In contrast, elections for the chairman of the Volgograd City Soviet took place in an open and highly competitive environment of formal institutions and rules. The chairman of one of the Volgograd district executive committees and a representative of one of the groups of urban managers, Yurii Chekhov, won this position and then managed to combine it with the position of chairman of the City Executive Committee. As a result of these developments the CPSU Gorkom (city party committee) lost control over the City Soviet.

However, this configuration of actors did not last long, for reasons, external to the region. Makharadze was soon appointed to a post in Boris Yeltsin's presidential administration. And in the aftermath of the August 1991 coup, Shabunin, who had supported Yeltsin, was the obvious choice to head the regional administration and Chekhov was appointed as head of the Volgograd city administration.

However, appointment as head of the regional administration did not in itself guarantee Shabunin the status of dominant actor in the region. To secure a sustained monopoly on power he had to establish an effective system of resource exchange. But this was problematic due to the shortage of economic and political resources in the region. His political-economic strategy was based on:

1 group patronage;
2 the redistribution of resources in favour of the agrarian group;
3 the attraction of external resources into the region.

After the abolition of the centralised state-planning system, the industrial director's interest in regional administrations increased sharply. In the course of the economic reform policy initiated in January 1992, Shabunin launched (in comparison to the majority of other regions in the country) the privatisation process for large industrial enterprises[29]; this led to a considerable share of state property being transferred to the managers of the enterprises.[30] At the same time, a number of giant factories were given direct and unsecured credits from the regional budget and some federal loans. In exchange the directors promised to passify their workers and to quell any protest movements. A Council of Directors was formed to support the interests of the industrial group in its relations with the regional administration. Promoting horizontal cooperation between large enterprises at the regional level, the regional administration proposed a series of programmes for regional social-economic development. At the same time Shabunin was the main lobbyist for enterprise directors' interests at the federal level. This period saw the emergence of a quasi-form of corporatism in the Oblast.[31]

The agrarians became the main recipients of regional budget funds, which is explained by Shabunin's previous leadership of the agrarian group as well as by other more pragmatic considerations. It was expected that the rural district administrators, as well as directors of the agricultural enterprises, would in exchange ensure social stability and economy growth (which in contrast to industry did not require large-scale investment). In the same period the regional administration launched a small private farming development, but this was to meet with little success.

At the same time small privatisation developed at a rapid pace, particularly in the city of Volgograd. At first Shabunin's access to resources for redistribution ensured him the loyalty of the city government, although it also later provided conditions for the city's subsequent autonomy. Despite the fact that the city of Volgograd as the main donor to the regional budget was interested in changing the budget relationship with the region in its favour, Chekhov did not press for changes here in exchange for Shabunin's political support. Finally, in addition to assuming patronage over the key elite groups, Shabunin attempted to forge selective patronage relationships with key social groups. In addition to a 25 per cent salary increase for certain categories of state employee, the regional administration also secured privileges for veteran groups. Relying on the support of the majority of the Oblast Soviet deputies and members of the city and regional executive, Shabunin was able to control the political situation in the region.

The political crisis of October 1993 further strengthened Shabunin's political leadership in the region. He managed to reach a peaceful agreement with the regional Soviet to hold new elections to the Volgograd Oblast Duma in December 1993 (in turn, the Oblast Soviet was not dissolved and survived until the new elections). Shabunin himself ran for a seat in the Federation Council and claimed victory with a convincing 56.8 per cent of the vote, giving him the electoral legitimacy he had previously lacked. His political partner and ally in the two-mandate constituency was Chekhov, who also won a seat in the Federation Council with 25.4 per cent of votes.[32] Among the thirty-two deputies elected to the regional Duma, the largest group were heads of industrial and agrarian enterprises, and heads of district administrations (of whom there were eight). On Shabunin's initiative, the head of administration of one of the districts of city of Volgograd, Leonid Semergey, was elected Chair of the Duma. In fact, the Duma (like the Oblast Soviet) represented the interests of the key elite groups and acted as a forum for formal decision making (the adoption of laws that confirmed decisions already adopted by the regional administration) and informal bargaining.

In this period the Volgograd Oblast seemed to have achieved stability and intra-elite consolidation. In the absence of political challengers, Shabunin was able to exercise personal control over the distribution of economic and political resources. Indeed, it seemed as if the basis for a monocentric political regime had been formed in the region. But the maintenance of the patronage system in Volgograd Oblast was rather costly in terms of resource expenses.[33] The economic crisis in the country and a sharp decline in the region's production in 1993–94 undermined the foundations of the new political regime.

An alternative strategy for preserving the regime on these terms was to attract resources from outside. In 1992–93 Shabunin made significant efforts to attract investments, but he was not very successful. Thus, in a situation of shrinking resources, the deterioration of social-economic development and a general decline in production, the patron–client system began to collapse. Structural cleavages were revitalised and a new reconfiguration of actors occurred. First of all, the city group (headed by Chekhov), unsatisfied by its subordinate position, escaped Shabunin's control and began to turn into an autonomous (and, later, alternative) political actor. According to the observations of Alexei Zudin, these strategies are common for patronage interactions between authorities and economic interest groups in Russia.[34] At the same time, the industrial group began to lose its influence over the elites and lost control of the workers. Shabunin was now faced with new mass protests from workers on the shop floor. Finally, a completely new political actor appeared on the political scene: the regional branch of the Communist Party of Russian Federation (KPRF).

Although former regional Communist leaders had already lost their political resources in 1990, the crisis in the ruling group made it possible to regain control over them. Led by its charismatic leader, Aparina, the regional KPRF organisation led social-economic protests and, with the beginning of the war in Chechnya, anti-military political demonstrations. After several KPRF candidates won seats, a communist faction was established in the Oblast Duma. Thus, by 1995, the KPRF had managed to set itself up as the only party able to address the question of social discontent (like the 'democrats' in 1989–90). The communists were also able to mobilise the support of the (former) industrial mass clientele, which had been excluded following the decline of the industrial directorate. At the same time the Communists managed to obtain the support of two other influential groups: the agrarians and the city managers. The former was longing to regain its status, and the latter was in search of allies to support its quest for autonomy.

Thus, a new opposition coalition of negative consensus was formed in the region; to a certain degree this mirrored the events of 1998–90 (although in this case with the communists replacing the 'democrats'). However, while the institutional changes of the perestroika period contributed to the breakdown of the previous regime and to a 'period of uncertainty', the institutional changes of 1995–96 led to an exit from uncertainty, the transfer of elite conflict to the arena of electoral politics and the rise of new actors on the political stage.

Exit from uncertainty and the dawn of a new regime

The institutional innovations of the 1980s and 1990s imposed by the federal centre on the regions were not the result of some consistent policy, but rather the spontaneous by-product of the shifting balances of forces in Moscow. The impact of these innovations reflected both on changes in the regional actors (hired and fired by federal authorities until 1995–96) and on institutional reforms which set the framework for political competition (or the lack of it). At the same time, however, the centre's ability to maintain control over the regions was limited by the structure of social cleavages and the configuration of economic actors. In other words, the region's resources allowed actors only limited space for their strategic choices. At the same time, the institutional changes initiated by the Centre created new political opportunities for regional actors.

In the 1990s the federal centre initiated a number of regional institutional reforms. The most significant institutional changes were:

1 the separation of legislative and executive branches of powers;[35]
2 the establishment of the system of local government;[36]
3 the installation of electoral practices.[37]

However, these innovations were applied rather inconsistently and depended on the shifting balance of forces at the centre and in the regions.

While the separation of powers in 1990–91 provided a framework for regional polycentric political regimes, in 1993–94, in contrast, they contributed to mono-centrism. The establishment of the system of local self-government that in theory was intended to promote municipal autonomy and polycentrism had rather limited impact in practice. Even elections, which were considered to be the key formal institution establishing the foundation for public contestation, led to the replacement of executive leaders in only about half of all Russia's regions.[38] The explanation for the contradictory impact of institutional changes on regional political practices may be due to differences in the structural character-istics of political development in different regions. Put simply, the seeds of insti-tutional innovations, imposed by the external actor, may or may not fall on fertile ground.[39] It is obvious that the consequences of institutional changes depended on the presence of powerful internal actors in the regions that had reasons to use these changes to their own advantage. The structures of political opportunities emerged in the regions as a result of previous changes, thus setting limits for possible innovations.

Structural cleavages and actors' ability to overcome them during the transi-tion were the most important factors determining institutional reforms. In those regions where cleavages were weak and clientelism was strong, institutional reforms tended to serve the interests of local elites. In those regions where the patron–client relations were weak, institutional reforms were more directly influ-enced by the structure of social cleavages.

In the course of conflict between regional political actors, those actors who did not have sufficient resources to claim a dominant position were forced to support the establishment of a formal institutional framework. In contrast, a dominant actor controlling excessive resources was not interested in creating formal institutional limitations on its strategies. Thus, for the 'weak' side of the conflict, formal institutions served as a weapon in the struggle for survival.[40] The opportunity to develop greater degrees of local government autonomy protected mayors against the danger of the arbitrary loss of power, while popular elections offered them a chance to enhance their political position.

The establishment of formal institutions considerably reduces actors' opportunities to engage informally, thus undermining clientelism. And the transfer of cleavages into the field of electoral politics forced actors to resort to mass mobilisation, which led to the formation of competitive 'administrative parties'. In addition, the stable nature of the cleavages did not allow electoral conflict to result in a 'winner take all' victory for one of the actors. The creation of strong and stable formal institutions (such as elections and assemblies), where actors now played according to the 'rules of the game' led to an exit from uncertainty.

Volgograd Oblast, 1995–99
The case of Volgograd Oblast conforms very well to the model of exit from uncertainty described above. The process can be divided into three consecutive stages:

1 the implementation of a system of local government in the region and the Volgograd mayoral elections (1995);
2 the election of the head of the regional administration (1996);
3 the establishment of a new regional political regime (after 1996).

Discussion of the law 'On the organisation of local government in the Volgograd Oblast' began in the Oblast Duma in 1994. Shabunin, who did not want to cede financial autonomy to the city of Volgograd, went on the defensive and tried to postpone the adoption of this law until a federal law on local government came into force at the federal level. Shabunin's usual strategy as head of administration included selective use of both formal and informal institutions. Often, formal institutions served only as a facade for 'behind the scenes' politics. However, Shabunin's attempt to impede the establishment of local government was unsuccessful; after eight months of conflict, the law was eventually signed by Shabunin and came into force in March 1995.[41] As a result, the city of Volgograd, led by Chekhov, had an opportunity to use the new formal institution of local government to escape their subordination to Shabunin. In June 1995, under Chekhov's influence, the regional Duma set elections for the Mayor of Volgograd and deputies of the city Duma on 1 October 1995. Prior to the elections Chekhov managed to form a coalition with the KPRF on a division of power. The Communists did not nominate their own candidate in the mayoral election and thus provided no obstacle to Chekhov's victory. In turn, with no serious competition from the urban managers, Communists won twenty-one of twenty-four seats in the City Duma elections. Chekhov was elected the mayor with 61.9 per cent votes, acquiring additional political resources and significantly consolidating his position as an autonomous actor.[42] The KPRF deputy, Nikolai Maksyuta, who was the director of a ship-building factory was elected chair of the City Duma.

The role of city elections in the transformation of the regional political regime was crucial. First of all, following the election of the mayor and the City Duma, informal 'behind the scenes' deals were replaced with open conflicts between actors. Second, the elections created a coalition of urban managers and the Communists to be set up in opposition to the regional administration. Thus, opposition actors had an opportunity to mobilise new resources and to undermine Shabunin's position. The latter, losing more and more administrative and economic resources, found himself in a situation close to that of the obkom in 1989–90. Finally, the Communists were now the group with the greatest influence over mass mobilisation. Through a series of election campaigns the communists steadily increased their resources, claiming victory in the State Duma elections (December 1995) and in the presidential elections in 1996.

The new intra-elite conflict in the region shifted into an open competition after the clash between the city and the regional authorities over the budget. At the beginning of 1996 Chekhov, supported by the City Duma (i.e. the KPRF) demanded a cut in the share of regional budget funds that were redistributed in favour of agriculture at the city's expense, and he threatened a legal suit against the regional administration (the threat, however, was not realised). The conflict culminated in the calling of a popular election for the head of the regional administration in December 1996.

Shortly before the election campaign, Shabunin was exposed to some pressure at the federal centre, which accused him of ineffective agriculture management in the region and of political disloyalty. Shabunin rejected the demands of the presidential administration to withdraw his candidacy. However, lacking presidential support he could no longer ensure the inflow of federal finances from the centre. At the same time, Chekhov, after securing the support of the Centre, unsuccessfully mobilised these federal resources in his own interest. Shabunin and Chekhov, both confident of victory, mobilised mainly administrative and economic resources. In contrast, the Communists who possessed only political resources, did not at first expect electoral success and nominated Maksyuta (not their leader Aparina) as the party's candidate for Governor.

Nevertheless, the Communists made highly effective use of mass mobilisation.[43] Shortly before the election campaign the Communists managed to secure if not the support then the favourable neutrality of the agrarian group who were dissatisfied by Shabunin's agricultural policy. In the first round of elections, Shabunin received 37.6 per cent of the vote, Maksyuta took 28.5 per cent and Chekhov gained 25.2 per cent. In the second round however, victory went to Maksyuta, who swept the rural areas and small towns, winning 50.95 per cent of the vote overall, with Shabunin polling 44.2 per cent. The communists had managed to mobilise structural cleavages: the 'periphery' – the rural voters and the (former) industrial mass clientele – gained a victory over the city 'centre'.

To a certain extent the events of December 1996, which signalled a tendency towards an exit from uncertainty in the region, mirrored the collapse of the former regime in February–March 1990 that had initiated the entry into uncertainty. In a similar manner to events six years earlier, the conflict between the urban and the regional administrations moved from a latent to an open phase, and with the mobilisation of the masses to a change of political regime. The city managers, who tried to reclaim the role of dominant actor, preserved only their autonomous position. The victory of the political opposition (Communists) was also the result of their successful coalition of 'negative consensus' with the agrarian group.

However, while the entry into uncertainty was followed by the breakdown of the institutions of the former political regime, the exit from uncertainty occurred after the formal institutions of the new political regime had been formed. Legal norms now prevailed (including the law on local government) and popular elections dictated who would be the head of the regional administration and mayor of Volgograd.

The KPRF victory in the gubernatorial elections did not lead to the emergence of a dominant actor in the region. On the contrary, the urban managers headed by Chekhov, based on significant economic resources, managed to preserve its relative autonomy, using formal institutions as a weapon in their struggle for survival. This situation did not allow the KPRF to fall back on strategies or force for removing their urban rivals. The Communists were now obliged to use formal institutions (mainly elections) as a weapon in their struggle. During the 'rotation' elections of the deputies of the Oblast Duma in March 1997 and December 1998, the Communists managed to obtain an absolute majority of the seats in the Oblast Duma (twenty-three mandates out of thirty-two)[44] The KPRF deputy Sergey Pripisnov has occupied the position of the Duma chairman since January 1999 to date. From his side, Chekhov was re-elected as city mayor in October 1999, taking 38 per cent of votes. The communist-backed candidate won 20 per cent. Moreover, in contrast to the 1995 City Duma elections, the Communists won six out of twenty-four seats, while the majority of newly elected deputies were loyal to Chekhov. Both key competitive actors were thus forced to conduct the struggle according to the rules – i.e. within the formal institutional framework – and to seek to maximise their control over regional resources with the help of compromise strategies. In other words, the structural pluralism among actors that was established in Volgograd Oblast served as a foundation for the consolidation of those institutions that supported the bicentrism of the political regime.

Paradoxically, the strengthening of the KPRF's positions as the key party in the region was accompanied by the preservation (and even strengthening) of its oppositional function at the federal level. Despite the inclusion in his administration of the Communist representatives (which had been part of the regional ruling group until 1990), in these circumstances Maksyuta was forced to choose a relatively autonomous course of action, as the region's dependence on the Centre rapidly increased. This condition raised tension between Maksyuta and the KPRF, although they still needed each other. The ambivalence of the situation can be explained by the restricted opportunities Maksyuta had for the mobilisation of resources. While showing his loyalty to the Centre, he was losing the support of the electorate which he had gained with the help of the communists, but his party 'label' prevented him from being given any recognition by the Centre.

On a wider scale, the contradictions between the governor and his party were essentially structural, related to the contradiction between the Communist Party's supposed principle of collective leadership and the position of a popularly elected chief executive. Thus, in Volgograd Oblast (as well as in several other Russia's regions, where the governors were elected with Communist support) we see a gradual distancing of the governors from the party.[45] Indeed, in the 1999 State Duma elections in the region one governor-backed candidate even competed with one of the local Communist leaders, and won. In any case, despite the presence of certain symbolic elements of continuity, there could not possibly be any talk of restoring the previous political regime.

Seeking if not stability then at least the prevention of economic collapse and his own survival as an actor in the region, Maksyuta continued to carry out in essence Shabunin's previous economic policy. First of all, he sought to preserve the patronage of the agrarian group. The support of the rural areas was publicly announced as his priority. The industrial directorate, which lost a considerable amount of influence and found itself as a subordinated actor, took the position of a 'servant of two masters'. The same representative of this group chaired the board of directors affiliated to the city and regional administrations. At the same time both Maksyuta and Chekhov, having an interest in minimising mass protest on the one hand and in keeping the industrial group's support on the other, fruitlessly sought to attract external resources to the region. Finally, the fuel and energy complex (FEC) significantly consolidated its position in the economic and political systems of the region. Lukoil, the most powerful of all the enterprises in the FEC sector, became the main source of subsidies to the agrarian sector as a result of an accumulation of credits provided by the administration. The FEC directorate in its turn won nine seats in the regional Duma in the 1997–98 elections and became a rather powerful and autonomous actor.

Conclusions

The 1988–99 regime transition in Volgograd Oblast can be described – with some limitations – as a case of more or less successful democratisation, at least in the minimalist 'procedural' sense.[46] However, three years after the exit from uncertainty, there is no reason to consider this process to be close to completion. It is too early to talk about the consolidation of the regime, at least until the end of the next cycle of regional elections. The principle characteristics of the new regional political regime in Volgograd Oblast are the instability of its major characteristics: the set of actors and dominant institutions. This instability can be seen at three levels:

1 the procedural;
2 the structural;
3 the one related to resources.

The procedural aspect of instability is connected to the fact that the set of formal institutions (institutional design) in the region does not constitute a guarantee against a 'seizure of power'.[47] There is also no political guarantee in the region against institutional changes which could change the competitive framework to a 'winner take all' system (for example, to replace popular mayoral elections with one in which the mayor is elected by the city Duma). More generally, if the political regime remains unconsolidated, the region could be 'doomed' to a permanent instability even where competing actors now play by the rules. As Philippe Schmitter noted:

> Democracy in its most generic sense persists after the demise of autocracy, but never gels into a specific, reliable, and generally accepted set of rules . . . Elections are held; associations are tolerated; rights may be respected; arbitrary treatment by authorities may decline – in other words, the procedural minimal are met with some degree of regularity – but regular, acceptable and predictable democratic patterns never quite crystallise. Democracy is not replaced, it just persists by acting in ad hoc and ad hominem ways as successive problems arise. [48]

The structural aspect of instability is connected to the specifics of structural cleavages and to the as yet incomplete reconfiguration of the actors. First, the continuing 'peripheralisation' of Russia's regions threatens an exhaustion or at least a reduction in the potential of regional capitals as 'centres' and their weakening in relation to the 'periphery'. This would mean shifts in structural cleavage lines in favour of the 'periphery'. Second, the high proportion of the agricultural sector in the economic structure of the region and the comparative advantage of the agrarian group induces regional leaders to continue the agrarian patronage policy, which also weakens Volgograd's role as a centre. Third, in terms of the continuing reduction in the regional resources base, the process of reconfiguration of political and economic actors is permanent, and there are no reasons to expect its rapid completion. Fourth, in spite of an abundance of election campaigns in the region, the comparatively stable structure of social cleavages, even when transferred into the field of mass politics, has not yet 'frozen' into a stable framework of inter-party competition. Still, it is difficult to say whether this configuration of political actors in the region will remain intact after the next cycle of regional elections.

The resource aspect of instability is due to the continuing economic decline in Russia in general and in the Volgograd Oblast in particular, and to the absence of short-term prospects for a significant inflow of resources into the region from outside. In this situation regional actors find themselves faced with the choice either to employ strategies or force in the struggle for vanishing resources, or to avoid open political competition by dividing the spheres of influence among themselves in an 'elite settlement'. Both of these options are feasible.

The structural instability of the political regime in Volgograd Oblast is deepened by the current instability of its actors. The prospects of the incumbent governor as an autonomous political actor seem to be doubtful in conditions of resource crisis in the region. At the same time, in anticipation of a new electoral cycle the ambivalent position of the KPRF as both opposition and ruling party challenges its future. Finally, it is still unclear whether strategies employed by competitive regional actors would strengthen or undermine their positions.

Thus, bicentrism in Volgograd Oblast is still unstable, and an exit from uncertainty is not yet completed. Nevertheless, the existence of a stable structural pluralism among actors in the region formed in the late-Soviet period and reproduced throughout all the subsequent stages of the transition process will continue to prevent any return to a monocentric regime, even in the event of a total victory for one of the competing actors in a 'zero-sum game'.

More generally, the case of Volgograd Oblast provides evidence of the impact of modernisation processes and the structural cleavages (both at the intra-elite and societal levels) on the process of regime transition. This impact can be represented in a three-stage 'path-contingent' model:[49]

1 Intra-elite cleavages setting the framework for a structure of political opportunities make competition between actors inevitable and indispensable.
2 The actualisation of intra-elite cleavages for the installation of formal institutions leads to the use of these institutions as a weapon in the struggle for political survival.
3 The translation of intra-elite cleavages and societal cleavages into the field of electoral competition and a consolidation of the configuration of actors who compete within a framework of formal institutions makes the democratisation process sustainable.

Notes

1 Translated by Andrei and Boris Rogatchevski.
2 The chapter is undertaken within the framework of the research project 'Russia of Regions', sponsored by Volkswagen Foundation. The author would like to thank Andrei Rogozhin for providing some of the data used in this study.
3 Vladimir Gel'man, 'Regime transition, uncertainty, and prospects for democratisation: the politics of Russia's regions in a comparative perspective', *Europe–Asia Studies*, 51:6 (1999), 939–56.
4 Neil Melvin, 'The consolidation of the new regional elite: the case of Omsk 1987–1995', *Europe–Asia Studies*, 50:4 (1998), 619–650; Nikolai Petro, 'The Novgorod region: a Russian success story', *Post-Soviet Affairs*, 15:3 (1999), 235–61; Andrei Tsygankov, 'Manifestation of delegative democracy in Russian local politics: what does it mean for the future of Russia?' *Communist and Post-Communist Studies*, 31:4 (1998), 329–44.
5 Arend Lijphart, 'Comparative politics and comparative method', *American Political Science Review*, 65:3 (1971), 691–92.
6 Dankwart Rustow, 'Transitions to democracy: toward a dynamics model', *Comparative Politics*, 2:3 (1970), 337–63.

7 Gel'man, 'Regime transition, uncertainty', 943–44.

8 Adam Przeworski, 'Some problems in the study of transition to democracy', in Guillermo O'Donnell, Philippe Schmitter and Lawrence Whitehead (eds.), *Transitions from Authoritarian Rule* (Baltimore, MD and London: Johns Hopkins University Press, 1986), vol. III, p. 59.

9 Olga Kryshtanovskaya, 'Transformatsiya staroi nomenklatury v novuyu Rossiiskuyu elitu', *Obshchestvennye Nauki i Sovremennost*, 1 (1995), 51–65; Olga Kryshtanovskaya and Steven White, 'From Soviet nomenklatura to Russian elite', *Europe–Asia Studies*, 48:5 (1996), 711–33.

10 Seymour Martin Lipset and Stein Rokkan, 'Cleavage structures, party systems, and voter alignment', in Seymour Martin Lipset and Stein Rokkan (eds.), *Party System and Voter Alignment: Cross-National Perspectives* (New York: Free Press, 1967), pp. 1–64; Stein Rokkan *et al.*, *Citizens, Elections, Parties: Approaches to the Comparative Study of The Process of Development* (Oslo: Universitetforlaget, 1970), pp. 72–144.

11 Giovanni Sartori, 'The sociology of parties: a critical review', in Peter Mair (ed.), *The West European Party System* (Oxford: Oxford University Press, 1990), p. 176.

12 Stein Rokkan, 'Toward a generalised concept of verzuilling, a preliminary note', *Political Studies*, 25:4 (1977), 563–70.

13 Angelo Panebianco, *Political Parties: Organisation and Power* (Cambridge: Cambridge University Press, 1988), pp. 33–67.

14 Vladimir Gel'man and Grigorii Golosov, 'Regional party system formation in Russia: the deviant case of Sverdlovsk Oblast', *Journal of Communist Studies and Transition Politics*, 14:1–2 (1998), 31–53.

15 G. O'Donnell, P. Schmitter, and L. Whitehead (eds.), *Transitions from Authoritarian Rule*; Adam Przeworski, *Democracy and the Market. Political and Economic Reform in Eastern Europe and Latin America* (Cambridge: Cambridge University Press, 1991); Samuel Huntington, *The Third Wave. Democratisation in the Late Twentieth Century* (Norman, OK and London: University of Oklahoma Press, 1991).

16 For an overview, see Vladimir Gel'man, 'Electoral research in Russia', in Hans-Dieter Klingemann, Ekkehard Mochmann and Kenneth Newton (eds.), *Elections in Central and Eastern Europe: The First Wave* (Berlin: Sigma, 2000), pp. 263–91.

17 Vladimir Kolosov and Rostislav Turovskii, 'Elektoral'naya karta sovremennoi Rossii: genezis, struktura i evolyutsiya', *Polis*, 4 (1996); Rostislav Turovskii, 'Politicheskoe rassloenie Rossiiskikh regionov (istoriya i faktory formirovaniya), in Victor Kuvaldin (ed.), *Partiino-Politicheskie Elity I Elektoral'nye Protsessy v Rossii* (Moscow: Tsentr Kompleksnykh Sotsial'nykh Issledovanii i Marketinga, 1996), pp. 37–52.

18 Samuel Eisenstadt, *Revolutions and Transformation of Societies: A Comparative Study of Civilisations* (New York: Free Press, 1978).

19 On 'urban breakthrough' during modernisation, see Samuel Huntington, *Political Order in Changing Societies* (New Haven, CT and London: Yale University Press, 1968), pp. 72–8.

20 Jerry Hough, *The Soviet Prefects: The Local Party Organs in Industrial Decision-Making* (Cambridge, MA: Harvard University Press, 1969); Peter Rutland, *The Politics of Economic Stagnation in the Soviet Union: The Role of Local Party Organs in Economic Management* (Cambridge: Cambridge University Press, 1993).

21 Mikhail Afanas'ev, *Klientelizm i Rossiiskaya Gosudarstvennost'* (Moscow: Moskovskii Obshchestvennyi Nauchnyi Fond, 1997).

22 M. Steven Fish, *Democracy from Scratch: Opposition and Regime in a New Russian*

Revolution (Princeton, NJ: Princeton University Press, 1995); Robert Orttung, *From Leningrad to St. Petersburg: Democratisation in a Russian City* (London: Macmillan, 1995); Michael Urban with Vyacheslav Igrunov and Sergei Mitrokhin, *The Rebirth of Politics in Russia* (Cambridge: Cambridge University Press, 1997).
23 Sidney Tarrow, *Power in Movement. Social Movements, Collective Action and Politics* (Cambridge: Cambridge University Press, 1994).
24 Joel C. Moses, 'Saratov and Volgograd, 1990–92: a tale of two Russian provinces', in Theodore H. Friedgut and Jeffrey W. Hahn (eds.), *Local Power and Post-Soviet Politics* (Armonk, NY and London: M. E. Sharpe, 1994), pp. 102–3.
25 Fish, *Democracy*, pp. 144–5, 153–5.
26 Terry Karl and Philippe Schmitter, 'Models of transition in Latin America, southern and eastern Europe', *International Social Science Journal*, 43:128 (1991), 275.
27 Albert Hirschman, *Exit, Voice and Loyalty: Response to Decline in Firms, Organisations, and States* (Cambridge, MA: Harvard University Press, 1970).
28 For example, on Nizhnii Novgorod Oblast see Vladimir Gel'man, '"Soobshchestvo elit" i predely demokratizatsii. Nizhegorodskaya Oblast', *Polis*, 1 (1999), 79–97.
29 Sergey Ryzhenkov, 'Volgogradskaya Oblast', in Ekaterina Mikhailovskaya (ed.), *Rossiiskii Sbornik* (Moscow: Panorama, 1995), pp. 73–120.
30 Andrew Barnes, 'Elite reaction and reform outcomes in Russian industry and agriculture: the case of Volgograd oblast, 1990–95'. Paper presented at the AAASS National Convention, Seattle, WA, 13–16 November 1997.
31 For a comparative analysis of corporatism in Russia's regions, see Kathryn Stoner-Weiss, *Local Heroes: The Political Economy of Russian Regional Governance* (Princeton, NJ: Princeton University Press, 1997), pp. 172–87.
32 Leonid Smirnyagin (ed.), *Rossiiskie Regiony Nakanune Vyborov–95* (Moscow, Yuridicheskaya Literatura, 1995), p. 123.
33 On patronage in Tatarstan and Sakha, see Mary McAuley, *Russia's Politics of Uncertainty* (Cambridge: Cambridge University Press, 1997), pp. 42–108.
34 Andrei Zudin, 'Rossiya: biznes i politika (strategii vlasti v otnosheniyakh s gruppami davleniya i biznesa)', *Mirovaya Ekonomika i Mezhdunarodnye Otnosheniya*, 5 (1996), 17–25.
35 Vladimir Gel'man, 'Regional power in contemporary Russia: institutions, regime and practice', *Russian Politics and Law*, 37:1 (1999), 5–29.
36 Sergey Ryzhenkov, 'Organy gosudarstvennoi vlasti v reforme mestnogo samoupravleniya', in Kimitaka Matsuzato (ed.), *Tret'e Zveno Gosudarstvennogo Stroitel'stva v Rossii. Podgotovka i Realizatsiya Federal'nogo Zakona ob Obshchikh Printsipakh Mestnogo Samoupravleniya v Rossiiskoi Federatsii* (Sapporo: Slavic Research Centre, 1998), pp. 130–99.
37 Vladimir Gel'man, 'Ucherditel'nye vybory v kontekste Rossiiskoi transformatsii', *Obshchestvennye Nauki i Sovremennost*, 6 (1999), 46–64.
38 Grigorii Golosov, 'Povedenie izbiratelei v Rossii: teoreticheskie perspektivy i rezul'taty regional'nykh vyborov', *Polis*, 4 (1997), 44–56; Steven Solnick, 'Gubernatorial elections in Russia, 1996–1997', *Post-Soviet Affairs*, 14:1 (1998), 48–80.
39 On the distinctions between discontinuous and incremental changes, see Douglas North, *Institutions, Institutional Changes, and Economic Performance* (Cambridge: Cambridge University Press, 1990), p. 89.
40 Barbara Geddes, 'Initiation of new democratic institutions in Eastern Europe and Latin America', in Arend Lijphart and Carlos Waisman (eds.), *Institutional Design in*

New Democracies: Eastern Europe and Latin America (Boulder, CO: Westview, 1996), pp. 18–19.

41 Ryzhenkov, 'Organy gosudarstvennoi vlasti', pp. 182–97.

42 Andrei Rogozhin, 'Mestnoe samoupravlenie v Volgograde: god posle vyborov', in Sergey Ryzhenkov (ed.), *Mestnoe Samoupravlenie v Sovremennoi Rosii: Politika, Praktika, Pravo* (Moscow: Moskovskii Obshchesvennyi Nauchnyi Fond, 1998), pp. 62–76.

43 Tarrow, *Power in Movement*, pp. 89–99.

44 *Vybory v Zakonodatel'nye (Predstavitel'nye) Organy Gosudarstvennoi Vlasti Sub'ektov Rossiiskoi Federatsii, 1995–1997: Elektoral'naya Statistika* (Moscow: Ves' mir, 1998), pp. 256–62. 'Rotation' elections were held in 16 of 32 single member districts of the Oblast Duma; thus, one half of the deputies were re-elected in 1997, and one half in 1998.

45 Rostislav Turovskii (ed.), *Politicheskie Protsessy v Regionakh Rossii* (Moscow: Tsentr Politicheskikh Tekhnologii, 1998), pp. 62–151.

46 Robert Dahl, *Polyarchy: Participation and Opposition* (New Haven, CT: Yale University Press, 1971), pp. 2–6.

47 Samuel Huntington, 'Democracy for the long haul', *Journal of Democracy*, 7:2 (1996), 9–10.

48 Philippe Schmitter, 'Dangers and dilemmas of democracy', *Journal of Democracy*, 5:2 (1994), 60–1.

49 Gel'man and Golosov, *Regional Party System*.

Bashkortostan: a case of regional authoritarianism

Why is it that after 1991 some regions inside the Russian Federation embarked upon a more democratic development than others? To what extent were regional developments dependent on the effects of federal institution building and other constraints created by the central government, and to what extent did local factors determine the outcome of regional attempts at democratisation? Addressing these general questions is the overall objective of this chapter, which concentrates, however, on the example of the Republic of Bashkortostan.

Discussions of the character of regional regimes in Russia have recently tended to emphasise the fact that while numerous deficiencies exist with regard to the quality of liberalism, civil society and institutional constraints, the formal shape of these regimes is still that of a democracy. Free and contested elections to chief executive offices and regional parliaments are cited as the most important feature that distinguishes political regimes in the regions from outright authoritarian rule. Moreover, regional elites can usually even be said formally to play by self-imposed rules defined in regional and federal legislation and governing the interaction of political forces and institutions. Using the terminology introduced by Guillermo O'Donnell,[1] political systems in Russia's regions do meet the minimal criteria of 'vertical accountability', meaning that every once in a while leaders have to face their electorate and win legitimacy for another term in office. Representative democracy, however, needs not only vertical, but also horizontal accountability. The latter refers to 'a network of relatively autonomous powers (i.e. other institutions) that can call into question, and eventually punish, improper ways of discharging the responsibilities of a given official.'[2] This, it has been argued, is exactly what is missing in Russia's regional regimes, which should therefore be regarded as cases of 'delegative democracy' rather than representative, or institutionalised, democracy.[3] But, as Jeffrey Hahn has pointed out in Chapter 6 in this book, 'if the species we are seeing is indeed delegative democracy, the genus is still democratic'.[4]

This author agrees with the general argument that, during the 1990s, Russia's regions have made considerable progress towards the introduction of key elements of democracy. However, such a 'benevolent' angle of analysis – that prefers to view the glass as half-full rather than half-empty – should not lead us to ignore the considerable differences that exist between different regional regimes and the fact that certain regions clearly stand out from the 'crowd'. This chapter demonstrates that the concept of delegative democracy does not capture the reality of all of Russia's regions. In particular, I argue that the Republic of Bashkortostan represents the example of a region that displays clearly authoritarian properties. An analysis of the process of institution building in Bashkortostan reveals how seemingly democratic institutions could be abused by local elites to establish a clearly non-democratic political regime on their territory.

Exploring the factors that help to explain such an untypical outcome, I argue that the institution of 'autonomy', inherited from the ethno-federal structure of the Soviet system, combined with a relatively modern and competitive industrial structure, provided republican elites with an unusually rich pool of political resources upon which they could rely. These resources enabled them largely to 'opt out' of Russia's general tendency towards greater local democracy and set up an authoritarian regime within a more democratic environment.

The chapter is structured in four parts. First, it analyses the process of political institution building in Bashkortostan in the 1990s. This part includes an overview of the formal structure of political institutions in the republic as it had developed by the beginning of 2000. The second part widens the perspective and distinguishes five structural elements of the Bashkir regime that are referred to as informal – in the sense that they do not derive from an written constitution – but are nonetheless fundamental for the character of the political institutions. The third part addresses the issue of autonomy and analyses how, in the case of Bashkortostan, the Soviet concept of autonomy has been translated into post-Soviet politics and political bargaining. Autonomy, it is argued, provided republican elites with a much broader scope of independent decision-making power than their counterparts in average Russian regions. The conclusions, finally, summarises why Bashkortostan should not be considered a case of delegative democracy and argues that autonomy, together with favourable economic preconditions, is the key to explaining the republic's divergent path.

The process of political institution building in Bashkortostan

The Republic of Bashkortostan is one of the most highly populated regions of the Russian Federation. With slightly more than four million people living in the region, Bashkortostan ranks first among Russia's twenty-one republics, overtaking even neighbouring Tatarstan, and seventh among all Russian regions. According to the 1989 Soviet census, ethnic Bashkirs account for 22 per cent of the population and constitute only the third largest ethnic group in the republic, while Russians and Tatars have a share of 39 per cent and 28 per cent, respectively. In the republic's capital, Ufa, more than half of the population is ethnic Russian. Mainly due to its oil resources and a powerful oil-processing industry,

Bashkortostan has for many years been among the small group of net contributors to the federal system of regional redistribution.

The process of political institution building in post-Soviet Bashkortostan can roughly be broken down into three periods:

1 a period of political change and struggle for power (from 1990 to late 1993);
2 a period of 'codification', or explicit institutionalisation (from late 1993 to late 1994);
3 since then, Bashkortostan has been in a third period of 'consolidated power', even though this period has included elements of additional institutionalisation.

Political change and the struggle for power

In Bashkortostan, the Communist Party organs were de facto deprived of power already in the spring of 1990, when the republic was still called the Bashkir Autonomous Soviet Socialist Republic. In February, shortly before the elections to the Soviets of all levels, the CPSU (Communist Party of the Soviet Union) oblast committee had voted its First Secretary out of office, since he was considered an old apparatchik unable to lead the party into the new era of *democratizatsiia* (democratisation). Moreover, he had lost the support of the influential republican enterprise directors who wanted greater economic independence from the Moscow ministerial bureaucracy and blamed the local party organs for not pushing their case.[5] For a couple of months, the party's leadership was paralysed. It entered the electoral contest without a new, strong leadership and, as a consequence, had to stand by and watch as the newly elected republican Supreme Soviet moved quickly to replace the party organs as the true centre of power in Bashkiria.

This process was driven by the new chairman of the Supreme Soviet, Murtaza Rakhimov. Rakhimov, in his mid-fifties by that time, had been the director of the Ufa oil-processing factory and spent his whole career in the oil sector.[6] When after the elections a new chairman of the Supreme Soviet was needed, Rakhimov was the ideal choice. For one thing, his candidacy was supported by the powerful directors of the local oil industry who were eager to increase their control over the state enterprises they managed.[7] The unofficial privatisation of state property had already begun in 1988 but threatened to bypass the republic as an extremely high percentage of its industry was still directly controlled by Moscow-based ministries rather than the local Bashkir authorities.[8] By placing one of their own people at the top of the republic, the directors could hope to reverse this situation to their own favour. As a top level manager, Rakhimov was of course also a party member, which helped him to secure votes among the high proportion of CPSU members who had been elected to the republican Supreme Soviet. At the same time he was a newcomer to politics, promising a new political style and, on top of it all, an ethnic Bashkir, which made him appeal to Bashkir nationalists who had only just begun to organise themselves.

Rakhimov espoused the idea of 'economic independence' (*ekonomicheskaia samostoiatel'nost'*) from Moscow and pursued a policy of 'sovereignisation'. His aim was not secession, but control; in other words: not symbolic power, but real power. Nonetheless, symbols played an important role, and Bashkiria joined the 'parade of sovereignty' on 11 October 1990 with its own 'Declaration of Sovereignty'. However, the text referred to Bashkortostan (which now became the official name of the republic) as a member of both the USSR and a 'renewed' Russian Federation, making it clear that secession was not on the agenda. Instead, much more important for local elites was the claim of the republic on its natural and economic resources as the 'exclusive property' of the 'multinational' people of Bashkortostan, as opposed to the Russian Federation.[9]

Rakhimov's main rival at that time was republican Prime Minister Marat Mirgaziamov. Mirgaziamov had been in office since 1986 and was much less inclined towards severing ties with Moscow than Rakhimov was, and rivalry between the two remained one of the top issues on the political agenda until 1992.

During the coup attempt in August 1991, the Bashkir leadership as a whole acted very cautiously, not fully implementing orders issued by the plotters' 'emergency committee', but at the same time not at all supporting President Boris Yeltsin's outright resistance. After the coup had failed both the Presidium of the Supreme Soviet of Bashkortostan and the government were harshly criticised for what was perceived to have been a tacit approval of the coup. The Ufa City Soviet, dominated by moderate reformist forces, was particularly dissatisfied with the republican authorities' performance and issued a vote of no confidence in the Bashkir leadership.[10] The republican Supreme Soviet, however, justified the behaviour of its Presidium and the government by pointing out that they had refrained from violating constitutional rights and introducing a state of emergency. Rather, a Supreme Soviet statement adopted on 23 August said that their actions had contributed to preserving civic peace and stability in the republic.[11]

While the declaration was enough to resist opposition from within the republic, external pressure grew when the Russian Supreme Soviet – on 11 October 1991, just exactly one year after the Bashkir declaration of sovereignty – took the decision to reintegrate the heads of the executive of the republics into a 'single system of executive power in the RSFSR [Russian Soviet Federative Socialist Republic]'.[12] Although the consequences of the resolution remained unclear, nervousness in Ufa increased and the Bashkir leadership came to the conclusion that only a strong republican chief executive – along the model of the presidency in Tatarstan – would insulate the republic from interference from Moscow. Thus, the Bashkir Supreme Soviet decided to hold elections to the office of a republican president quickly in order to win new legitimacy for the Bashkir leadership.[13]

It turned out, however, that the federal government was much keener on achieving agreements with regional leaders than on redrawing the map of Russia's emerging asymmetrical federalism. For the Yeltsin–Gaidar team, the consequences of a major centre–periphery conflict with a strong ethnic component were far too unpredictable to appear as a viable option. Therefore, pressure towards recentralisation passed the republics.

Meanwhile, Bashkir Supreme Soviet leader Rakhimov came to realise that his prospects for victory in the presidential elections scheduled for December were far from secure. Both republican Prime Minister Mirgaziamov and a successful banker by the name of Rafis Kadyrov were potential opponents to be reckoned with, and the outcome was largely considered open. At that point, Rakhimov decided that the best thing to do was not to have elections at all. With the USSR just about being buried and with major changes lying ahead, the Bashkir Supreme Soviet chairman managed to persuade a majority of deputies that this was not a good time for elections, since the republican authorities should be capable of acting rather than being paralysed by an electoral contest. The elections were cancelled, all changes previously made to the constitutional structure were nullified, and a general moratorium was declared on elections throughout the republic.[14]

During the following year, tensions between Rakhimov and Mirgaziamov grew constantly, and Bashkortostan found itself in a situation of *dvoevlastie* (dual power). In particular, both contenders tried hard to assert control over the heads of local administrations. Finally, in November 1992, Rakhimov succeeded in staging an intrigue inside the government against the Prime Minister. Several cabinet ministers were encouraged to leave the government as a sign of protest against Mirgaziamov. When the Supreme Soviet failed to deliver a vote of confidence in the Prime Minister, Supreme Soviet chairman Rakhimov announced that this meant Mirgaziamov's dismissal. Although such an interpretation of the Bashkir constitution was at least disputable, Mirgaziamov realised that he had lost the struggle for power and gave up. Rakhimov had managed to get rid of his main rival.

In Moscow, in October 1993, *dvoevlastie* between the legislature (Russian Supreme Soviet) and the executive (President Yeltsin) resulted in the legislature's violent defeat. In that respect, the outcome of the rivalry at the top of the Bashkir leadership one year earlier seemed to follow a different pattern. Here, the head of the legislature emerged victorious. However, it is noteworthy that in both cases the winner was the person who could claim a higher degree of legitimacy than his competitor. While the Russian Supreme Soviet's election dated back to 1990, Yeltsin had been elected in a direct vote in 1991. And while Prime Minister Mirgaziamov had no popular vote to refer to, Rakhimov's position was based on the Bashkir Supreme Soviet's election in 1990.

It seems fair to conclude that – beside other factors – democratic legitimacy was one important resource of power which competing actors could make use of. Therefore, the next logical step in Rakhimov's attempt at consolidating his power was the adoption of a new, post-Soviet constitution for Bashkortostan, promising additional legitimacy for the republican leadership. Consequently, a Supreme Soviet committee, charged with drafting a new basic law and chaired by Rakhimov himself, intensified its work in 1993. However, a number of issues relating to the distribution of powers between state authorities remained disputed among deputies and prevented them from reaching a swift agreement. Throughout most of 1993, for example, the question of whether Bashkortostan should become a presidential republic or adopt a rather soviet-style parliamentary system of government remained undecided. Publicly, Rakhimov announced repeatedly that he did not like the institution of a presidency at all and that Bashkortostan did not need it. The events in Moscow in September–October 1993, however, made him change his attitude again.

After President Yeltsin had secured victory in the violent conflict with the Russian Supreme Soviet, he seized the initiative to finally destroy the system of soviets at all levels. Rumours were spread that the Russian president threatened to appoint powerful representatives to those republics that were still governed by the presidium of a soviet.[15] Very much like two years earlier, Moscow politics posed a threat to the existing constellation of power in Bashkortostan, and again the institution of a strong presidency seemed best fit to protect the interests of the republican elite. In November 1993 the laws nullified in 1991 were reinstated and elections were called for 12 December, together with the Russian parliamentary elections and the referendum on the federal constitution.[16] This time, other than in 1991, Rakhimov could be secure of his victory. First, he now enjoyed the longstanding advantage of quasi-incumbency as the head of republic, including control over local administrations and most of the local media. Second, the period of time left for the election campaign was extremely short, depriving any opponent of a fair chance.

Under these circumstances, the adoption of a new republican constitution that took full account of the new form of government, which was introduced, with the election of a president, was postponed until after the election. In addition, unlike the adoption of the new Russian constitution, approval of the new basic law for Bashkortostan was not to become an exercise of the people but of the old Soviet. For Rakhimov, the scenario that emerged was like a double-checked reinsurance policy. If he was elected, he could use the interim period before his inauguration to chair the Supreme Soviet's session that would adopt the new constitution, and then enter office under new, tailor-made conditions. In the unlikely event that he was not elected, he could keep his position as the chairman of the Supreme Soviet and of the constitutional committee and use it to amend the draft constitution in a way that served the interests of the soviet rather than the president.

In fact, Rakhimov was elected with almost a two-thirds majority (64.0 per cent) in the first round, leaving his only opponent, banker Rafis Kadyrov, a mere 28.5 per cent. The constitution was adopted on 24 December 1993. One day later, Rakhimov was sworn in as the new president under a new constitution.

'Codification'

The new constitution for the Republic of Bashkortostan was in many respects very similar to its Russian counterpart.[17] At first glance – with its many references to democracy, human rights, civil rights, protection of minorities, etc. – the document seemed to open the way for a democratic development. However, when it came to power, its organisation and distribution, the Bashkir constitution contained a number of interesting peculiarities. Its most important aspects include, first, the position of the president, second, the role and composition of parliament and, third, local self-government.

The position of the president
Although the Bashkir presidency was largely modelled on the presidency of the Russian Federation, there were a few significant differences. Unlike the Russian president, the head of Bashkortostan is elected for a five-year term. He may not serve more than two consecutive terms, but there is no limit to the absolute number of terms the same person may serve. The Bashkir president needs parliamentary approval not only for the appointment of a new prime minister, but also for his (or her) dismissal. Under no circumstances is he allowed to dissolve parliament. In fact, he is explicitly prohibited from doing so. So far, the Bashkir presidency looks weaker than the Russian one. This disadvantage, however, is made up for when the president is granted the right to appoint and dismiss heads of local government at will. In addition, he is entitled to dismiss members of the executive branch if they violate laws, while procedures regulating such an offence are not defined. Finally, the constitution established language, residency and age requirements for presidential candidates that – if applied to the reality of Bashkortostan – excluded roughly three quarters of all eligible voters in the republic from the office.

The parliament
The Bashkir legislature, the 'State Assembly', was designed as a two chamber parliament. Both houses, the 'Legislative Chamber' and the 'Chamber of Representatives', are elected for four-year terms. Compared to the Russian Federal Assembly, the main distinguishing feature of the State Assembly is its right to issue a binding vote of no confidence in the government as a result of which the president has to dismiss the government. A right to dissolve the parliament, as mentioned above, does not exist. Strangely enough, however, the constitution remained silent about how the members of the two chambers were to be elected and how their functions would differ from each other. In the absence of constitutional norms, these questions were left for normal legislation. Subsequent events make it hard to believe that this had been done without a good deal of political calculation on the part of the ruling elite around Murtaza Rakhimov.

Local self-government
Local self-government was in principle guaranteed by the Bashkir constitution. Nevertheless, the heads of local government were not to be elected by the people but selected by the president. Moreover, besides local 'self-government', the

constitution established 'local state government' at the city and raion (region) level, but failed to explicate the difference between the two. Again, details were left for normal legislation, suggesting that interesting things were still to come.

As a result, the constitution itself provided for a very strong presidency, but also for a potentially strong and independent legislature. This, however, depended on the results of legislation that was to be hammered out during 1994 under the threat of a presidential veto. And the result was stunning: Local self-government, it turned out, was to be restricted to the level of villages and settlements below cities and raions.[18] If only for lack of financial resources, it was obvious that this level would never be able to play an important role in checking republican power from below. Local state government at the level of cities and raions, by contrast, was fully subordinate to the republican executive. The only important right left to the soviets at that level was to approve of budgets drafted by the heads of administrations.

Even more interesting was the design of the two-chamber parliament, laid down in two consecutive laws in March and October 1994, respectively.[19] According to these documents, the Legislative Chamber was to consist of forty professional deputies elected on the basis of constituencies of roughly equal size of population. A Chamber of Representatives, by contrast, was to be elected as a non-professional body from the republic's seventy-seven administrative units with two representatives from each of them and no restriction as to their main profession. The first obvious result was an extreme over-representation of the rural population in the upper chamber. Thirty-seven per cent of voters living in the three biggest cities of the republic were represented by only eighteen out of 154 representatives (or 11.7 per cent). In addition, candidates were required to collect signatures of 5 per cent of eligible voters in their respective constituency, which was five times more than in the 1993 State Duma elections. This was also in violation of federal legislation, which set a maximum limit of 2 per cent.[20] The higher the barrier, however, the greater the chances of already well known figures to be elected. In sum, the electoral system was biased in favour of a conservative electorate and of 'official' candidates, i.e. the heads of local administrations.

Consolidated power

The new parliament was elected in March 1995. The results confirmed the most serious concerns that the legislation had provoked. All heads of local administrations ran for the Chamber of Representatives and won their seats. Almost all members of the government, including the Prime Minister, had also been given promising constituencies and won them (twenty-six seats). Altogether, at least three quarters of the members of the Chamber of Representatives held offices that made them directly dependent on the President, not to count representatives running de facto state-controlled businesses and enterprises.

In the Legislative Chamber, independent candidates accounted for a higher proportion, with only one third having been professionally affiliated to the state executive. Unsurprisingly, however, there was nothing like a political structure inside this small chamber.

Even such a composition, however, was not sufficient for Rakhimov to be sure of his power. In January 1996 he managed to have a bill approved by parliament that finally did away with all pretence of democratic checks and balances: Separate voting of the two chambers as the normal procedure was replaced by the 'possibility' of joint voting whenever it seemed appropriate. At joint sessions, however, the president's quasi-institutionalised majority in the Chamber of Representatives could easily neutralise any potential opposition from the ranks of the much smaller Legislative Chamber. Basically now, the executive was checked by itself.

In the following years, President Rakhimov needed little more than occasional legislative amendments to maintain control over all branches and levels of power in the republic. In 1998, when presidential elections were due, the existing legislation was instrumental in disqualifying four serious oppositional candidates from the electoral race. Neither State Duma deputies Aleksandr Arinin (Our Home is Russia) and Valentin Nikitin (Communist Party) nor veterans Marat Mirgaziamov and Rafis Kadyrov succeeded in having their names registered on the ballot. Even an urgent Russian Supreme Court ruling that demanded registration for Arinin and Mirgaziamov was not implemented. Instead, republican forestry minister Rif Kazakkulov played the formal role of the necessary 'challenger' to the incumbent, barely hiding the preference he himself gave to Rakhimov. In the end, on 14 June 1998, Rakhimov won a 70.2 per cent vote, with 9.0 per cent of the votes cast for his 'contender' Kazakkulov and 17.1 per cent 'against all'. Five weeks later, another Russian Supreme Court ruling concluded that the exclusion of Arinin and Mirgaziamov from the ballot had been illegal. The Bashkir authorities answered that Russian courts had no jurisdiction over their republic. Meanwhile, the federal government accepted Rakhimov's re-election and sent its official representatives to the inauguration of the president of Bashkortostan.[21]

On 14 March 1999, the people of Bashkortostan re-elected the republican State Assembly. Due to the merger of several administrative districts, the number of seats in the Chamber of Representatives had been reduced to 144. By way of 'compensation', the Legislative Chamber had also been reduced by ten seats and comprised merely thirty deputies. Thus, the relative weight of the potentially less controllable chamber was even further marginalised. The structure of the new parliament was almost identical to its predecessor. Again, all heads of local administrations and many cabinet ministers as well as other high-ranking officials had been elected, and voting in the State Assembly remained completely dominated by state officials subordinate to the president.[22]

Although the above account described important features of the formal architecture of the Bashkir regime, there are other elements of a more informal type that are no less important for keeping the 'building' together and preventing it from breaking apart. Five such elements are identified as:

The structure of the new Bashkir elite

Rakhimov has promoted a striking over-representation of ethnic Bashkirs in political and administrative offices throughout the republic. This over-representation does not at all, for example, conform with higher levels of education or professional training. Rather the opposite is true. Consequently, even if one does not assume primitive mechanisms of ethnic affiliation at work, many members of the new Bashkir elite know that they owe their jobs to the president and that their future is tied to him personally. At the same time, dependence and loyalty go far beyond what one would normally expect: In early 1996, for example, Rakhimov dismissed eight heads of local administrations whose work had failed to satisfy him for various reasons. As things were, each of them could still have remained a member of the Chamber of Representatives to which he had been elected in 1995. Not so in Bashkortostan: In a prompt reaction to their dismissal, all eight 'voluntarily' gave up their seats in parliament.[23]

State control over the republic's economy

Another important element of President Rakhimov's power is his control over large parts of the republican economy. While Russia in general moved towards a substantial increase in private economic activities, authorities in Bashkortostan established more or less direct state control over vital parts of the economy. Forcing enterprises with tax arrears to sell additional shares at nominal value to the republic, Rakhimov raised the government's share in the oil-processing sector from 51 per cent to 90 per cent in 1996. Today, almost the whole oil sector (crude oil production and processing) is controlled by the government and run by people close to Rakhimov. Oil and petrochemical exports from the state holding company Bashneftekhim are overseen by Rakhimov's son, Ural. Similarly, the banking sector is completely dominated by a republican bank (Bashkreditbank) that gained its position not on the market but through a host of privileges granted by republican authorities. Since the republic refused to dissolve kolkhozy and sovkhozy at the beginning of the 1990s, the agrarian sector, too, lacks private initiative and depends largely on budgetary funds.[24]

Control over the security organs

Much more than in most other regions of Russia, the security organs are subordinate to republican rather than federal orders. While officially the federal centre is still in charge, Moscow condoned the fact that Rakhimov appointed the republican prosecutor, helped the Bashkir president to remove an uncooperative head of the republican state security organ and has not challenged his claim to appoint judges himself. While some of these features that are in contradiction to the federal constitution may be subject to change in the future, they have helped Rakhimov a great deal in establishing control over the republic.[25]

State control over ideology and information

Over the years, President Rakhimov has placed himself at the centre of an ideology that blends elements of Bashkir nationalism with a more conciliatory tone in relations with Moscow and a state-centred economic policy with elements of the market. At the same time, he usually denounces all his critics as extremists and shows no respect for political opposition. In addition, as in most regions of Russia, the media in Bashkortostan is neither independent nor free to criticise the republican leadership. There is widespread agreement, however, that the situation in Bashkortostan is amongst the most pitiful of all. Election campaigns at all levels since 1993 have repeatedly demonstrated that the Bashkir leadership does everything to prevent oppositional opinions from being voiced freely and effectively. Journalists have been threatened, beaten up or arrested, newspapers and radio stations have been shut down, central television news programmes have been taken off the air.[26] In 1999 a project commissioned by the Russian Union of Journalists assessing the level of freedom of the press in Russia's regions ranked Bashkortostan dead last.[27]

Rigged elections

One of the most crucial features of the political regime of Bashkortostan, finally, is the fact that there are no free and fair elections in the republic. Whatever official OSCE election observation missions have concluded about Russian elections in general, local observers in Ufa were usually stunned by the level of state interference in the process, the absence of a free press, the arbitrariness of electoral commissions' rulings with regard to oppositional candidates, and many similar phenomena.[28] If this applied to State Duma and Russian presidential elections, the situation with republican elections is even worse, although much less transparent. The 1998 presidential elections were only the most prominent among a long series of examples. Although republican electoral legislation already comes close to an institutional guarantee against a change-over of power, the ruling elite of Bashkortostan has also resorted to outright manipulations and falsifications in the electoral process. In the 1995 State Assembly elections, for example, one of the liberal candidates was able to prove fraud in favour of a competing republican deputy health minister in one of the Legislative Chamber constituencies in Ufa. More recently, however, electoral commissions and courts in the republic have usually applied double standards and turned a blind eye to violations by 'official' candidates, while deregistering their contenders on minor or even very doubtful grounds.

What constitutes Bashkortostan's autonomy?

During Soviet times, republics inside the Russian Federation were called 'autonomous'. Under the system of 'democratic centralism', however, autonomy amounted to little more than some particular emphasis on cultural affairs of the titular ethnic group of a given republic. Only after 1989, when the USSR was falling apart and new options for republican elites became viable, did the formally autonomous entities began to claim self-determination not only in a cultural, but also in a political and an economic dimension. To distinguish their effort from the past, they usually replaced the term 'autonomy' with 'sovereignty'. Yet in fact it was not independent statehood, but political and economic autonomy that elites in most of these republics were interested in.

In the case of Bashkortostan, the republican elite's quest for 'sovereignty' meant federal non-interference in internal (political) affairs and economic self-determination. Between 1989–90 and 1994 the foundation was laid for the republic's status as an autonomous entity inside the Russian Federation with very special rights. This period included the adoption of a number of important documents both at the level of the republic and between Ufa and Moscow. After 1994, relations between Bashkortostan and the federal government entered a period of consolidation and cooperation on the basis of what had been agreed upon before. Only since Vladimir Putin took over power in the Kremlin in May 2000 has a partial revision of Bashkortostan's special rights seemed to be on the agenda.

The first important document concerning Bashkortostan's relations with the federal centre was the republic's Declaration of Sovereignty adopted by its Supreme Soviet on 11 October 1990.[29] The document announced 'state sovereignty of Bashkortostan on its whole territory in the existing borders'. Unlike neighbouring Tatarstan, however, Bashkortostan was acknowledged to be a member of both the USSR and a 'renewed' Russian Federation. On the whole, the declaration combined three rather different components, each of which made it appeal to a different set of interest groups inside the republic. First, 'sovereignty' with a focus on economic self-determination was in the interest of enterprise directors; second, the ethnic component of self-determination of the Bashkir nation referred to the demands of the Bashkir national movement; third, references to human rights, the rule of law, democracy and the division of power made the declaration acceptable among urban activists of democratisation.

In March 1992, Bashkortostan signed the Federation Treaty between Moscow and the republics only after the federal government had agreed to accept an additional 'attachment' by the Bashkir side that laid down the terms under which the republic was prepared to join the treaty.[30] This document repeated Bashkortostan's claim over control of the economic resources of the republic, tax sovereignty and judicial independence from Moscow. For the Bashkir authorities it served as a basis for a boycott of the federal tax system that lasted until 1994.

The Russian and the Bashkir constitution of December 1993 revealed differing approaches to the problem of federal relations in Russia, although both documents were not irreconcilable. The Russian constitution – which failed to achieve the support of a majority in Bashkortostan during the referendum – displayed the model of a moderately asymmetric constitutional federalism with contractual elements. The Bashkir constitution, by contrast, pursued the idea of a voluntary and theoretically reversible integration based on contracts and recognising the constituent parts' statehood. In its more concrete provisions, however, the text of the Bashkir constitution referred only to what had already been agreed upon between Moscow and Ufa. Therefore, the two constitutions of

December 1993 did not change the existing relationship between republic and federation but rather resembled a ratification of the status quo.

In August 1994, finally, the two sides concluded a bilateral power-sharing treaty.[31] The treaty was preceded by ten inter-governmental agreements signed in May 1994 on issues such as economic cooperation, agro-industry, international (economic) relations, state property, fuel and energy, customs, military-industrial complex and others. The document, signed on 3 August by the 'organs of state power' of the Russian Federation and the Republic Bashkortostan, was basically a compromise agreement repeating what had already been agreed upon in previous years. Unsolved problems, like the true meaning and scope of words like sovereignty, statehood or foreign relations, had been concealed behind a vague rhetoric that allowed both sides to interpret the agreement as a confirmation of their respective position. The document's main importance was the fact that both sides agreed to seek cooperation rather than confrontation in the future. It was not by coincidence, therefore, that Bashkortostan resumed transferring federal taxes only after the treaty had been signed.

The 1994 power-sharing treaty paved the way for a new period in the relations between Moscow and Ufa that was essentially characterised by the willingness on both sides to cooperate. In order to improve his personal ties with the federal authorities, President Rakhimov allied himself with the pro-government bloc Our Home is Russia (NDR) and joined the Political Council of the organisation that was led by Russian Prime Minister Viktor Chernomyrdin. When Chernomyrdin was dismissed in 1998, Rakhimov was among the initiators of the All Russia (*Vsya Rossia*) movement and looked like a logical backer of the Fatherland – All Russia (OVR) electoral bloc at the 1999 Duma elections. However, as the Kremlin-backed Yedinstvo (Unity) movement came to appear more and more as the likely winner of the elections, Rakhimov toned down his campaign for OVR, and only hours after the vote, together with Tatarstan president Mintimer Shaimiev, he began switching allegiances and deserted OVR, only to become a strong supporter of Vladimir Putin in the March 2000 presidential elections.

The concessions Moscow made in its relations with Bashkortostan were much more than with most other regions. They were clearly linked to the fact that politically motivated social unrest in one of the largest republics of the country was the last thing the federal government needed. Bashkortostan's ethnic composition as well as its export-oriented oil and petrochemical industry were two important factors that prevented Moscow from choosing a high-risk strategy in its dealings with the republic. To the Yeltsin administration, a strategy of mutual give and take seemed more rational. While the federal government granted special rights to Ufa (or turned a blind eye to some developments), the Bashkir leadership promised social stability, political predictability and electoral support in exchange. Local democracy and civil rights, by contrast, were a lesser priority for Moscow, not worth risking a serious conflict with the leadership of a densely populated region that was a net donor to the federal system of regional redistribution.

Since Putin's election in March 2000, however, federal relations in general have entered a new stage. The new president has repeatedly insisted that all subjects of the Russian Federation implement federal legislation in full and that diverging regional laws are brought in line with federal norms. With Putin's 13 May decision to appoint seven presidential representatives as heads of federal districts, Bashkortostan has for the first time since 1990 been fully incorporated in the system of federal executive power. For the time being, President Rakhimov, together with his Tatarstan counterpart Mintimer Shaimiev, seems to be hoping for compromise solutions once negotiations reach the level of concrete bargaining. Nonetheless, he may soon find himself in a situation where he will have to decide between loyalty and confrontation.

Conclusions

The process of political institution building and the character of the political regime in the Republic of Bashkortostan reveal clearly authoritarian properties. Behind a democratic facade, the republican elite under President Rakhimov has systematically deprived opposing political forces of any fair chance to compete for power. Formal and informal elements of the regime have contributed to the emergence of a system that is characterised by the absence of both horizontal and vertical accountability. In that respect, Bashkortostan differs from most other regional regimes in Russia. If we apply the definition given by O'Donnell, the republic does not qualify for the label 'delegative democracy'.

The key to explaining Bashkortostan's diverging path – that has been shared by only a few other regional regimes in Russia – is autonomy. An almost meaningless institution of formal ethno-federalism in Soviet times, autonomy was used by local elites after 1990 as an instrument to pursue their own interests, which lay much more in all-encompassing control than in democracy and pluralism. At the same time, Bashkortostan's economic potential was a necessary precondition for such a path to be successfully pursued in a republic of such considerable size.

The lesson to be learnt from the Bashkir case is that where skilful regional elites were able to make use of certain structural conditions inherited from the Soviet past, the institutionalisation of local democracy reached its limits. While democratisation at the regional and municipal levels remained a general objective throughout the Yeltsin presidency, efficient regional government and elite consensus between Moscow and the regions were higher priorities for Russia's ruling elite. Where federal resistance to regional deviations from democratic standards threatened to be politically costly for the centre, Moscow preferred tacit approval to open conflict as long as its regional counterparts were able and willing to deliver general political stability and electoral support in exchange.

Notes

1 G. O'Donnell, 'Delegative democracy', *Journal of Democracy*, 5:1 (1994), 55–68.
2 *Ibid.*, 61.
3 V. Ya. Gel'man, 'Regional'nye rezhimy: zavershenie transformatsii?', *Svobodnaya mysl'*, 9 (1996), 13–33; A. Tsygankov, 'Manifestations of delegative democracy in Russian local politics: what does it mean for the future of Russia?' *Communist and Post-Communist Studies*, 31:4 (1998), 329–44; see also Chapter 6 in this book.
4 See Chapter 6 of this book, p. 114.
5 'Laboratoriya strategicheskikh issledovanii Tsentra sotsial'nogo vzaimodeistvitiya "Kontakt plus"', M. *Rakhimov: Ego strategiya sozdaniya suverennogo Bashkortostana* (Ufa: mimeo, 1993).
6 *Kto est' kto v Respublike Bashkortostan. Vypusk 1. Po sostoyaniyu na 1 avgusta 1995g.* (Ufa: Izvestya Bashkortostana, 1995), p. 5.
7 I. Rabinovich and S. Fufaev, *Khozyain (shtrikhi k politicheskomu portretu Murtazy Rakhimova)*, (Moskow: Moskovskii Tsentr Karnegi, mimeo, 1997).
8 The 1988 USSR law on the cooperatives opened the door for a 'wild' privatisation of state assets that was based mainly on tacit agreements between enterprise managements and their respective counterparts in the state bureaucracy. See O. Kryshtanovskaya and S. White, 'From Soviet *nomenklatura* to Russian elite', *Europe–Asia Studies*, 48:5 (1996), 711–33.
9 'Deklaratsiya o gosudarstvennom suverenitete Bashkirskoi Sovetskoi Sotsialisticheskoi Respubliki, 11 Oktyabrya 1990 goda', in *Bashkortostan: Vybor Puti: Interv'yu, Vystupleniya, Stenogrammy, Dokumenty* (Ufa: Kitap, 1995), pp. 108–10.
10 *Sovetskaya Bashkiriya* (21 August 1991) and (24 August 1991).
11 'O polozhenii v respublike i vypolnenii postanovleniya Prezidyuma Verkhovnogo Soveta RSFSR ot 23 avgusta, 1991 goda "O deyatel'nosti Sovetov narodnykh deputatov RSFSR vo vremya gosudarstvennogo perevorota"' (Postanovlenie Verkhovnogo Soveta Bashkirskoi SSR, 23 August 1991), in *Zakony Respubliki Bashkortostan: vypusk II* (Ufa: 1992), p. 169 (quoted from www.bashinform.ru/win, 5 April 1998).
12 'O glavakh ispolnitel'noi vlasti respublik v sostave RSFSR' (Postanovlenie Verkhovnogo Soveta RSFSR, 1741-1, 11 October 1991), in *Rossiiskaja gazeta* (19 October 1991), p. 1.
13 'Ob uchrezhdenii posta Prezidenta Bashkirskoi SSR' (Zakon Bashkirskoi SSR, 15 October 1991), in *Zakony Respubliki Bashkortostan: vypusk II*, p. 169 (quoted from www.bashinform.ru/win, 5 April 1998).
14 Rabinovich/Fufaev, *Khozyain*; *IGPI Monitoring Bashkortostan*, November 1993.
15 *Segodnya* (14 October 1993), quoted in *Current Digest of the Post-Soviet Press*, 45:41 (1993).
16 *IGPI Monitoring Bashkortostan*, November 1993.
17 *Konstitutsiya Respubliki Bashkortostan. Prinyata Verkhovnym Sovetom Respubliki Bashkortostan 24 dekabrya 1993 goda* (Ufa: 1995).
18 *Zakon Respubliki Bashkortostan o mestnom gosudarstvennom upravlenii v Respublike Bashkortostan. Prinyat Verkhovnym Sovetom Respubliki Bashkortostan 12 oktyabrya 1994 goda; Zakon Respubliki Bashkortostan o mestnom samoupravlenii v Respublike Bashkortostan. Prinyat Verkhovnym Sovetom Respubliki Bashkortostan 20 dekabrya 1994 goda* (Ufa:1995).

19 Zakon Respubliki Bashkortostan o Gosudarstvennom Sobranii Respubliki Bashkortostan. Prinyat Verkhovnym Sovetom Respubliki Bashkortostan 2 marta 1994 goda (Ufa: 1994); Zakon Respubliki Bashkortostan o vyborakh deputatov Gosudarstvennogo Sobraniya Respubliki Bashkortostan. Prinyat Verkhovnym Sovetom Respubliki Bashkortostan, 13 oktyabrya 1994 goda (Ufa: 1994).

20 Federal'nyi zakon ob osnovnykh garantiiakh izbiratel'nykh prav grazhdan Rossiiskoi Federatsii. Ofitsial'noe izdanie (Moscow: 1995).

21 For details of this highly controversial campaign, see D. Lussier, 'Bashkortostan's president re-elected in campaign plagued by violations', East–West Institute, *Russian Regional Report (Internet Edition)*, 3:25 (1998) (hereafter, EWI, *Russian Regional Report*); T. Lankina, 'Showcase of manipulated democracy: elections without choice in Bashkortostan', *Transitions*, 8 (1998), 62–4; *Kommersant Daily* (7 May 1998) p. 5; *Russkii telegraf* (25 July 1998), p. 2.

22 *Kommersant* (16 March 1999), p. 3; EWI, *Russian Regional Report*, 18 March 1999.

23 R. R. Gallyamov, 'Politicheskie elity rossiiskikh respublik: osobennosti transformatsii v postsovetskii period', *Polis* 2 (1998), 108–15; I. Rotar, 'Development, Bashkir-Style: Ufa's Internal Policy Benefits The Kremlin', *Prism. A Bi-Weekly On The Post-Soviet States (Internet edition)*, 4:2, part 3 (1998).

24 A. Khabibullin, 'Bashkirskaya ekonomika: chto za vitrinoi regional seenogo kapitalizma. Respublika porazhena tyazhelym krizisom', *Nezavisimaya gazeta* (5 March 1998), p. 4; R. Nazarov, 'Monopoliya na kapitalizm v odnom otdel seeno vzyatom regione: Rukovodstvu Bashkirii udalos see skontsentrirovat see osnovnye finansovye resursy respubliki v kontroliruemom vlastyami Bashkreditbanke', *Nezavisimaya gazeta* (18 November 1997), pp. 1,4; *Monitoring Bashkortostan*, January 1996; *IEWS Russian Regional Report*, 8 May 1997.

25 *Monitoring Bashkortostan*, May 1995, June 1996, December 1996, January 1997, February 1997.

26 A. Paretskaya, 'Bashkortostan authorities assault the independent press', *OMRI Analytical Brief*, 428, 1 November 1996; *Novoe vremia*, 25 (1998), 12.

27 The ranking is taken from (www.freepress.ru/win/main.htm), 5 November 1999. See also EWI, *Russian Regional Report*, 4:44 (1999).

28 In December 1993 the author was a European Union election observer in Ufa. He is grateful to OSCE election observers who shared their views with him on election campaigns in Ufa in 1996, 1999 and 2000.

29 'Deklaratsiya o gosudarstvennom suverenitete'.

30 *Prilozhenie k Federativnomu Dogovoru ot Respubliki Bashkortostan* (Moscow, mimeo, 1992).

31 Dogovor Rossiiskoi Federatsii i Respubliki Bashkortostan 'O razgranichenii predmetov vedeniya i vzaimnom delegirovanii polnomochii mezhdu organami gosudarstvennoi vlasti Rossiiskoi Federatsii i organami gosudarstvennoi vlasti Respubliki Bashkortostan', *Rossiiskie vesti* (22 February 1996).

11   *Midkhat Farukhshin*[1]

Tatarstan: syndrome of authoritarianism

The regions of the Russian Federation are very diverse. As well as having some common features they possess many features that are specific to individual regimes. In order to compile a comprehensive picture of Russia's internal processes it is necessary to study the correlation of common and specific features in each unit of the Russian Federation. This chapter considers some of the more important aspects of political life in the Republic of Tatarstan.

Authoritarianism under the guise of greater sovereignty

One of the more notable outcomes of the political development of the Republic of Tatarstan since the collapse of the USSR has been a manifest movement away from declared democratic values towards a regime based on personal authority. Initially the political elite of Tatarstan was keen to acquire an image as a champion of democratic change and to promote a democratic path of development in the republic. This desire was influenced by the fact that in the early 1990s the republic was under considerable pressure from the centre to democratise its political system. The new institutions of power were relatively weak and unstable. The republic's ruling elite was confused about its immediate future and which measures it should take in order to preserve its own power. The general mood of the population was almost euphoric as people cherished the hope of replacing authoritarianism with freedom and democracy. This situation forced the leading elites to cover their real intentions and engage in obfuscation

Although an image as champions of democracy did not accord with the past conduct of the party and state nomenklatura, the situation in the republic forced them to pay at least lip service to certain democratic principles. Such democratic principles were declared in the Constitution of the Republic of Tatarstan, adopted on 6 November 1992. The Constitution proclaimed the establishment of a democratic and social state embracing the rule of law, separation of powers, universal equality of rights, freedom of political activity and supremacy of human rights.

The envisaged institutional structure was to include an independent and fairly prominent role for the Parliament, which was the Supreme Soviet (now named

The State Council) of the Republic of Tatarstan. The executive branch, headed by the president, had clearly defined functions and powers. An independent judiciary was to be created, commencing with a constitutional court. This declaration of universally recognised democratic principles was intended to demonstrate that the republican leadership was in tune with the liberal democratic values advocated by the public, loyalty to which was also espoused by the federal power.

However, as soon as the Tatarstan ruling elite established its power and increased its independence from the federal centre, it became clear that its expressed support for democratic norms and principles was a fig leaf which disguised strong authoritarian tendencies. Some of the declared democratic 'rules of the game' were even formally abolished while others simply were never implemented. At the same time some policies were introduced which signified a 'renaissance' of conspicuous features of authoritarianism.

In their fight with the weakened federal centre, under the banner of greater sovereignty, the local political elite – and primarily the republican leader – were hoping to achieve much more power than their predecessors had possessed before the early 1990s. The degree of authority they won, essentially independence from the federal centre, was used to establish a regime based on personal power.

At present, the political scene in Tatarstan shows no signs of political pluralism. The main feature is an overwhelming domination by the executive power. The main actor is the President of the Republic of Tatarstan. All formally existing legal restrictions on his power are skilfully bypassed. The President de facto enjoys autocratic power.

The President has the power to make all appointments. Any appointment to a position of power, not only in the executive but also in the legislature and judiciary, has to be approved by the President. The same applies to leadership positions in the state mass media, directors of state and partially privatised enterprises and even the heads of territorial offices of federal bodies. The lists of candidates from the party of power who intend to run for the State Duma or the republican parliament – the State Council – also require presidential approval. The president selects who will be Prime Minister and appoints and dismisses ministers and heads of city, town and district administrations. The President even interferes in the award of academic and other honorary titles arbitrarily separating people into 'worthy' and 'unworthy'. All this creates a strong impression that the President of Tatarstan himself believes that he can make no mistakes, that he really is the wise father figure of the nation, which his flattering courtiers and servile mass media try to present. Even the President's wife's birthday has been turned into a republican holiday. Local mass media publish sycophantic stories about it.

According to our calculations the present political elite of Tatarstan comprises about one hundred people. It is important to note that it consists mainly of the rural dwellers, mostly of the representatives of one ethnic group – Tatars

– and largely of the members of the former party-state nomenklatura. Their leader is also a typical representative of the same nomenklatura at the obkom (the oblast party committee) level who suddenly remodelled himself into a 'democrat' and 'free marketeer' and started to make anti-communist pronouncements. Additionally, the majority of the present political elite in Tatarstan have a degree in agriculture or veterinary medicine. It is a paradox that a republic with developed industries and high technical potential is headed by experts in agriculture. What makes things worse is that they are agrarians not just by education and main professional experience, but in mentality as well.

The political elite gives the impression of being a monolith united by the 'iron fist' of the 'father of the nation'. However, its obedience and servility does not necessarily imply unanimous approval of the president's policies. Among the elite there are a number of independently thinking people, but their influence is severely limited. They remain silent for the time being for fear of losing their positions if they voice any doubts about the president's actions. The deputies to the Tatarstan parliament (with very few exceptions) have also had to adjust to the power of the President. The deputies are prepared to support any motion proposed by the President in order to preserve their position at the next elections or to secure an important post in the executive.

The regional elite has seen proof that any attempt to voice an independent opinion will be nipped in the bud. In May 1998 several heads of local administration and state officials attempted to support an alternative candidate for the post of Chairman of the State Council. This 'rebellion of the kneeling' was immediately suppressed. The heads of local administration who were bold enough to express an independent opinion were sacked. The head of the presidential office and the minister for home affairs were also dismissed and the unsuccessful candidate had to emigrate from the republic.

In order to secure his personal power after his re-election for a second term, the President supported the proposal to remove from the text of the Constitution the democratic statement that 'the same person cannot serve as President of the Republic of Tatarstan for more than two successive terms' (Article 108). This has created a constitutional basis for a life-long presidency. President Mintimer Shaimiev also supported the inclusion in the republican Constitution of an article which allows for uncontested elections, despite the fact that it directly contradicts federal legislation. Such uncontested elections were held for Shaimiev himself (the presidential elections in 1991 and 1996) and for twenty-one heads of local administrations (the parliamentary elections of 1995). The existing electoral system and, even more importantly, the wide use of administrative resources and fraud means that in any elections held in Tatarstan there is practically a 100 per cent chance of re-electing the incumbent.

At present there are no independent centres of power and influence. The parliament (the State Council) is an obedient tool of the executive. This situation was achieved with the help of an original electoral system. State Council elections are conducted in two types of constituencies: administrative-territorial and territorial. The boundaries of administrative-territorial constituencies coincide with the boundaries of towns and districts where heads of local government exercise full control. In preparation for the elections to the State Council on 19 December 1999, sixty-three single-mandate administrative-territorial constituencies were created. The State Council consists of 130 deputies, so sixty-seven single-mandate territorial constituencies were then added.

Initially the main difference between the two types of constituencies was that the candidates who were elected in the administrative-territorial constituencies could combine their main job with parliamentary activity. This was done to allow heads of local government to become members of the republican parliament. Bearing in mind that the heads of local government are appointed and dismissed by the President, it becomes obvious that they were convenient and obedient deputies.

As for the deputies elected in the territorial constituencies, they originally had to sign an obligation to take up a full-time job in the parliament if elected. As a result, in the 1995 elections to the State Council, directors of enterprises and other top managers who did not wish to give up their jobs did not run. However, later, this restriction was lifted, and at the next elections of 1999 directors and bankers rushed to take part.

The current State Council comprises exclusively members of the nomenklatura. Out of the 130 deputies fifty-two were heads of local government, five were deputy heads, forty-five were directors general or directors of various enterprises and companies, three headed banks, twelve were re-elected from the previous State Council (including the Speaker who had demonstrated total loyalty to the executive and personally to the President). The remaining deputies of the State Council are: the Prime Minister, the Head of the Presidential Office, the deputy chairman of Kazan' city legislature, three heads of hospitals, one hospital consultant, one editor-in-chief of a journal, one trade union boss, one university associate professor, one head of department in a research laboratory, one deputy head of department in the Interior Ministry and the chairman of the Writers Union.

Not once in the recent history of Tatarstan have elections been held without the use of administrative resources and direct fraud. There is ample proof of this allegation. The President of Tatarstan is in the habit of announcing long before federal elections take place the outcome of the elections for various public offices or political blocks. On the whole, the final results coincide with the ones previously announced by the President. The most recent incident concerns the State Duma elections, which were held in December 1999. In September 1999 Shaimiev promised 50 per cent of the votes to the block 'Motherland – All Russia'. The final result was just that. In January 2000 Mintimer Shaimiev abandoned Yevgenii Primakov and Yurii Luzhkov and promised Vladimir Putin that 70 per cent of voters in Tatarstan would support him in the March 2000 presidential elections. He kept his word.

These presidential 'predictions' prove at least three main points. First, Shaimiev demonstrates to the federal centre that he is totally in control of the situation in the republic and can always secure the desired outcome of elections. This gives him a certain leverage over the central authorities. Second, by naming the winner and indicating the final outcome of the elections, he sends a signal to the heads of local government setting them target figures they should provide in the area under their control. Third, voters can never vote the head of the exec- utive out by means of elections. They will be prevented from doing this by Shaimiev and his satrapies who pre-determine the outcome of all elections.

The wide use of administrative resources to influence elections is indirectly confirmed by the recent situation in Tatarstan. At the elections to the State Duma on 19 December 1999 approximately 50 per cent of the voters supported the block 'Fatherland – All Russia headed by Primakov and Luzhkov, who were the opponents of Putin. However three months later the picture was totally reversed and a considerable majority of the same voters transferred their allegiance to Putin in the presidential elections.

A former chairman of the Writers' Union of Tatarstan, member of the State Duma in 1993–95, and member of the State Council of Tatarstan in 1995–99, Rinat Mukhamadiev, decided to run in the State Duma elections of 1999 in the Nizhnekamsk constituency. The following dialogue took place when he visited the Head of the Presidential Office, Gubaidullin:

G. 'You are not on the list. This time you won't be a deputy, neither to the State Duma nor to the State Council.'
M. 'Why?'
G. 'You no longer hold a managerial post.'
M. 'This is the end of October. How do you know who will be elected?'
G. 'Why do you think we are sitting here? You are not a novice in Tatarstan and do not need any explanation of how things are done. You know very well that it will be the way we say.'

When the writer declined the ultimatum to withdraw his candidacy, the head of the Presidential Office said: 'This is up to you, but you stand no chance. Ziyatdinova will be elected.'

M. 'I am not sure people in the rural areas know her better than me.'
G. 'That is of no consequence. It is enough that we support her.'[2]

Gubaidullin was right. Fluera Ziyatdinova, head of the Protocol Department of the Presidential Office, was elected.

Not long before the elections to the State Council of Tatarstan there was an information leak from the Presidential Office. On 1 December 1999 the news- paper *Vechernaya Kazan* published a list of 130 people who the authorities wanted to be elected to the State Council. 109 of them were elected.[3]

A parliament elected in this way is totally subservient to the executive. The role of this parliament is to rubber-stamp the laws and decrees submitted by the executive. To date, every single proposition put forward by the executive has been approved by the parliament. The State Council now is no different from the

Supreme Soviet in the Soviet period. Having no real power, it comes together from time to time to demonstrate its approval of the actions of the executive. Practically all deputies realise that they owe their position in the republican parliament to the executive. It is only natural that with a guaranteed and well-controlled majority in parliament the ruling elites resist any attempt to create an opposition, and oppose even partial introduction of a proportional electoral system based on 'party lists'.

The electoral system adopted in Tatarstan has several consequences. First, combining the role of deputy with the role of head of local government (or Prime Minister, or Head of the Presidential Office: they were also elected to the parliament) violates the democratic principle of the division of powers declared both in the Constitution of the Russian Federation and the Constitution of the Republic of Tatarstan. The fact that the head of a local administration is, as a rule, also head of the local legislature violates the above-mentioned principle in two respects. In practice, there is no guarantor of the Constitution. Or rather, there is one on paper, but not in real life.

Second, as a consequence of the present electoral system the republic suffers from having a non-professional parliament. In 1995 an amendment was introduced into the Constitution of Tatarstan stating, among other things, that 'a deputy elected to the State Council of the Republic of Tatarstan from a territorial constituency as a rule works full time in the parliament.' Thus it was implied that the deputies elected from administrative-territorial constituencies may work in the parliament through periodical 'raids'. It was hoped that at least the deputies from the territorial constituencies would work in the parliament full time. Unfortunately, as often happens in Russia, the formula 'as a rule opened the way to exceptions, which soon became the norm. In the newly elected State Council only twenty-nine deputies agreed to work full time.

Third, the present system violates the principle of equality of votes. Administrative-territorial constituencies represent very varied numbers of voters. Tatarstan legislation stipulates that the difference in the numbers of voters in various electoral constituencies should not exceed 15 per cent. In reality this rule is constantly violated. Thus, at the time of the elections to the parliament of Tatarstan in 1995 the Kazan' city constituency had 788,900 voters, while, for example, the Zainsk town constituency had only 26,800 voters. In other words, the vote of one Zainsk citizen carried more weight than the votes of twenty-nine citizens of Kazan'. In 114 out of the 130 constituencies from the list approved by the Central Electoral Committee for the December elections of 1999 the number of voters was either higher than the maximum envisaged by the law or lower than the minimum envisaged by the law. For example, Kazan' constituency No. 1 had over 800,000 voters registered, while Elabuga constituency No. 38 had only about 8,000 voters.[4]

There is also a difference in representation between the deputies elected from the territorial constituencies, on the one hand, and the administrative-territorial ones, on the other. One might argue that a similar thing happens in the Council of the Federation, where each unit of the federation, irrespective of its size, is represented by two senators, or in the American Senate, where each state is represented by two senators also irrespective of its size. However, the crucial difference is that in these cases we are dealing with a consistent pattern of representation to a second (upper) chamber of the parliament, while in Tatarstan the deputies who represent such varied numbers of voters all sit in a single-chamber parliament.

Fourth, as voters in Tatarstan are now entitled to at least two votes, one of which they give to a candidate in their territorial constituency and another to a candidate in their administrative-territorial constituency, each voter is represented by at least two deputies in the same single-chamber parliament. In the city of Kazan' electors are represented by three deputies, one of whom is returned from the city administrative-territorial constituency, another from the administrative-territorial constituency of the district within the city ('raion'), as well as a further one from the territorial constituency. (The Tatarstan ruling elite should patent this original invention!)

Finally, by ruling out any elements of a proportional electoral system, the present mechanism of election to the State Council hinders the consolidation of political parties and the formation of a party system within the republic. Everything possible is done to prevent the appearance of an organised political opposition.

Notably, practices of Soviet times are being revived in Tatarstan. When the head of a district or town administration resigns, he (or she) simultaneously and 'voluntarily' resigns his seat as a deputy of the State Council. This seat is inherited by the new head of administration. Just as it used to be that the first secretary of the local committee of the Communist Party of the Soviet Union (KPSS) would have a seat on the Supreme Soviet of the Tatar Autonomous Republic, now the heads of local government are, ex officio, deputies to the State Council from the corresponding administrative-territorial constituency.

Another branch of power dependent on the executive is the judiciary. The Constitution of the Russian Federation states that judges are independent and subordinate only to the law, and Federal Law stipulates that the appointment of judges is the prerogative of the federal centre. However, district, town and republican judges in Tatarstan are in fact selected and appointed by the Tatarstan republican parliament. The courts and Procurator's offices in Tatarstan are interwoven into the regime of personal power and do not raise objections despite the numerous contradictions between local laws and federal legislation.

The ruling elite of Tatarstan has removed any opposition which might arise from within the institutions of power. They adhere to the traditional Russian point of view that 'any opposition is undesirable, and, if circumstances permit, it should be eliminated. If it has to be endured, it should be contained by rules imposed from above, which should be constantly adjusted accordingly to the balance of forces in the society as a whole.'[5]

At present, an organised opposition as traditionally understood is non-existent, although a social background for its creation does exist. The level of alienation between the population and the institutions of power is high, and there are few contacts between them. However, popular opposition to the authorities is not adequately institutionalised. The level of popular participation in political and civic organisations is low.

There are practically no political parties that could aggregate the interests of citizens or social groups to form relatively independent centres of influence. The absence of conditions which would favour the development of a multi-party system can be accounted for by the following factors:

1 The electoral system in Tatarstan does not permit the election of even a proportion of the deputies on party lists. It does not facilitate party organisation and activity, and prevents the institutionalisation of parties and the creation of a multi-party system. As a consequence, the State Council has no party factions.
2 Such political parties in the republic are organisationally weak and practically ignored by the mass media. Without this they cannot reach the population.
3 Political parties lack financial support. Because of this they do not have their own publications, do not have mass events on a regular basis and cannot afford political advertising.
4 Neither the republican branches of national parties, nor Tatarstan's own regional parties, can boast a charismatic and popular leader. Surprisingly, nationwide parties and movements seem unaware of the local situation and appoint or elect inappropriate leaders to their regional branches.

The local economic elite could present an independent influence and a certain check on the Tatarstan ruling elite. However, contrary to the situation in many other units of the Russian Federation, the economic elite of Tatarstan is not an independent force and cannot offer any resistance to the decisions of the authorities. This could partly be explained by the fact that the economic elite consists, as a rule, of close associates (children, close relatives and subordinates) of those high-ranking officials who form the political elite. Another reason why the economic elite does not form an independent group results from the peculiarities of Tatarstan's privatisation procedures, which were controlled by the authorities for their own benefit. It is no surprise, therefore, that the economic elite is under the total control of the authorities.

This analysis of the situation in Tatarstan raises questions about the nature of the republican regime. There are numerous indications that the current leadership of Tatarstan has not yet succeeded in establishing a classic authoritarian regime. It is more like the 'authoritarian situation' which has been described both in Russian and Western political science literature. The main symptoms of this situation in post-Soviet society are:

1 the existence of a dominant actor (for example, the leader of the executive);
2 the dominance of informal institutions (for example, in appointment procedures);

3 the obstruction or elimination of the opportunity to depose the carriers of real power (presidents, heads of executive) through elections;
4 the domination of the executive over all other institutions of power;
5 the limiting of the role of parliament to rubber-stamping pre-existing decisions;
6 a judiciary which is formally independent but not free in its verdicts;
7 election committees which are under the control of the executive;
8 a mass media which is formally free but within which the main radio and television companies and most influential newspapers are established and/or owned by the state or companies controlled by the groups close to the executive;
9 political parties which play no role because the regime does not permit party politics.[6]

If we refrain from blaming the people of Tatarstan, who were practically powerless to prevent the development of authoritarian tendencies in the political life of the republic, the responsibility for the authoritarian situation in Tatarstan, and in a number of other regions of Russia, lies with the federal centre.

Sovereignty and the results of socio-economic policy

In some countries (for example, Chile and South Korea) authoritarianism has led to considerable economic development and higher living standards. The populations of these countries paid for economic progress through limits on their freedom and democracy. Has the population of Tatarstan been similarly compensated for the growth of authoritarian tendencies in the political life of the republic? I do not think so.

The pompously presented 'State Programme for the economic and social development of the Republic of Tatarstan' is not being implemented and few people are aware of its existence. The 'Tatarstan economic model' comprises banal cliches and very little content. Statistics, even official statistics, provide the best evidence of the situation in which the population now finds itself. What matters to the population is not empty talk about the rate of industrial growth, but evidence that their life is changing for the better.

The indicators of living standards in Tatarstan display no consistent pattern, but during the last few years they have revealed a general decline, despite the hypocritical statements of the republic's leaders that 'the interests of the people are of utmost importance to us'. The standard of living, calculated by dividing average earnings by the minimum subsistence wage, has fluctuated as follows in Table 11.1.

The average per capita monetary income in the Republic of Tatarstan in 1998 was 77.3 per cent of the average for Russia; in 1999 it is estimated to be 77.6 per cent. On this indicator Tatarstan was ranked thirty-second among the units of the Russian Federation in 1998. In November 1999 the republic was ranked fortieth.

Table 11.1 Standard of living in Tatarstan, based on average earnings over minimum subsistence wage, 1993–99

1992	1993	1994	1995	1996	1997	1999
1.9	4.2	2.9	2.2	2.9	3.0	2.3

Source: Republic of Tatarstan, 1997: Statistical Information (Kazan', 1997), pp. 58, 63.

With respect to the old-age pension, taking into account compensational pay-outs, in 1998 the Republic of Tatarstan was ranked eightieth in the Russian Federation. In the first quarter of 1999 it was ranked seventy-ninth. With respect to the purchasing power of the population Tatarstan was ranked sixteenth in 1998 when purchasing power was 92.5 per cent of the average in Russia. In 1999 there was a considerable drop in the purchasing power of the population and the republic fell to twenty-fourth place with only 90.8 per cent of the average in Russia.[7] This shows the true value of the boastful statements of the leadership that in Tatarstan people are better off than in other areas of the Russian Federation. However, these data are not to be found in the official statements of the republican elites or in the mass media which supports them.

It would be interesting to compare a few indicators of living standards in the Russian Federation as a whole, in the Republic of Tatarstan and in Samara Oblast. The latter is chosen for comparison on good grounds. In Soviet times it was usual to organise socialist competition between Kuibyshev Oblast and the city of Kuibyshev (now Samara), on the one hand, and the Tatar ASSR and the city of Kazan' on the other. Both areas were considered to make low provision for their populations, to share the comparable soils and climate of the Middle Volga, and to have approximately the same territory, population and comparable economic potential. One of the crucial differences of the last ten years is that Samara Oblast, unlike Tatarstan, did not fight for greater sovereignty. So what are the comparable economic indicators of the sovereign Tatarstan and the non-sovereign Samara?

In February 2000 the minimum subsistence wage in Tatarstan was 2,497.7 roubles per adult. In October 1999 the republican interdisciplinary committee stated that during 1998–99 wages in the Republic grew by only 270 roubles per month, while in the neighbouring regions the growth was 700 roubles per month.[8] With respect to the value of average earnings the Republic of Tatarstan ranks thirtieth in the Russian Federation, while Samara region ranks twenty-third. With respect to the cost of the minimum consumer basket per capita Tatarstan and Samara rank seventy-third and thirty-sixth respectively among the units of the Russian Federation.[9]

Other interesting comparisons are the data on real monetary income per capita. After the first quarter of 1999 monetary income per capita in Tatarstan was 1,238.2 roubles, while in Samara it was 2,034.3 roubles. Tatarstan was ranked twenty-fifth in Russia on this indicator, while Samara Oblast was ranked ninth.[10]

Table 11.2 Housing provision (end of corresponding year, m^2 per citizen)

	1990	1992	1994	1995	1996	1997	1998
The Russian Federation	16.4	16.8	17.7	18.1	18.3	18.6	18.9
The Republic of Tatarstan	16.0	16.3	16.6	16.9	17.1	17.4	17.7
Samara Region	16.6	17.0	18.7	19.1	19.0	19.3	19.4

Sources: The Republic of Tatarstan, 1997: Statistical Information (Kazan': 1998),
p. 509; *Russian Statistical Yearbook* (Moscow: Goskomstat, 1999), pp. 172, 175.

In June 1999 the number of enterprises that had not paid their employees their salaries in full was 4,368 in Tatarstan and 679 in Samara Oblast. The general debt on salaries and wages on the 1 January 2000 was 1,135.4 million roubles in Tatarstan compared with 241.3 million roubles in Samara Oblast.[11]

An important indicator of the standard of living of the population is the turn-over of trade and services. In 1999 trade turnover was 32,937.2 million roubles in Tatarstan and 67,380.9 million roubles in Samara Oblast. The per capita turn-over of trade in Tatarstan was 8,700 roubles (ranking twenty-ninth in the Russian Federation). In Samara Oblast it was 20,400 roubles (ranking second in the Russian Federation). For the same period the monetary volume of services was 6,426.8 million roubles in the Republic of Tatarstan and 9,247.1 million roubles in Samara Oblast. The ranking among the units of the Russian Federation on this indicator are ninth for Samara Oblast and eighteenth for Tatarstan.[12]

Another important indicator of living standards is housing provision and its cost. The figures for this indicator in the units of the Federation under comparison is illustrated in Table 11.2.

Significantly, in 1990 housing provision for the population of Tatarstan was practically the same as in Samara Oblast, but by 1998 Samara had almost two metres per person more than in Tatarstan. According to the Ministry of housing of Tatarstan, the average cost of 1 m^2 of municipal housing in Kazan' is 1.97 roubles, while in Samara it is 0.88 roubles.

In the period between January and May 1999 in Tatarstan 103,300 m^2 of new housing was built, while in Samara Oblast the corresponding figure is 172,400 m^2. Tatarstan was ranked a modest forty-third according to the amount of new housing built per 1,000 people, while Samara Oblast was ranked eleventh.[13]

Overall the standard of living calculated by dividing the average income per capita in mid-1999 by the cost of the minimum consumer basket was approximately 1.4 in Tatarstan compared to over 1.8 in Samara Oblast.

The above data indicates that in order to achieve a particular goal, such as a growth in living standards of the population, one does not have to be involved in a struggle for sovereignty so typical of the Tatarstan political elite. Samara Oblast has achieved much more impressive results without insisting on greater sovereignty and, incidentally, while paying more taxes to the federal budget than the republic of Tatarstan. The statistical data quoted above convincingly prove that the struggle of the Tatarstan elite for a larger share of power under the banner of greater sovereignty had very little to do with increasing people's living standards, but was conducted in order to secure the power of the local elite and to free it from the control of the federal centre.

The political future of Tatarstan: possible scenarios

There are three possible scenarios for the future political development of Tatarstan:

1 stabilisation over an indefinite time of the present 'authoritarian situation';
2 a shift towards classic authoritarianism, which might prove rather difficult in the context of the general democratisation of Russian society; or
3 an evolution towards democracy.

This latter scenario could prove equally difficult in view of the position adopted by the local political elite, its apparent monolithic nature and the weakness of democratic forces in the republic.

The experience of Tatarstan and some other units of the Russian Federation provides convincing proof that in the absence of democratic traditions in Russian society, and in the presence of strong traditions of authoritarianism and a patrimonial political culture, introducing a presidential form of government with a strong presidency has a negative effect. The absence of control 'from below' and a total lack of control 'from above' enable strong individuals to rein-state the tradition of authoritarianism in the political life of units of the Russian Federation and prevents the formation of truly democratic 'rules of the game'.

The future of democratic change in Tatarstan is dependent on changes in the composition and policies of the regional elite. The latter depends in turn on the maturity of the population of the Republic, on the degree of conflict within the elite, and on the pressure imposed by the federal centre (assuming the presiden-tial elections in Russia bring to power people who do share democratic values).

At present, inside the Republic of Tatarstan, there are practically no institution-alised forces that could challenge Shaimiev's regime. It seems unrealistic to hope that just by voting against those currently in power the population could achieve radical changes in the composition and policies of the ruling elite. The results of any elections could be easily falsified if the outcome is unfavourable to the exist-ing authorities. The regime could be challenged from inside or outside the politi-cal elite only if certain external conditions are in place. These conditions include:

- the refusal of the federal authorities to placate the regional elites and their leadership whilst simultaneously giving strong support to the forces which are opposed to the ruling regime;
- increasing the control exercised by the federal centre over the local elite, and, as the first step in this direction, appointing a Presidential Representative to the Republic;

- political, economic and legal pressure on the republican authorities to secure their compliance with the superior single political, legal and economic space of the federal state. One possible measure in this direction would be the federal authorities to turn to the Constitutional Court of the Russian Federation in order to secure the compliance of the Tatarstan legal system with federal legislation;
- objective (and that implies critical) monitoring by the central mass media of the processes which are taking place in the republic.

The final objective in order to create the necessary conditions for viable political and economic development in the republic is to secure social and demographic changes in the republican elite. These changes should see the arrival of a younger generation which has mastered the concept of democratic values, the replacement of many of the representatives of the rural population by urban residents in the elites, and a wider representation of people from industry, banking, the law, science and technology. This will be a long and difficult journey but there is no alternative in view of the burning economic and political needs of Tatarstan and its multinational and, unfortunately, long-suffering people.

Notes

1 Translated by Elena Hore.
2 *Vechernaya Kazan'* (14 January 2000).
3 *Vechernaya Kazan'* (1 December 1999).
4 *Vechernaya Kazan'* (5 October 1999).
5 *Vlast i Oppozitsya. Rossiiskii politicheskii Protsess XX Stoletya* (Moscow: Rossiiskaya Politicheskaya Entsiklopediya (ROSSPEN) 1995), p 5.
6 V. Gel'man, *Transformatsiya v Rossii: Politicheskii Rezhim i Demokraticheskaya Oppositsiya* (Moscow: Moskovskii Obshchestvennyi Nauchnyi Fond, 1999), pp. 123–9.
7 *Monitoring: Dokhody i Uroven Zhizni Naseleniya. Ozone Pokazateli Dokhodov I Urovnya Zhizni Naseleniya po Sub'ektam Rossiiskoi Federatsii, II kvartal 1999* (Moscow: 1999), p. 78; *Monitoring: Dokhody i Uroven Zhizni Naseleniya, IV kvartal 1999 (Oktiabr–Dekabr)* (Moscow: 1999), pp. 70, 82.
8 Sotsialno-Ekonomicheskoe Polozhenie Respubliki Tatarstan No. 2: Yanvar–Dekabr (Kazan': Goskomstat, Respubliki Tatarstan, 2000), p. 81.
9 *Nekotorye Statisticheskie Pokazately Sotsialno-Ekonomicheskogo Polozheniya Respubliki Tatarstan i Otdelnykh Regionov Rossiiskoi Federatsii za Yanvar–Dekabr 1999* (Kazan: Goskomstat Respubliki Tatarstan, 1999), p. 44.
10 *Monitoring: Dokhody i Uroven Zhizni Naseleniya, IV kvartal 1999 (Oktiabr–Dekabr)* (Moscow: IGPI, 1999), p. 54; *Nekotorye Statisticheskie Pokazately Sotsialno-Ekonomicheskogo Polozheniya Respubliki Tatarstan i Otdelnykh Regionov Rossiiskoi Federatsii za Yanvar–Dekabr 1999* (Kazan': Goskomstat Respubliki Tatarstan, 1999), p. 44.
11 *Nekotorye Statisticheskie Pokazately Sotsialno-Ekonomicheskogo Polozheniya Respubliki Tatarstan i Otdelnykh Regionov Rossiiskoi Federatsii za Yanvar–Mai 1999*

(Kazan: Goskomstat Respubliki Tatarstan, 1999), p. 34; *Nekotorye Statisticheskie Pokazately Sotsialno-Ekonomicheskogo Polozheniya Respubliki Tatarstan i Otdelnykh Regionov Rossiiskoi Federatsii za Yanvar–Dekabr 1999* (Kazan': Goskomstat Respubliki Tatarstan, 1999), p. 34.

12 *Nekotorye Statisticheskie Pokazately Sotsialno-Ekonomicheskogo Polozheniya Respubliki Tatarstan i Otdelnykh Regionov Rossiiskoi Federatsii za Yanvar–Dekabr 1999* (Kazan': Goskomstat Respubliki Tatarstan, 1999), pp. 23–5.

13 *Nekotorye Statisticheskie Pokazately Sotsialno-Ekonomicheskogo Polozheniya Respubliki Tatarstan i Otdelnykh Regionov Rossiiskoi Federatsii za Yanvar–Mai 1999* (Kazan': Goskomstat Respubliki Tatarstan, 1999), pp. 15–16.

Putin reforms the federal system

As other chapters in this book recount, President Boris Yeltsin deliberately set out to devolve power to Russia's republics and regions and to build a federation 'from the ground up'. In the opinion of many Russians, Yeltsin was too successful: his successor President Vladimir Putin and other members of the elite thought Yeltsin had, in his eagerness to sweep away the rubble of the USSR, allowed the state to grow dangerously weak. This chapter outlines Putin's early moves to assert central control over regional leaders and to turn the country into 'a single economic and legal space'. This Putin did by creating a new, extra-constitutional layer of bureaucracy between the presidential apparatus and the regional governments. In the process, he effectively tore up the unorthodox bilateral treaties that had been the building blocks of Yeltsin's federal system. He also sidelined the upper house of the Russian parliament, on which regional leaders held ex officio membership. It became clear that Putin had a dual purpose in mind: not only to bring the regional barons to heel but also to assert presidential control over the federal government, similarly seen as having control during the Yeltsin years. Although Russia remained a federation in name, Putin seemed to be turning it back into a unitary state.

Yeltsin's legacy

The Russia that emerged in 1991 from the rubble of the USSR was a federation in name alone. As the USSR crumbled under the impact of Mikhail Gorbachev's assault on the Communist Party, Yeltsin won the support of Russia's eighty-nine constituent republics and regions by urging them to 'take as much autonomy as you can swallow'. Once the USSR collapsed, Yeltsin set about building a new Russian federation.

A decade later, many Russians felt that Yeltsin had allowed Russia's regions to escape too far from central control. This was partly because of Yeltsin's increasing age and frailty. It was also because Yeltsin had, in the early years of his leadership, consciously tried to turn the unitary state of the Soviet era into a true federation. The geographer Leonid Smirnyagin observed all this at first hand between 1994 and 1997, when he served in Yeltsin's presidential administration. At a conference in Dundee in 2000, Smirnyagin told contributors to the present volume of Yeltsin's desire to build a new kind of federation founded on consent. A democratic Russia, Yeltsin believed, would be a more stable Russia. Key elements in his project were the 1992 Federal Treaty and the series of bilateral treaties that Yeltsin signed, on behalf of the Russian Federation, first with Tatarstan in 1994 and then with over half of the other constituent republics and regions of the Russian Federation.

Devolution did not, however, make Russia more democratic. In some regions, such as liberal Novgorod, that may have been the case but it was not so everywhere. Instead there was a tendency, as other chapters in this book demonstrate, towards regional authoritarianism. Regional governors, closely linked with local financial elites, controlled key regional industries plus the press, courts, mass media and law-enforcement agencies on their territories. According to official sources, up to 30 per cent of the legislation passed by regional legislatures was in conflict with federal law.

Particularly alarming from the federal government's point of view were moves by regional governors to reduce the flow of tax revenues to the federal budget. Tax collection was a federal function: bases and rates for all the main revenue-raising taxes were set by the federal authorities and the regions had only very limited tax-raising powers of their own. Taxes were collected by federally-controlled tax services, tax police and customs. A federal treasury system, through which the moneys flowed, operated in all regions except Tatarstan and supposedly made it impossible for regions to withhold tax revenue from the centre.

Regional leaders were nonetheless forced to find ways of retaining in their regions at least part of the revenue that should have been remitted to the centre. The cash-strapped federal government of the Yeltsin era delegated responsibility for much social-welfare spending to sub-national governments without providing adequate funding with which to meet their new responsibilities. Regions accordingly had little incentive either to collect tax vigorously or to rationalise and account for their spending. The republics and regions with the greatest political and economic clout used their strength to negotiate special tax breaks: these were enshrined in bilateral treaties signed with the federal centre. Tatarstan led the way by securing the right to retain all the tax and export revenues collected on its territory. As a result, Tatarstan was able to keep prices low, pay wages regularly and maintain a relatively high standard of living for its residents.[1] The bilateral treaties were problematic, however. Opaque and unequal, they were no substitute for the rule of law or a coherent constitutional order. Sooner or later, they were bound to come under challenge.[2]

While the stronger regions negotiated advantageous bilateral treaties, the weaker had to find other ways to avoid remitting taxes to the federal centre. Taking advantage of the fact that the federal budget accepted only money, regional leaders made widespread use of barter, money surrogates and tax offsets. These enabled regional leaders to withhold funds from the centre and to bail out local enterprises that would otherwise have been forced into bankruptcy; they also provided almost limitless scope for corrupt, crony dealings from which regional and local officials benefited.[3]

According to Smirnyagin, Yeltsin tolerated these and other regional shenanigans because, in the president's words, 'Every day of stability is another nail in the coffin of accursed Bolshevism!'

Putin redraws the federal map

Putin lost no time in abandoning this live-and-let-live policy. He repeatedly stated his determination to establish 'a single legal and economic space'. By this he seemed to have in mind the eminently sensible aims of ensuring that the regions were all subject to the same body of laws, abolishing the inequitable tax advantages enjoyed by some of them, and dismantling the protectionist trade barriers that others regions had tried to erect between themselves and their neighbours. However, Putin's aim was not merely to restore federal control over wayward regional leaders and governments. Equally important, as this chapter tries to show, was his determination to assert presidential control over the federal government. 'Russia', Putin told interviewers shortly before his election, 'was founded as a super-centralised state from the very start. This is inherent in the genetic code, traditions and popular mentality.'[4]

Putin moved to curtail the powers of the governors by creating an entirely new level of bureaucracy between the governors and the federal centre. In a presidential decree dated 13 May 2000, Russia's eighty-nine republics and regions were divided into seven new 'federal districts'. These new units, whose borders corresponded closely with those of Russia's existing military districts, were each to be headed by a 'plenipotentiary representative' or 'envoy' appointed personally by the president. (For the composition of the new 'super-regions', see Appendix 12.1.) The federal districts reminded some of the six *guberniyas* into which the territory of tsarist Russia was divided until the 1917 revolution. The institution dated back to Peter the Great, when governors general were the country's most powerful regional officials, directly subordinate to the tsar.

Many of the powers that the regional governors had accumulated during the Yeltsin decade were to be transferred to these presidential representatives. Security and law enforcement were to be key elements of their work. This was underscored by the fact that five of the seven new appointees had backgrounds in the army or security services (see Appendix 12.1). They were to have the right to attend meetings of the federal government as non-voting members when questions regarding their districts were to be discussed. More important, they were to be ex officio members of the Security Council, an executive body responsible directly to the president and headed by Putin's most trusted associate, Sergei Ivanov. Putin and Ivanov had served together in the KGB, the Soviet intelligence agency, and in its successor organisation, the Federal Security Service (FSB). It was reportedly the Security Council that drafted the 13 May decree and Ivanov who determined which regions should belong to which federal district. The main tasks of the presidential representatives included:

- reporting to the president on the security, political, economic and social situation in their districts, and making policy recommendations;
- monitoring the implementation of federal government policy in their districts and reporting to the president on any discrepancies between federal and regional legislation;
- monitoring the work of the regional departments of key federal ministries and agencies on the territory of their districts. These were to include, among others, the justice ministry, finance ministry, courts, police, procuracy, security service and tax police. Units for combating organised crime were also to be set up in each of the federal districts. These agencies were to be reorganised along the lines of the new districts and funded at that level;
- approving personnel appointments to positions in the territorial branches of all federal agencies in their districts.

At a stroke, regional governors lost the power they had acquired during Yeltsin's leadership over the execution of law and order on their territories. They also lost their right to be consulted by the Kremlin over the appointment of heads of federal agencies, such as regional police chiefs, on their territories. This marked a sharp reversal of the practice of the Yeltsin period, when these bodies grew increasingly dependent on regional governments for financial support that was not forthcoming from the federal centre. Plans were also floated to give the presidential representatives the power to elaborate economic programmes for their districts.[5]

Putin was reasserting control not only over the regional elites but also, through its numerous regional branches, over the federal government itself. The number of federal employees working at regional level (some 310,000 in the late 1990s) far outweighed those in Moscow (about 30,000). In Tatarstan, there were branches of no fewer than forty-seven federal agencies.[6] During the Yeltsin period, as Leonid Smirnyagin has pointed out, this vast army of federal employees were formally subordinated to the federal ministries but were in fact out of the control even of the prime minister, to say nothing of the president. Putin's purpose was to create a new chain of command that would bring them under presidential scrutiny. The newspaper *Nezavisimaya gazeta* was the first to point out, in an article published on 16 May 2000, that Putin's reform represented the first step in the Russian Federation's transformation back into a unitary state.

A bold plan, this incorporated many ideas that had been in the air for much of the Yeltsin leadership but that Yeltsin had lacked the energy and motivation to implement. As Cameron Ross has detailed, the idea of re-dividing Russia's eighty-nine regions into a smaller number of 'super-regions' had been around for a long time.[7] In reducing the number to seven, Putin's plan went further than earlier proposals, most of which envisioned a total of around twenty regions.

Putin's plan had the particular advantage that it could be implemented without the necessity of amending the constitution, something that Russia's 1993 constitution rendered extremely difficult. Putin began instead to construct parallel state institutions alongside those described in the constitution. Also new was the determination with which Putin moved to implement his reforms and the speed with which he tackled those institutions, such as the regional governors, that he saw as a threat to strong presidential rule.

Next, Putin stripped the governors of the right to sit in the Federation Council, the upper house of the Russian parliament. In a series of newspaper interviews, Kremlin spin-doctor Gleb Pavlovsky identified the governors as one of the most important threats to Putin's leadership. Regional officials managing regional budgets were 'the real oligarchs', he told an interviewer.[8] The Federation Council, Pavlovsky went on, was 'the legal foundation of the shadow regime, a stock exchange where the centre cut political and financial deals with the regions. . . . Senators were paid in fund transfers, offsets, taxes and non-interference in their acts of tyranny . . .' This constituted 'a giant market of corrupt services, which turned billions of dollars of budget money into the budget of the shadow state'. The primary aim of Putin's reforms, he stated, was to do away with this shadow economy. Putin's redrawing of the federal map, Pavlovsky declared, was 'only the beginning of reforms to restore federal control'.

In removing the governors from parliament's upper chamber, Putin exploited the ambiguous wording of the 1993 constitution, which stated merely that the Federation Council 'was formed' of two representatives from each republic and region of the Russian Federation without specifying how the representatives were to be chosen. From 1995 onwards, the governor of each region and the speaker of the local parliament sat in the upper house as ex officio representatives of their regions. This increased the leverage regional leaders were able to exert over federal policy and provided them with immunity from criminal prosecution. Since electoral laws varied from region to region, however, it also meant that the composition of the upper chamber was effectively determined not by federal norms but by regional ones.

On 17 May 2000, Putin submitted to parliament a package of three bills designed to 'strengthen the unity of the state'. The first bill proposed depriving the governors and speakers of their automatic right to sit in the Federation Council and replacing them by full-time legislators. The latter would be nominated for a four-year term by the governors and speakers and approved by the regional parliament in a secret ballot.

A second bill proposed that the president be given the power to remove governors from office and to dissolve regional legislatures. This was a particularly controversial proposal since it meant that the president would have the right to dismiss executives and legislators who had been popularly elected. To sweeten the pill, a third bill proposed giving governors the right to dismiss municipal leaders (mayors) of cities on their territories. Relations between governors and mayors, particularly of regional capitals, had typically been tense during the Yeltsin period, and the governors had long hankered after the power to rid themselves of such troublesome officials.

From their seats in the Federation Council, the governors resisted these reforms as best they could. First, they managed to postpone their ejection from the Federation Council from 2001 to 2002 (by which time the terms in office of many of them would have expired). Next, the bill allowing the president to dismiss governors was fenced around with restrictions. Putin's original draft would have given the President the power to sack a governor virtually at will. The final version as approved by both houses of parliament allowed the president to sack a governor only in certain circumstances. One was if a court had ruled that the governor had failed to bring regional legislation into line with federal law. Alternatively, the president could dismiss a governor against whom criminal charges had been brought, but only in the case of a 'serious' crime and only if the prosecutor general provided supporting evidence in support of the charges. And, before the president could dissolve a regional legislature, the president must present appropriate legislation to the State Duma.

Putin offer a further sweetener to the governors when he proposed the establishment of the State Council of the Russian Federation. This was yet another extra-constitutional body and, as befitting a body set up in such a way, it was to have only advisory, not law-making powers. The governors and presidents of all Russia's regions would have ex officio membership. The regional bosses declared themselves well satisfied with this arrangement, which they saw as giving them back the voice they would lose when they relinquished their seats in the Federation Council in 2002. Once the carrot had been dangled before their noses, they abandoned their resistance to Putin's reforms and sanctioned the passage of his bills through parliament. They were signed into law in July 2000.

There was, however, a sting in the tail. In early September 2000 Putin signed a decree establishing the State Council. He also announced that the new body's presidium, or governing body, would consist of governors representing each of the seven federal districts, appointed on a rotating basis to serve for six-month terms. Putin hinted that the State Council might receive greater powers in the future, although he said it would be 'improper' to give it anything other than advisory functions as long as the Federation Council continued 'to function fully'. Sergei Samoilov, head of the Kremlin department dealing with regional affairs, let the cat out of the bag when he told a newspaper interviewer that 'decisions of the State Council' would be signed into law by the president 'in the form of decrees, instructions and protocols'.[9] The purpose of this novel arrangement appeared to be to allow the president to circumvent the upper house of parliament, on which the representatives nominated by the governors were to sit, and to turn it into a mere talking-shop. The arrangement would, by the same token, circumvent the constitutional arrangements for law making.[10]

The meekness with which the governors relinquished their privileges astonished many observers. Putin's ability – which dated from the December 1999

parliamentary election – to command a majority in the State Duma strengthened his hand because it meant that the lower house of parliament would be able
to override any attempt by the upper house to veto legislation, but there was
surely more to it than that. Perhaps the governors thought that, if they kept their
heads down, Putin's reforms would blow over in the same way that so many legislative initiatives by previous Russian leaders had done. The strongest among
them may have sensed that they had the support of their regional elites and
would be hard for the Kremlin to dislodge. Alternatively, the governors may have
judged membership of the Federation Council to be insignificant compared to
the necessity of maintaining good relations with the Kremlin.

The financial weakness of many regions certainly played a role. The majority
of Russia's regions were dependent on the federal government for state subsidies
to keep rust-belt industries on their territory in operation. When push came to
shove, they were unable to resist Kremlin pressure to toe the line. According to
one media report, this pressure was applied to the governors not directly, but
through the tycoons who controlled the largest enterprises on their territory.
These tycoons threatened the governors that, if they did not support Putin's
moves, the tycoons would withdraw funding from vital social-welfare programmes at regional level. According to rumour, the tycoons had, in turn, been
pressured to act by Kremlin threats to review the circumstances in which their
enterprises had been privatised.[11]

The governors' meekness may have resulted from Russia's continuing lack of
political pluralism. Governors who would shortly be facing re-election may not
have dared oppose the Kremlin. The humiliating defeat meted out in the
December 1999 elections to Moscow Mayor Yurii Luzhkov's OVR regional coalition by the pro-Putin Yedinstvo (Unity) movement may have warned other
governors not to step out of line.

Finally, Putin may have threatened regional bosses with compromising
material (*kompromat*) about them, derived from his FSB connections. It may
well have been sufficient that regional leaders believed Putin could make use of
such *kompromat* if he wished.

Putin also moved to rescind the tax concessions that Yeltsin had granted to some
of Russia's most powerful regions. He scored a significant victory when Tatarstan's
President Mintimer Shaimiev confirmed that, as of 1 January 2001, Tatarstan
would relinquish its substantial tax privileges and that it would thereafter pay over
to the federal government 50 per cent of value-added tax plus all excises on oil, gas-
oline and vodka.[12] This was an important concession on Tatarstan's part. Under
an unpublished protocol to the 1994 bilateral treaty, Tatarstan had been permitted
to retain as much as 20 per cent of the republic's budget. What pressure Putin put
on Shaimiev to secure this concession was not known. But other regional leaders,
seeing Tatarstan forced to forego one of its most cherished privileges, would
doubtless think twice before defying Putin themselves.

Next, Deputy Prime Minister Aleksei Kudrin announced the government's
intention of adjusting, in 2001, the division of tax-take between the federal

government and the regions from the existing ratio of 52:48 to one of 56.4:43.6 in the centre's favour. Kudrin also announced that the government intended to centralise the collection of value-added tax. Governors complained that this decision would make for a ratio of 70:30 in favour of the centre. Kudrin insisted, however, that the government was centralising revenue collection only in order to ensure a more equitable redistribution catering for the needs of poorer regions.[13] Though the re-division of the tax-take was expected to be opposed by the Federation Council, the pro-government majority in the State Duma was not expected to have difficulty ensuring passage of the relevant legislation.

Putin's measures to strengthen central control over the regions could, the British economist Philip Hanson argued, produce benefits for the economy. This was because the entrenched power of regional elites bore much of the blame for Russia's relative lack of success in building an efficient market economy. For example, non-monetary settlements in transactions between Russian firms – and between Russian firms and the state – had developed as a form of concealed subsidy to inefficient producers, inpeding competition and structural adjustment. Much of the responsibility for this development, Hanson argued, lay with sub-national governments, and these unsound practices were reinforced by the governors' crony relations with local business elites. A more top-down system of government – with the federal treasury network placed firmly beyond regional control and judges appointed in districts that did not coincide with regional boundaries – 'could help to reduce government over-reach and corruption.'[14]

Conclusions

In the first months of his presidency, Putin demonstrated a clear determination to reduce the power of the regional leaders and to strengthen that of the centre. In pushing through the measures necessary to achieve this objective, he did not have things all his own way. He made some apparent concessions to regional leaders, such as inviting their representatives to sit on the State Council. At the same time, many of his measures were not strongly resisted, indicating that a new and vigorous president with strong popular and Duma support could not be easily opposed by regional elites.

Insofar as regional governments had been a major source of state intervention in the economy, impeding competition and promoting cronyism, corruption and hidden subsidies, a diminution of the power of the regional bosses was at first sight a step in the right direction as far as economic liberalisation was concerned. This would be the case even if economic liberalisation turned out not to be the main purpose of Putin's recentralising moves.

Several possible scenarios presented themselves whereby Putin's strategy for increasing the efficiency of central government might be thwarted. One would see the regional elites proving capable of continuing to go their own way regardless of the new formal arrangements. In this case, the federal districts would become just another ineffective layer of bureaucracy.

Putin's intentions might also be thwarted if the federal districts turned, over time, into effective power centres in their own right, pursuing their own interests. Such an outcome would support the foreboding of those Yeltsin advisers in the early 1990s who warned that a smaller number of larger regions could be more threatening to the central control than that system inherited from the old Soviet order.

The direction of Putin's changes was clearly back towards a de facto unitary state. At the time of writing, however, the ability of the president and his regional representatives to reduce the real authority of regional elites had yet to be put to the test.

Appendix 12.1   The seven federal districts

Russia is an asymmetrical federation consisting of eighty-nine 'subjects of the federation': twenty-one republics, six krais (territories), forty-nine oblasts (regions), one autonomous oblast, ten autonomous okrugs (districts), and the cities of Moscow and St. Petersburg. Under a presidential decree dated 13 May 2000, the eighty-nine regions were administratively divided as follows into seven 'federal districts'.

Central District

- Presidential Representative: Lieutenant-General Georgii Poltavchenko (formerly presidential representative to Leningrad Oblast; before that, headed the St. Petersburg tax police – where he knew Putin – and worked in the St. Petersburg Federal Security Service FSB)
- District capital: Moscow
- Made up of Belgorod, Bryansk, Ivanovo, Kaluga, Kostroma, Kursk, Lipetsk, Moscow, Orel, Ryazan', Smolensk, Tambov, Tver', Tula, Vladimir, Voronezh and Yaroslavl' Oblasts; and the City of Moscow.

Far Eastern District

- Presidential Representative: Lieutenant-General (retired) Konstantin Pulikovsky (former chief of staff to General Anatolii Kvashnin, Chief of the General Staff; ran Putin's presidential election campaign in his native Krasnodar Krai)
- District capital: Khabarovsk
- Made up of the Republic of Sakha; Khabarovsk and Primorskii Krais; Amur, Kamchatka, Magadan and Sakhalin Oblasts; the Jewish Autonomous Oblast; and the Koryak and Chukchi Autonomous Okrugs.

North-West District

- Presidential Representative: Lieutenant-General Viktor Cherkesov (formerly first deputy head of the FSB; served in St. Petersburg in the 1980s; said to be close to Putin)
- District capital: St. Petersburg
- Made up of the Republics of Karelia and Komi; Arkhange'sk, Kaliningrad, Leningrad, Murmansk, Novgorod, Pskov and Vologda Oblasts; the Nenets Autonomous Okrug; and the City of St. Petersburg.

Siberian District
- Presidential Representative: Leonid Drachevsky (career diplomat, formerly Minister for the Commonwealth of Independent States)
- District capital: Novosibirsk
- Made up of the Republics of Altai, Buryatia, Khakassia and Tyva; Altai and Krasnoyarsk Krais; Chita, Irkutsk, Kemerovo, Novosibirsk, Omsk and Tomsk Oblasts; and the Evenk, Taimyr and Ust'-Orda Buryat Autonomous Okrugs.

Southern District

- Presidential Representative: General Viktor Kazantsev (formerly commander-in-chief of the combined federal forces in Chechnya; also served in Afghanistan)
- District capital: Rostov-on-Don
  Made up of the Republics of Adygeya, Chechnya, Dagestan, Ingushetia, Kabardino-Balkariya, Kalmykia, Karachaevo-Cherkessia and North Ossetia; Krasnodar and Stavropol' Krais; and Astrakhan, Rostov and Volgograd Oblasts.

Urals District

- Presidential Representative: Colonel-General (Police) Petr Latyshev (formerly Deputy Interior Minister; led investigation of corruption in the St. Petersburg city administration)
- District capital: Yekaterinburg
- Made up of Chelyabinsk, Kurgan, Sverdlovsk and Tyumen' Oblasts; and the Khanty-Mansii and Yamal-Nenets Autonomous Okrugs.

Volga District
- Presidential Representative: Sergei Kirienko, a native of Nizhnii Novgorod; Prime Minister, March–September 1998; subsequently leader of the Union of Right Forces (URF) political movement
- District capital: Nizhnii Novgorod
- Made up of the Republics of Bashkortostan, Chuvashia, Marii El, Mordovia, Tatarstan and Udmurtia; Kirov, Nizhnii Novgorod, Orenburg, Penza, Perm', Samara, Saratov and Ulyanovsk Oblasts; and the Komi-Permyak Autonomous Okrug.

Source: *RFE/RL Russian Federation Report*, 18 and 19, 2000, compiled by Julie Corwin.

Notes

1 East–West Institute, *Russian Regional Report* (12 February 1998) (hereafter, EWI, *Russian Regional Report*).
2 John Gibson and Philip Hanson (eds.), *Transformation from Below: Local Power and the Political Economy of Post-Communist Transitions* (Cheltenham: Edward Elgar, 1996), pp. 30–1, 312–13. The author is grateful to Philip Hanson for comments on an earlier draft of this chapter.
3 Philip Hanson *et al.*, 'Federal government responses to regional economic change', in Philip Hanson and Michael Bradshaw (eds.), *Regional Economic Change in Russia* (Cheltenham: Edward Elgar, 2000).
4 'Ot pervogo litsa,' www.vagrius.com

5 RFE/RL *Russian Federation Report* (23 August 2000).
6 EWI, *Russian Regional Report* (28 June 2000).
7 See Cameron Ross, 'Federalism and regional politics', in Mike Bowker and Cameron Ross (eds.), *Russia after the Cold War* (London: Longman, 2000).
8 *Komsomolskaya pravda* (26 July 2000).
9 *Komsomolskaya pravda* (8 September 2000).
10 I am grateful to Duncan Allan for drawing this point to my attention.
11 *Novaya gazeta* (31 July 2000).
12 EWI, *Russian Regional Report* (25 June 2000).
13 *ITAR-TASS* (9 August 2000), cited in *RFE/RL Russian Federation Report* (23 August 2000).
14 Oxford Analytica, *Daily Brief*, 23 May 2000 (published anonymously).

Index

Lightning Source UK Ltd.
Milton Keynes UK
11 February 2010

149865UK00001B/4/P